MW00737192

HOLLYWOOD TEEN MOVIES

80 FROM THE 80S

The Good, The Bad & The Forgotten

Above: Molly Ringwald & Michael Schoeffling in "Sixteen Candles" (1984)

TONY & DOUG PICHALOFF

Copyright © 2011 Tony & Doug Pichaloff

All rights reserved. No part of this publication may be reproduced, stored in a retrieval system or transmitted in any form or by any means, electronic, mechanical, photocopying, recording or otherwise, without the prior written permission of the publisher.

The information, views, opinions and visuals expressed in this publication are solely those of the author(s) and do not reflect those of the publisher. The publisher disclaims any liabilities or responsibilities whatsoever for any damages, libel or liabilities arising directly or indirectly from the contents of this publication.

A copy of this publication can be found in the National Library of Australia.

ISBN: 9781742841557

Published by Book Pal
www.bookpal.com.au

Dedication

"There are many teen movies out there that are really smart, believable and intuitive to what makes a young person tick"

.....this book is dedicated to them.

Above: Ralph Macchio & Elisabeth Shue in "The Karate Kid" (1984)

Table of Contents

ABOUT THE AUTHORS

The Guys from www.hollywoodteenmovies.com

Hi, welcome to our first book, "Hollywood Teen Movies: 80 from the 80s". Our names are Doug and Tony Pichaloff; we are a father and son team and creators of the website known as Hollywood Teen Movies (www.hollywoodteenmovies.com). In simple terms we are a couple of movie buffs or film historians that have a passion for movies and appreciate film as an art-form. Doug's working background is in high school teaching while Tony's qualifications are in International Tourism and Travel. It was 2001 when we decided to take our interest in film to another level by building our very first website. Hollywood Teen Movies stemmed from Tony's over-enthusiastic interest in the teen movie genre, in particular, teen movies of the 1980s. After some discussions we decided to build what we believe would be the ultimate teen movie website that would cover all teen movies throughout the decades, from the 1950s to the new millennium. Everyone has seen a teen movie, everyone has a favourite teen movie and everyone has been affected by a teen movie in some form or another. Teen movies have always proven to be a great source of fun and enjoyment. They are often viewed at an impressionable age, have a significant impact and often leave a lasting impression on its audience. That is the reason for the development of the Hollywood Teen Movie website and now for this book. Here are some personal comments from each of the two authors:

"My interest in film began in the late 1950's and intensified during the 1960's where as a child I lived across the road from the local cinema. I attended without fail the double features at the Saturday matinee each week. There I became hooked on a healthy dose of, Westerns, Tarzan adventures, Italian strongman epics, James Bond spy films and of course teen films. In my youth there were a handful of teen movies that left lasting impressions, they include, "Gidget Goes Hawaiian", the Cliff Richard teen musicals "The Young Ones" and "Summer Holiday", the Frankie Avalon / Annette Funicello "Beach Party" movies, and of course the countless Elvis Presley pictures. In the 1980s I was able to share my love of film with my son Tony with regular cinema visits that still continue to this day – Doug Pichaloff (2008)

"With Dad being the movie maniac that he is it had to rub off onto somebody and that somebody was me. My interest in film began in the 1980's where as a young child I was fortunate enough, with the advent of the

VCR to see movies that were initially released well before I was born. The 1980's were a golden age for teen movies and it was during this period that films began to make an impact on my life. Although I was not yet a teenager in the 1980's I still managed to see quite a few teen movies at the cinema. Those that I missed, I was fortunate enough to catch on video in my teenage years during the 1990's. I have many pleasant and happy memories of watching these films, often with my Dad. Some of my favourite 1980s teen movies include, "The Karate Kid", "Back To The Future", "Sixteen Candles", "Valley Girl", "Pretty In Pink", "The Breakfast Club", "Ferris Bueller's Day Off", "Can't Buy Me Love", "Say Anything" and of course the Porky's sex comedies. – Tony Pichaloff (2008)

We now work full-time developing our internet network of movie related websites of which Hollywood Teen Movies is the cornerstone. Some of the other websites in our "internet movie media network" are: Hollywood Cult Movies (www.hollywoodcultmovies.com), 80s Cinema (www.80scinema.com), Internet Actors Database (www.internetactorsdatabase.com) and Pick Of The Flicks (www.pickoftheflicks.com), at which Tony is the resident film critic. Our daily life has now become a combination of creating and designing new movie related websites together with viewing and writing about films. Also, from August 2008 until July 2011 we owned & operated a Movie Collector's Store / Video Editing business called "The Movie Experts". Our shop was situated in N.S.W. Australia & after 3 great years was forced to cease trading due to a re-development of the shopping centre in which we were located.

Now in 2011, with a bit more time up our sleeve, we are happy to release this book that is based on what inspired us to set up Hollywood Teen

Movies in the first place and that is Teen Movies from the Totally Awesome 80s. We hope that you enjoy reading this ode to 1980s Teen Movies and if all goes well we may return with more movie related books in the near future, two of which are already on the drawing board, "Hollywood Teen Movies: Another 80 From The 80s" and "Hollywood Teen Movies: 90 From The 90s". **Picture at Left:** The authors, Doug & Tony Pichaloff at Universal Studios Hollywood (2008).

ABOUT THE MOVIES

Hollywood Teen Movies – A Brief History

Let's take a quick stroll down memory lane with a brief history of the worldwide phenomenon known as "The Teen Movie". During the Hollywood of the 1930s and 1940s movies specifically about teens were rare, the exception being the long running Andy Hardy film series starring then-teenager Mickey Rooney. It was 1937 when the first Andy Hardy film, "A Family Affair", hit the big screen. Released by MGM in glorious black and white, who would have guessed that this minor film would spark off an entire film series that would run for nearly 10 years and produce an output of at least 15 big screen entries?

The term "Teen Movie" hadn't even been coined yet, when the Andy Hardy character came to life on film. During this rather tame and innocent pre-1950s period, the Andy Hardy films examined the life of an American family, but as the Andy Hardy character rose in popularity, filmmakers were bold enough to take the teenager and place him in the foreground for most of the remaining films in the series. The plots usually revolved around Andy's romantic entanglements and youthful misadventures. It took only 3 popular films before the name Andy Hardy was quickly introduced or should I say promoted to the next film's title, "Love Finds Andy Hardy" (1938). The film co-starred Hollywood darling Judy Garland and was one of the most popular entries in the series. "Love Finds Andy Hardy" is arguably the first bona-fide romantic teen comedy. According to internet source Wikipedia, "In 2000, "Love Finds Andy Hardy" was selected for preservation in the United States National Film Registry by the Library of Congress as being "culturally, historically, or aesthetically significant". One thing is for sure, the Andy Hardy film series certainly had an impact; it made Mickey Rooney a major Hollywood star and became a pre-cursor to a genre of film that would quickly explode in the next decade.

For many, the 1950s was the decade which marked the birth of the Hollywood Teen Movie. Leather jackets, motorcycles, rock 'n' roll and rebellious youths were introduced to the world. It was a period that launched the careers of Marlon Brando ("The Wild One", 1953), James Dean ("Rebel Without A Cause", 1955) and of course Elvis Presley ("King Creole", 1958). Juvenile delinquency had arrived in film when the groundbreaking high school drama, "Blackboard Jungle" (1955) burst onto the screen, with a lively opening credit sequence that featured the Billy Haley smash hit "Rock Around The Clock". Arguably the first JD film ever made, "Blackboard Jungle", left its mark on teen audiences with its jolting sound and gritty depiction of troubled youth. The film and its soundtrack made such an impact that it inspired a string of teen rock 'n' roll musicals that featured popular singers of the day. Rocker Bill Hayley led the pack with "Rock Around The Clock" (1956) and its sequel "Don't Knock The Rock" (1956). Other notable films laced with Rock 'n' Roll music include "Rock, Rock, Rock" (1956), "Mister Rock n Roll" (1957) and "Go, Johnny Go!" (1959), all three films being helmed by legendary 50's Disc Jockey Alan Freed. Another DJ that joined the band-wagon in 1957 was Dick Clark, with the release of the teen musical "Jamboree". The film provided minimal plot but maximum music, proving to be a 21 song extravaganza that showcased big name rockers such as Fats Domino, Jerry Lee Lewis and Carl Perkins, just to name a few. "Jamboree" also marked the first on-screen film appearance of a Philadelphia kid called Frankie Avalon. For Frankie, this film was the launching pad he needed for film prominence in the 1960s. Another Philadelphia kid that hit the scene at the end of the decade was the "Fabulous" Fabian Forte. At a time when Elvis Presley hysteria was in full swing, Fabian, with his pompadour Elvis inspired hair style made his film debut in the teen romance drama "Hound-Dog Man" (1959), a film that was not dissimilar to Presley's first starring vehicle "Love Me Tender" (1956). By 1959 there was no sign of the teen movie genre slowing down when two of the decade's biggest contributions hit the screens, "Gidget" and "A Summer Place". Both these films starred the new cute blonde sensation Sandra Dee, a fresh faced beauty that would soon become the female face of teenage pop culture.

The 1960s marked the beginning of the "Teen Beach Party Movies" which made household names of stars like Frankie Avalon, Annette Funicello, Fabian Forte and Deborah Walley. The original "Beach Party" (1963) released through American International Pictures and starring Frankie and Annette made such a splash with its fusion of color, skimpy bikinis, sand, surf and blue-screen wave riding that numerous sequels and spinoffs followed throughout the decade. It was a formula of music, romance and comedy that teens loved but unfortunately made real wave riders cringe in their seats. To satisfy the hardened surf crowd, Colombia Pictures attempted to up the ante with a

more authentic approach to the surf film when they released the Hawaiian based, teen wave epic "Ride The Wild Surf" starring Frankie's rival, Fabian Forte. Aside from the catchy Jan and Dean title track, what "Ride The Wild Surf" (1964) lacked was music and comedy but it more than made up for it with solid drama and some real wave riding. The "Beach Party" series continued to flourish and reached a peak with "Beach Blanket Bingo" (1965). By 1966 Frankie and Fabian joined forces to maximize their popularity when they starred opposite each other in the teen hot-rod flick "Fire-Ball 500", a sequel of sorts "Thunder Alley" followed with only Fabian and Annette returning. The 1960s was also the decade that took the success of the 1959 smash hit "Gidget" to the next level with two popular film sequels starring two new Gidget's; "Gidget Goes Hawaiian" (1961) with Deborah Walley and "Gidget Goes To Rome" (1963) with Cindy Carol, the common dominator in all three Gidget films being heartthrob and crooner James Darren as Moondoggie. The Gidget phenomenon didn't just stop there when in 1965, a spin-off "Gidget" TV series starring Sally Field hit the small screen. However, by the end of the 1960s the fun in the sun had come to an end and teens had hung up their surfboards. Teens were now getting ready for long-hair, flared pants and subsequently the disco boom.

The Teen Movies of the 1970's were a real mixed bag, from the emotional drama of "Love Story" (1970), to the nostalgic George Lucas classic "American Graffiti" (1973), to the Motown high school comedy "Cooley High" (1975), to The Beatles inspired time capsule "I Wanna Hold Your Hand" (1978), to the crazy antics and raunchiness of "National Lampoon's Animal House" (1978), to the cool riders and huge waves of "Big Wednesday" (1978), to the hot-rod hilarity of "Hometown USA" (1979) and to the Bill Murray summer camp epic "Meatballs" (1979), the 1970's certainly had it all. Juvenile delinquency also found its place during the decade with a string of teen movies falling into the "street gangs" sub-genre. Films such as the low-budget gang-flick "The Lords Of Flatbush" (1974) introduced cinemagoers to leather-clad-greasers, Sylvester Stallone and Henry Winkler, while the gritty violence of "The Warriors" (1979) unleashed a youthful Michael Beck as a Coney Island gang leader. The slickest of them all, however, would probably be the tuneful, gang-rivalry classic, "The Wanderers" (1979), with brooding beefcake Ken Wahl steaming up the screen and the forever-cool Dion title track leaving a lasting impression. All these "street gangs" films found their audience but the decade soared to even greater heights when the blockbuster teen musical returned with a bang, in the form of two classic John Travolta dance flicks, "Saturday Night Fever" (1977) and "Grease" (1978). Apart from these musicals the two landmark teen films of the 1970s that deserve special mention would have to be "American Graffiti" and "National Lampoon's Animal House". "Graffiti" was a throwback to the 1960s and focused on a group of teens coming of age after their high school graduation. The entire film sees the teens cruising in and around Mel's Diner, during one night in the summer of '62. It was a unique film-going experience with all of the happenings taking place to the backdrop of Wolfman Jack's radio show which busted out more than 40 pulsating rock n roll tracks. Shot in less than a month and on a budget of less than a million dollars, "American Graffiti" still stands out as the trailblazer of the era having grossed more than $115 million in the US alone. Future A-list Hollywood stars, Harrison Ford and Richard Dreyfuss, not to mention future Oscar winning Director Ron Howard all made their mark in this film. Graffiti's slew of critical plaudits and Oscar nominations, including both Best Picture and Best Director nods, led to an eventual sequel "More American Graffiti" (1979). Unfortunately, some great films are best to stand alone as the "Graffiti" sequel received mixed reactions from both critics and audiences. The other blockbuster, the frat-house favourite, "National Lampoon's Animal House" grossed over $141 million, not bad considering its budget was a mere $3 million. It starred the unforgettable, toga-wearing John Belushi as Bluto. To this day, Belushi still stands as one of the most vulgar and possibly biggest slobs to ever appear in a teen movie, although "Ogre" from "Revenge Of The Nerds" may give him a run for his money…. which leads us to the teen movies of the 1980s.

<u>**Above:**</u> Christopher Atkins & Brooke Shields in "The Blue Lagoon" (1980)

The 1980s were a peak period for teen movies and the main reason for this book. The decade kicked off slowly with only a handful of teen movies released in 1980 and 1981, most of them showcasing the popular young starlets of the day. The most notable being, "Foxes", the female JD flick starring future Academy Award winner Jodie Foster, the summer camp classic "Little Darlings" with Tatum O'Neal and Kristy McNichol and of course the Brooke Shield's romance dramas "The Blue Lagoon" and "Endless Love". Kristy McNicol, Brooke Shields and Jodie Foster were all nominated for "Best Young Actress" at the "Young Artist Awards" for their solid performances in these film but they all lost out to another young starlet by the name of Diane Lane, for her role in the Elvis Presley pen pal drama "Touched By Love". However, it wasn't until 1982 that the teen movie genre truly exploded when "Porky's" was launched on an unsuspecting public. The film was not only a $100 million grossing teen film, but with its raunchiness breaking new ground, it firmly established itself as a comedy classic that would soon become one of the very first teen movie franchises.

Another franchise of sorts were the John Hughes teen comedies, although not connected by name, the films featured a contingent of young actors who were quickly becoming faces of the era. One of the youngest to emerge was the talented Molly Ringwald, who stood out from the crowd after her heartfelt performances in a string of high profile Hughes films. Molly was box office gold in classic hits such as "16 Candles" (1984), "The Breakfast Club" (1985) and the unforgettable "Pretty In Pink" (1986) which established her as the "Teen Queen of the 1980s". Molly was so popular that she even had the honour of gracing the cover of Time Magazine in 1986. Another phenomenon that emerged from the decade was the infamous "Brat Pack" which consisted of a group of young actors of the era who worked together on a number of high profile teen films. The core of this group of actors are usually culled from two prominent films of the mid-1980s, "The Breakfast Club" (1985) and "St. Elmo's Fire" (1985), with an earlier film, "The Outsiders" (1983) often thrown in as an honourable mention. The main Brat Packers were Emilo Estevez, Rob Lowe, Judd Nelson, Anthony Michael Hall, Andrew McCarthy, Molly Ringwald, Demi Moore and Ally Sheedy with some of the honourable mentions being, C. Thomas Howell, Matt Dillon, Ralph Macchio, Patrick Swayze and Tom Cruise.

Above: Estevez, Lowe, Howell, Swayze & Cruise in "The Outsiders" (1983)

By the mid-1980s Teen movies were in high demand, so much so, that the multiplexes were flooded with an abundance of new product weekly. There were so many teen movies on offer that viewers just couldn't keep up with all of them. Some films hit pay dirt with lengthy cinema runs as they broke new ground by appealing to both adults and teens ("The Karate Kid", 1984 and "Back To The Future", 1985), while others flew in and out of the cinemas in a flash ("Losin' It", 1983 and "The Heavenly Kid", 1985). On the other hand, with the advent of the VCR many that got overlooked in the cinematic shuffle ("The Last American Virgin", 1982 and "Girls Just Want To Have Fun", 1985), found a new lease of life on VHS. Whatever the case, many teen movies during the 1980s were like fast-food; cheap to produce, easy to digest and left you feeling satisfied. While many were of the fast-food variety some were leaning more towards fine dining. The flavoursome taste sensations of the era, that deserve special mention are: "Fast Times At Ridgemont High" (1982), "Valley Girl" (1983), "WarGames" (1983), "Risky Business" (1983), "Footloose" (1984), "Ferris Bueller's Day Off" (1986), "Can't Buy Me Love" (1987), "Some Kind of Wonderful" (1987), "License to Drive" (1988), "Say Anything" (1989) and the list could go on and on and on.

The teen films of the early 1990's were a mish-mash of sorts, ranging from straight to video films featuring former teen stars of the 80s that had now lost some of their shine together with a handful of popular big screen cinema releases showcasing a number of new faces. That's right; Corey Haim and Corey Feldman were back but this time in a string of low-budget video films. For Haim it was "Dream Machine" (1990), "Fast Getaway" (1991), "The Double O Kid" (1992),"O What A Night" (1992), "Just One Of The Girls" (1993) and "Life 101" (1995). For Feldman it was "Rock n Roll High School Forever" (1991), "Meatballs 4" (1992), "Round Trip To Heaven" (1992) and "Voodoo" (1995). The two Corey's even teamed up again on a few occasions for "Blown Away" (1992), "National Lampoon's Last Resort" (1994) and "Dream A Little Dream 2" (1995). The decade also saw the emergence of newcomers Christian Slater ("Pump Up The Volume", 1990), Winona Ryder ("Welcome Home, Roxy Carmichael, 1990), Richard Grieco ("If Looks Could Kill", 1991), Brendan Fraser ("Encino Man", 1992) and Kristy Swanson ("Buffy The Vampire Slayer", 1992), to mention just a few. However, it wasn't until 1995 when Alicia Silverstone exploded onto the screen in the box office smash hit "Clueless", that the teen movie was back in style again and this time with a new vernacular and a new superstar. This film did not only catapult Alicia's career but also sparked off a new wave of teen movies in the late 90s that would introduce audiences to even more fresh faces. The teen thriller "Disturbing Behaviour" brought TV stars Kate Holmes and James Marsden to the big screen, while the romantic high school comedy "She's All That" (1999) gave us a trio of rising young stars in the form of Freddie Prinze Jr, Paul Walker and Rachael Leigh Cook. The critically acclaimed Shakespearean update of "The Taming Of The Shrew", titled "10 Things I Hate About You", introduced us to the brilliance of Australia's Heath Ledger and America's Julia Stiles, while "Drive Me Crazy" saw

Melissa Joan Hart from TV's "Sabrina The Teenage Witch" team up with cinema's newest pretty boy Adrian Grenier. Finally, when we thought the teen sex comedy had run its course after the countless "Porky's" knock offs in the 1980s, we got served a slice of "American Pie", a raunchy little film that caused a stir at the box office and did for 90s audiences what Porky's did in the 1980s. "American Pie" was a success story that launched its own franchise, introduced some new faces and opened the door for more of the same hi-jinks in future films of the new millennium.

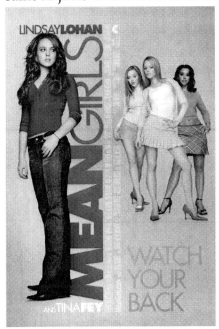

The teen movie craze has continued to flourish into the new millennium with films such as, the Kirsten Dunst cheerleader comedy "Bring It On" (2000), the Reese Witherspoon academic farce "Legally Blonde" (2001), the comic-book teen superhero "Spider-Man" (2002), the Amanda Bynes fish-out-water romance "What A Girl Wants" (2003), the Lindsay Lohan high school smash "Mean Girls" (2004), the uniquely likeable geek-fest Napoleon Dynamite (2004), the Hilary Duff fairytale "A Cinderella Story" (2004), the soccer-filled gender-bender "She's The Man" (2006), the Brittany Snow revenge flick "John Tucker Must Die" (2006), the Hitchcockian teen thriller "Disturbia" (2007), the outrageously raunchy "Superbad" (2007), the critically acclaimed Oscar winner "Juno" (2008), the cheerleader camp pom-pom farce "Fired Up" (2009) the Emma Stone, rumor-fuelled high school romp "Easy A" (2010) and of course, the "Goonies-like" sci-fi fantasy "Super 8" (2011) .

Big-screen franchises, appealing to both tweens and teens made their mark in the new millennium like never-before. Warner Bros. has already notched up about 8 "Harry Potter" movies which have turned Daniel Radcliffe into a teenage celebrity. Disney has also added their special stamp to the teen genre with the three song and dance "High School Musical" (2006-2008) spectaculars. The first two films were Disney Channel favourites, while the third film emerged as a big screen release making household names of Zac Efron and Vanessa Hudgens. Another dance franchise that has proven popular with teens is the exciting "Step Up" trilogy (2006-2010), with the 3rd instalment hitting the screens in 3-D. Dreamworks splashed out the bucks by bringing the popular 1980s Hasbro toy line to the big screen with 3 extravagant special effects fantasies, "Transformers" (2007), "Transformers: Revenge Of The Fallen" (2009) & "Transformers: Dark Of The Moon" (2011). These robotic blockbusters have sent teens into a special-effects tailspin, with stars Shia LaBeouf and Megan Fox constantly hitting the tabloids. Another success story is Disney's it-girl Miley Cyrus, daughter of country singer Billy Ray Cyrus, who took her successful TV Show "Hannah Montana" to the big-screen, firstly with the 3-D concert movie "Hannah Montana & Miley Cyrus: The Best Of Both Worlds" (2007) and secondly, singing up a storm in "Hannah Montana: The Movie" (2009). However, Miley's transition from tween to teen was put to the test with her dramatic skills on show in the teen romance drama "The Last Song" (2010). In 2011 Miley challenged herself yet again, this time playing a street-smart private eye in the action comedy "So Undercover".

Also, in the new millennium, the "Twilight Film Saga" broke new ground in teen entertainment. With 5 films (Twilight, New Moon, Eclipse & Breaking Dawn 1 & 2) now in the can and possibly more still to come, these romance / vampire / fantasies have quickly emerged as one of the biggest teen movie franchises ever. The film's vampire romanticism has struck a chord with girls and is the primary draw-card for its predominately female audience. Usually females and vampire films don't mix and have no common-denominator but with newcomers, Kristen Stewart, Robert Pattinson & Taylor Lautner setting pulses racing, in a love-story-like-no-other, the box offices keep ringing to the tune of millions while teenage girls spend their pocket-change on merchandise as they wait in anticipation for the next installment.

As "Twilight" cements its place as the new money-spinner, the cast spread their appeal with appearances in other teen projects, most notably, Robert Pattinson in the romance drama "Remember Me" (2010), Kristen Stewart in the amusement park comedy "Adventureland" (2009) and Taylor Lautner in the high-octane action thriller "Abduction" (2011).

We are now more than 10 years into the new millennium and the amazing thing is 1980s teen movies are back in vogue with filmmakers choosing to revisit some of the classics by remaking them. Will they be bigger and better than the originals? Only time will tell.... Who would have thought that "Fame" (2009), "The Karate Kid" (2010) "Footloose" (2011) and "Fright Night 3-D" (2011) would have found their way back into the multiplexes of the new millennium. That's right, this is an impressive collection of teen movies on a return engagement and they are all leaving their mark with cinemagoers all over again. There is also chatter regarding a remake of "Dirty Dancing" but as some purists believe certain movies are best left alone.

Finally, one movie that we haven't mentioned at this point but is certainly worthy of note is "Not Another Teen Movie" (2001). Although not a great flick, "Not Another Teen Movie" is a spoof of teen movies and when they do a spoof of a genre, you know that the genre has come-of-age and entered into the lexicon of the film-going public. Now, with the next-decade of the new millennium beginning, the future certainly looks bright for the teen movie. CGI is in full-throttle and cinema technology is at a peak. Who knows, our next big-budget teen movie may be in an IMAX theatre in 4-D, only time will tell. The teen movie genre today is definitely

in a healthy state and looks certain to stay that way for a long time to come as Hollywood's new breed of young actors and actresses continue to strut their stuff on the silver screen be it in 2-D, 3-D, 4-D or whatever!

ABOUT THE BOOK

Introduction & Overview

Welcome to "Hollywood Teen Movies: 80 From The 80s", the first edition of hopefully a number of books based on the popular website Hollywood Teen Movies (www.hollywoodteenmovies.com). Teen Movies have been around now for well over 50 years and this book is dedicated, not only to them, but also to the filmmakers and millions of fans that love and appreciate these movies. Why the 1980s, you may ask? Simple, it was the decade of the Teen Movie. There were more teen movies made during this period than in any other. This book will take you on a journey through the 1980s; the decade that we feel teen movies were not only most prevalent but possibly reached a peak in terms of quality and popularity. Who can forget; "Porky's", "Sixteen Candles", "The Karate Kid", "The Breakfast Club", "Back To The Future", "Pretty In Pink", "Ferris Bueller's Day Off" and "Can't Buy Me Love" to name just a few. This book will provide you, the reader, with the ultimate collection of information on 80 Teen Movies from the totally awesome 80s. Yes, that's right, "The Good, The Bad And The Forgotten", they're all here for you to read about. All the information you want about the teen movies you like; the most popular, the critically acclaimed, the cult favorites, the forgotten gems and the bombs, they're all here for your enjoyment. Also, find out who were the "Teen Idols" and "Teen Queens" of the era. They came in all shapes and sizes; hunks, babes, pretty boys, bimbos, jocks, cheerleaders, rebels, beach girls, surfers and nerds. "Hollywood Teen Movies: 80 From The 80s" is loaded with posters, movie stills and movie reviews that are jam-packed with stats, history, trivia, quotes, taglines and detailed film analysis.

Above: Lea Thompson & Michael J. Fox in "Back To The Future" (1985)

"Hollywood Teen Movies: 80 From The 80s" is a unique book in that the reviews are written by two people, a father and son team representing two generations. Each review is a collaboration of ideas, thoughts and compromises. Opinions have been tossed up and thrashed out before pen was put to paper. It's been a delicate balancing act at times deciding exactly what to write about each film. With two writers from two different generations writing the same review, well as they say....something's gotta give. Often, one would begin a sentence or idea and the other would complete it. The writing style, whatever it may be, is a unique mix of two minds and two opinions, blending into one. Some reviews may have a slightly stronger influence by one party than the other but in general, whenever there was a conflict of opinion we tried very hard to reach a middle ground. One thing that does come through in some of the reviews is that there are often throwbacks and comparisons made to films of an earlier era. Also, the movie reviews in this book have been presented in chronological order deliberately so that when reading the book the transcript comes across almost like a history of 1980s teen movies rather than a disjointed list of reviews which would be the case if they were presented in alphabetical order.

Above: The colorful cast of "The Last American Virgin" (1982)

What makes a teen movie, you may ask? Well most teen movies feature some of the following key ingredients: the classroom, the lockers, the change room, the gym, the cafeteria, the prom, the sporting grounds, the local diner, the shopping mall, the drive-in, the beach, the fast car, the gangs and the motorbikes. What types of characters are featured in a teen movie? Teens of course! But what type of teens? Here are just a few, the strong guy, the fat guy, the genius, the loner, the geek, the jock, the rebel, the bully, the pervert, the dreamer, the hero, the dumb blonde, the bimbo, the princess, the virgin, the cheerleader, the sensitive new age guy, Mr. and Mrs. Popularity and of course the lovers. If you take any combination of the above ingredients and sprinkle them with a generous helping of alcohol, sex and music, you will more than likely get a teen movie.

In general, a teen movie centers on characters that are teenagers who in most cases attend some form of educational institution. Some movies, however, can still be classified as teen movies even though the central characters are older, usually 20 something, the reason being is that teens still flock to these films because their favorite teen stars appear in them. In this book we have tended to favor films of the traditional teenage variety, that is, movies about teenagers that are usually set in schools, rather than young adult films that are popular with teens. Some actors become so synonymous with the teen movie genre that they often find it hard to break free of their teen star status, two good examples of this are Andrew McCarthy and Michael J. Fox.

Andrew McCarthy had success in teen movies like "Class" and "Pretty In Pink" but by the end of the 1980s the school books were gone and he was starring in 20-something young adult roles in films such as "Mannequin" (1987) and "Weekend At Bernies" which were both adored by teenage audiences because of the overflow effect. Michael J. Fox hit it big in teen movies such as "Back To The Future" and "Teen Wolf" but his next major film "The Secret Of My Success" was a young adult role that appealed to the teenage crowd. Once again, these young adult films that were extremely popular with teenagers could in a sense be classified as teen films but have nevertheless been excluded from this book because of the criteria explained. Another popular movie with teens of the 80s, the Brat Pack classic "St. Elmo's Fire", has also been excluded from the book for similar reasons. In "St. Elmo's Fire" the brat packers have left high school or college behind them and are now embarking on adulthood. It seems that for every great teen movie that a popular teen actor appears in, there is also a great follow-up young adult film with similar appeal. Such films, plus sequels and rarities may be included in a future book, titled "Hollywood Teen Movies: Another 80 From The 80s", the book may even be subtitled "Sequels, Rarities and When Teens Grow Up".

Many of the films chosen for this book were viewed in cinemas on their initial release by both Doug and Tony, while some may have been viewed in cinemas by one or the other. A small minority were viewed on video, cable television or DVD. Whatever the case, all of the films have been viewed at least once, while many have been watched countless times over the years. There was even a big debate on the selection of the 80 films that were to be included. We discarded all sequels and any made for TV films. This is not to say that we tried to pick the best 80 films from the era. In fact we tried very hard to include a nice blend and variety of films in the mix. We even made way for some lesser known films because we felt that they deserved some attention for one reason or another, it may have been because the film included a cult actor, an unusual theme or a variation on the genre that was unique.

Some examples of the lesser known films included in the book are, the John Stamos secret agent flick "Never Too Young To Die" (1986), the Jim Youngs soccer epic "Hotshot" (1987) and the fun in the sun Johnny Depp sex comedy "Private Resort" (1985). "Never Too Young To Die" was included for two reasons. Number one, it is possibly the first teen secret agent film of its type and number two, it starred teen pin-up-boy John Stamos whose biggest claim to fame was not in movies but rather in the TV series "Full House". "Never Too Young To Die" did not do very well at the box office but Stamos was nevertheless a face of the era. On the other hand, the teen sports film, "Hotshot" starring Jim Youngs of "Footloose" fame, is a unique entry, as it is one of the few teen films about soccer and as a bonus features the world's greatest soccer player, Pele. Also, Jim Youngs did not appear in many films as a lead so this one is a bit of a rarity. As for "Private Resort", it was a teen sex comedy that was completely ignored during its original release but nevertheless deserves a special mention because of its two stars, Johnny Depp and Rob Morrow. Depp was a relative newcomer at the time and so was his co-star Morrow. As we all know now,

Depp has since become an A-list Hollywood superstar with the "Pirates Of The Caribbean" films, while Morrow went on to find fame on TV's "Northern Exposure" in the 90s and more recently the TV crime drama "Numbers" (2005-2008). "Private Resort" is light and breezy teen entertainment that has now developed a cult following of sorts because of its stars.

The teen movie genre has lasted the test of time. One of the secrets to its ongoing appeal is that it has been able to successfully cross the boundaries of all popular film genres, never more so than in the 1980s. Film genres such as; action ("The Karate Kid"), comedy ("Ferris Bueller's Day Off"), romance ("Pretty In Pink"), drama ("Tex"), adventure ("The Goonies"), fantasy ("Back To The Future"), sci-fi ("The Last Starfighter"), horror ("The Lost Boys"), thriller ("Class of 1984"), sports ("All The Right Moves"), dance ("Footloose") and western (Young Guns) were all catered for within the 1980s teen movie spectrum.

Above: Jeff Cohen, Sean Astin, Corey Feldman,
Jonathan Ke Quan in "The Goonies" (1985)

"Hollywood Teen Movies: 80 From The 80s" is a book more than 10 years in the making. In 2000 Tony wanted to write a book about teen movies. Sadly, it didn't happen but the subsequent result was the website www.hollywoodteenmovies.com established in 2001. By 2003, the website was in full swing and was gaining popularity at a steady rate. The thought of a book returned and pen was soon put to paper. Hours of viewing began and notes were compiled at an alarming rate. However, by the end of 2003 we got sidetracked again developing other websites. Our focus had changed and our writing came to a standstill. The book was once again put on the back-burner, but not forgotten. From 2004 to 2006 an occasional piece of writing came into play in small spurts but not with the same intensity. It wasn't until 2007 that our interest in the book was rekindled again. A burst of energy for about 12 months from early 2007 right through to early 2008 was our biggest leap forward. In fact by mid-2008, after numerous name changes and formats, we had finally completed our 80 reviews and the book was almost finished. As strange as it may seem, we got sidetracked again, this time with the opening of our very own DVD store called "The Movie Experts". Finally in 2011, our thoughts returned to the book. All the loose ends were tidied up and as they say….here we are in print.

To all the people involved in the making of the Teen Movies featured in this book, be it, actors, actresses, directors, make-up artists, script writers, editors, special effects people, stunt-men, cameramen, general assistants etc….this book is dedicated to you all, in appreciation for the joy and happiness that you have given to the millions of fans out there who love and adore your movies. Finally, this book is a celebration of teen movies and was created with the purpose of giving pleasure to fans that love and adore 1980s teen movies. The 80s was truly a special decade for the genre. We hope this book is interesting, entertaining, informative and above all, enjoyable to all the teen movie fans from around the world that take the time to read it. All the best & have fun watching Teen Movies….

STAR RATING GUIDE

An Explanation To The Ratings System

★ ★ ★ ★ ★ Masterpiece

The 5 Star Rating is the top rating and indicates that the film is a Masterpiece. It is exceptionally well produced, acted and directed. It's an enjoyable movie, often groundbreaking and in most cases has something important to say.

★ ★ ★ ★ ½ Outstanding

The 4 ½ Star Rating is an intermediate rating that indicates that the film is Outstanding and lies somewhere between Excellent and Masterpiece.

★ ★ ★ ★ ★ Excellent

The 4 Star Rating indicates that the film is Excellent and generally of high quality in all departments. It is usually a film that stands out and should not be missed but for one reason or another doesn't match up to the 5 Star Rating.

★ ★ ★ ★ ★ Very Good

The 3 ½ Star Rating is an intermediate rating that indicates that the film is Very Good and lies somewhere between Good and Excellent.

★ ★ ★ ★ ★ Good

The 3 Star Rating indicates that the film is Good. It is an entertaining film with sufficient quality in most areas and will certainly keep you interested throughout.

★ ★ ★ ★ ★ Not Bad

The 2 ½ Star Rating is an intermediate rating that indicates that the film is Not Bad and lies somewhere between Fair and Good.

★ ★ ★ ★ ★ Fair

The 2 Star Rating indicates that the film is Fair and is worth some interest, but probably has noticeable drawbacks such as mediocre acting, mediocre directing or a thin plot.

★ ★ ★ ★ ★ Not Good

The 1 ½ Star Rating is an intermediate rating that indicates that the film is not good and lies somewhere between Bad and Fair.

★ ★ ★ ★ ★ Bad

The 1 Star Rating indicates that the film is Bad. It falls short in all departments and is of poor quality. It is usually a boring movie that is not worth watching.

★ ★ ★ ★ ★ Bomb

The ZERO Star Rating is the bottom rating and indicates that the film is a Cinema or DVD Bomb. It is of extremely poor quality and has nothing to offer at all. The film should be avoided at all costs.

Chapter 1:

TEEN MOVIES OF 1980

Foxes **

US Release Date: 29th February 1980
Running Time: 106 min
US Classification: R
Director: Adrian Lyne
Starring: Jodie Foster, Scott Baio, Sally Kellerman, Randy Quaid, Cherie Currie, Marilyn Kagan, Kandice Stroh, Adam Faith, Robert Romanus

Taglines:

* The City Had It Coming.
* Daring To Do It

Film Review:

Before "Fatal Attraction", "Indecent Proposal" and "Unfaithful", English Director Adrian Lyne moved from TV underwear commercials to his feature film debut with this unsettling look at the teenage subculture of its time. Set in the San Fernando Valley, "Foxes" is predominately a female JD flick focusing on the troubled lives of four rebellious teenage girls who seem to spend most of their time sleeping at each other's houses, going to parties and dabbling in alcohol and drugs. The leader of the pack is Jeanie, played by future Academy Award winner Jodie Foster; she's the smartest of the group and a little more sensible than the others. Jeanie has adopted the position of mother figure and feels a responsibility to look out for the safety of her more imbalanced friends, Annie (Cherie Currie), Madge (Marilyn Kagan) and Deirdre (Kandice Stroh). Yet, Jeanie has her own problems, living with a young divorced mother (played by Sally Kellerman) who is still trying to pick up the pieces of her own missteps in life.

The male characters in the film are minor in comparison to the four "Foxes". 1960s British pop star Adam Faith makes a small appearance as Jodie Foster's father, while Scott Baio drops in and out of the film as a skateboard kid. Baio's appearances are brief except for one exciting chase sequence that sees him duck and skate under a truck to escape a gang of hoods. "Foxes" also marked the re-teaming of Foster and Baio who had worked together previously in the kids gangster musical "Bugsy Malone" (1976). Randy Quaid of "Vacation" fame plays the only boyfriend who develops a serious relationship with one of the girls. In one interesting scene Quaid's house is trashed when the girls decide to host a dinner party that goes wrong. Also, appearing in his film debut is Robert Romanus (Fast Times) in a small role as Foster's boyfriend.

Although released in 1980, the film has a real 1970s period flavour with regards to fashion and music. The Donna Summer track "On The Radio" pops up throughout and the song "20th Century Foxes" by Angel is featured in a concert sequence. Los Angeles Times described "Foxes" as "intimate, astonishing and powerful". The film grossed $7,470,348, ranked 73rd in the overall yearly box office and Director Adrian Lyne got enough notice with the film to win the directorial job on the dance musical "Flashdance" (1983) which went on to become a mega-hit for Paramount.

"Foxes" is not the most pleasant of teen films; it has its flaws just like its characters. Foster and Kellerman come out of it the best while the other female stars struggle at times. Scott Baio is somewhat wasted and could have been used to better effect. Production values and locations are great but the pace of the film is at times uneven and the editing disjointed. The script is fair but far from outstanding. As an entertainment it appeals to teenage girls who can identify with the "Foxes" of the title but the film as a whole lacks mass audience appeal because the average moviegoer finds it difficult to connect with these characters, the disturbing themes and the dark portrait of teenage life. Nevertheless, today, "Foxes" stands as a gritty, realistic 1980 time capsule of teenage girls growing up tuff, in L.A.'s fast lane.

Little Darlings ***

US Release Date: 21st March 1980
Running Time: 96 min
US Classification: R
Director: Ronald F. Maxwell
Starring: Tatum O'Neal, Kristy McNichol, Armand Assante, Matt Dillon, Cynthia Nixon

Taglines:

* The bet is on: whoever loses her virginity first - wins.
* Don't let the title fool you.

Film Review:

Take two talented young actresses, one an Oscar winner (Tatum O'Neal) and the other an Emmy winner (Kristy McNichol) put them head to head in a coming of age teen film involving a competition about the loss of one's innocence and you have a recipe for success. The movie poster displays the two pretty young starlets, back to back with smiley grins on their faces, the tagline states; "The bet is on: whoever loses her virginity first – wins". The film title "Little Darlings" is displayed in red text with a small caption underneath stating, "Don't Let The Title Fool You". On first impression the tacky tagline may give the indication that the film is a cheap, sexploitation flick, appealing only to young teens and of little value to a mature audience; but nothing is further from the truth. "Little Darlings" is an engaging teen summer camp movie featuring a superb screenplay from writers Kimi Peck & Dalene Young, competent direction from Ronald F. Maxwell (his first theatrical film) and outstanding performances from the two leading ladies.

The film's premise is simple but effective; two 15 year-old-girls attend Camp Little Wolf for the summer and learn more about themselves than any classroom could ever offer. Each comes from a different class background. Kristy McNichol shines as Angel, the streetwise chick from a tough neighbourhood whose rough exterior (denim jacket, black tank top and Marlboro cigarettes) hides an innocent sensitivity of a young girl approaching adulthood. One thing is for sure Angel, who was raised by her mother, knows how to handle herself when it comes to boys, or so she thinks. In the opening scene she kicks one in the groin and later tries to seduce another by getting him drunk, only to discover that the alcohol puts him to sleep, "You're supposed to get turned on, stupid, not pass out" she says to her boyfriend. Tatum O'Neal plays Ferris, the rich girl with the divorced father. She is the complete opposite of Kristy's character. When Tatum arrives late at the bus departure terminal in her dad's limousine, the door is opened for her like a princess, she is dressed in a white suit and beret, complete with a stylized haircut, she is a real lady and certainly the most prim and proper girl at the camp. On the other-hand Kristy arrives with her mother in an old beat-up convertible that backfires when it comes to a halt. As the camp bus girls drool over discussions about Andy Gibb, John Travolta and the number of times they have watched "Last Tango In Paris", the two leads meet for the first time when they are forced to share a seat on the bus. Their obvious differences spark an immediate scuffle to the thrill of the other onlookers including "Sex And City's" Cynthia Nixon in a supporting role. When they arrive at the camp and go to their cabins, McNichol and O'Neal are egged on by the other girls and made to believe that they are the only virgins in camp and so the mindless "virginity" bet is on. The prize: $100 to the one who loses their virginity first. The male targets become, a very hairy Armand Assante, as the camp coach and a young Matt Dillon (like you have never seen him before, with hair as long as his female co-star) as Randy the boy from Camp Tomahawk on the other-side of the lake.

All the fun and games you would expect in a summer camp film is present, laughter, lies, seduction, first love, tears and more. The girls get into all kinds of mischief, like taking the school bus for a joyride, stealing a condom machine from a boy's bathroom, blowing condoms up like balloons, faking drowning to be rescued by the hunky coach and of course viewers are treated to the ultimate food fight in the mess-hall, sparked by the two leads. The serious nature of the drama kicks in during the last quarter of the film. For the director, it's a balancing act of slapstick fun, romantic situations and sensitive coming of age drama. A striking quality of the film is that the innocence and integrity of the male characters is maintained. Neither of the boys is trying to take advantage of the girls. They are never portrayed to be the villains of the piece, then neither are the girls, they are just naïve and going through the stages of puberty. When O'Neal finds her way into Assante's cabin he states "I'm not a prince. I'm a teacher. You know, in a year you're gonna look at me and you're gonna wonder how you could have even thought of loving me". He knows she's an innocent girl with a crush and he has no intention of taking advantage of her. McNichol's scenes with Dillon are a standout. After their sexual encounter the emotional power of the scene kicks in when she states "it made me feel like you could see right through me." Dillon later declares his love for her, "I don't know. I think I love you". Her reply, "You don't have to, you know." His reply is, "I know". When she is leaving the camp at the end of the film, her final statement to Dillon is "I will never forget you… ever" and we, the audience believe she won't as McNichol's performance is nothing short of brilliant. The girls in this film learn a big lesson in life on their own terms and in their own way without the intervention of parental figures.

Little Darling's was shot in Georgia with Hard Labor Creek State Park used as the location for Camp Little Wolf. Rumour has it; Tatum O'Neal had first choice over which character she would play. She chose to play Ferris and I think she made the right choice. As it turned out Kristy McNichol was perfect in the other role and many believe stole the show. She even took up smoking as preparation for her part but couldn't quit the habit after work on the film ended. One of the puzzling things about the film is that it received an R Rating in the United States. The film does not contain the profanity, nudity or sex scenes that were prevalent in other teen movies of the decade with the same rating such as "Porky's" and "Fast Times". Maybe it's because the PG-13 rating did not exist at that time. In 1980 films had to be rated PG or R, there was no in-between rating, and "Little Darlings" must have just missed out on the PG. The PG-13 rating was first introduced in 1984 with the release of the teen military flick "Red Dawn". Nevertheless, children under 17 were allowed to see "Little Darlings" in the cinema, provided they went with their parents. It seems many teens did just that, as the film was a solid performer at the US box office, earning $34,326,249 and gaining 20th position in the overall yearly box office ranks. When the film was first broadcast on US television in 1983 all references to "virginity loss" disappeared. Scenes were either edited out or dubbed over. Also, over the years the film has been subjected to some soundtrack changes due to copyright issues. Most fans of the film prefer the original theatrical cut which featured "Oh My Love" by John Lennon on the sequence which begins with Kristy picking up Matt in the canoe and "Let Your Love Flow" by The Bellamy Brothers on the film's closing credits.

The final moments of "Little Darlings" are captivating. The film hits a home run of emotions. The two girls who were once rivals are brought together and develop a close friendship when they open up and share their true feelings about each other and their experiences with the boys. They discover that telling the truth is important and that sex is a personal thing between two people who love each other. Summer camp has certainly been a life changing experience for these two girls. When McNichol is reunited with her mother it is like the roles of parent and child have been reversed. She says to her mother, "What's this crap about sex being nothing? You've been hanging around creeps! I'm gonna keep my eye on you". McNichol has reached a maturity level where she is now able to give her mother advice on life's complexities. In the film's moving finale McNichol introduces O'Neal to her mother stating, "This is my friend Ferris Whitney... my best friend." "Little Darlings" is a sweet little teen film, a quality production that scores well on all levels. It succeeds in engaging audiences with its combination of summer camp fun and thought provoking teen issues. The film's message is spot on and by the film's end the girls and the audience fully understand the consequences of the bet.

*Fame ****

US Release Date: 16th May 1980
Running Time: 134 min
US Classification: R
Director: Alan Parker
Starring: Irene Cara, Lee Curreri, Laura Dean, Antonia Franceschi, Boyd Gaines, Albert Hague, Gene Anthony Ray

Taglines:
* If they've really got what it takes, it's going to take everything they've got.
* Remember my name...

Film Review:
When "Fame" hit cinemas in 1980 it immediately created a buzz among moviegoers. It had no big stars yet it was still able to grab audiences with its energy, its grit, its realism and its style. It was different to any musical movie that came before it. It was far from conventional and certainly not your traditional storytelling. It was a landmark film that provided audiences with a window into the lives of students attending a New York City High School for the Performing Arts. The film doesn't try to follow the exploits of a central character as many films do, but instead it jumps from one student or one classroom situation to another and gives you a real overview of what life at the school is really like. "Fame" is predominately a series of fragmented scenes that capture, the sights, the sounds, the trials, the heartaches, the determination and the pain of the actors, the musicians, the dancers and the singers as they strive for stardom or "Fame" as the title suggests. It is not until well into the film that you begin to really know the characters and by the time the film is over you not only know what makes the characters tick but you feel that you have been part of the school experience yourself.

"Fame" won critical acclaim and grossed over $21 million at the US box office. Two of the film's songs, "Fame" and "Out Here On My Own" were nominated in the "Best Song" category at the Academy Awards. This marked the first time ever that two songs from the one film were nominated for the same award. The title track "Fame" understandably won the Oscar. It was inevitable that the film's success would spill over to the small screen and in 1982 the "Fame" TV series was launched. Its popularity kept it on the air until 1987. Four of the film's original stars (Debbie Allen, Lee Curreri, Gene Anthony Ray, and Albert Hague) reprised their roles in the TV series.

For viewers, "Fame" leaves a number of imprints on the brain. Most notably, "Fame" (the title, the way it is written, the font or logo is captivating), the catchy title song itself (Irene Cara's voice has never been more powerful), the presentation of the title song in the movie (performed in NY streets and on-top of a car) and of course who can forget Gene Anthony Ray's dynamic dance moves (complete with black sports shorts and leotards). Since "Fame" the music and film industries have moved forward in leaps and bounds. Films such as "Flashdance, "Footloose" and "Dirty Dancing" have all put their own stamp on how music and dance should be put on film. In the new millennium teens are fed a daily diet of over-the-top MTV Music videos and reality TV talent shows are the norm. For today's teens "Fame" may be a little outdated but the film will always stand as one of the groundbreaking movies of the music genre. As for the film's title track, it still sounds as fresh today as it did back in 1980. It is simply timeless.

The Blue Lagoon **

US Release Date: 20th June 1980
Running Time: 104 min
US Classification: R
Director: Randal Kleiser
Starring: Brooke Shields, Christopher Atkins, Leo McKern, William Daniels

Taglines:

* A story of natural love.
* Two children shipwrecked alone on a tropical island. Nature is kind. They thrive on the bounty of jungle and lagoon. The boy grows tall. The girl beautiful. They swim naked over coral reefs. They run in a cathedral of trees. And the warm winds, the tropic moon, the silk sand conspire to enchant them. When their love happens, it is natural as the sea, and as powerful. Love as nature intended to be.

The director of "Grease," Randal Kleiser, brings to the screen a sensual story of natural love.

Two children, shipwrecked alone on a tropical island. Nature is kind. They thrive on the bounty of jungle and lagoon. The boy grows tall. The girl beautiful.

When their love happens, it is as natural as the sea, and as powerful.

Film Review:

Moviemakers and audiences alike have obviously been fascinated with this story. The British were the first to put it on the screen in 1923 as a black and white silent film. In 1949 the British decided to remake the film, this time in colour and with sound. Donald Houston and the beautiful Jean Simmons were cast in the lead roles and many believe that this is the best version of the story. It was inevitable that the film would be updated again. The next time round the American's gave it a shot. In 1980 Director Randal Kleiser, fresh off the success of his hit musical "Grease" took on the task. Casting agents were leaving nothing to chance when they began their search for the perfect young couple to play the shipwrecked teens. Rumour has it Lori Loughlin and Matt Dillion were the original choices for the lead roles but for one reason or another Brooke Shields and Christopher Atkins became the lucky couple that got the gig and as they say… the rest is history.

Brooke Shields came into this film with a reputation as being the prettiest girl in the world. Add to the mix, Christopher Atkins, a handsome young boy in his feature film debut. Put them together on a deserted island with some of the most breathtaking scenery audiences are ever going to see and what do you get, box office gold. For audiences Brooke and Christopher proved to be the idyllic couple. Some parents even took their young teens to cinemas believing that the film might provide a modern-form of sex education. "The Blue Lagoon" was a huge success at the US Box office ranking 9th in its year and bringing in $58,853,106. It seemed audiences loved it but critics weren't so kind and who can blame them, the film is predominately an exploitation flick centering on the sexual awakening of young teens. At least the producers had the sensibility to cover up 15-year-old Brooke and use a body double when required. Roger Ebert from the Chicago Sun-Times called it, "The dumbest movie of the year". Film critic Leonard Maltin stated that even "Nestor Almendros' photography can't save it". Despite the critical panning of the film it still proved popular enough for it to resurface again about 11 years later in the form of a sequel "Return To The Blue Lagoon" (1991). This time round, there was no Brooke Shields and no Christopher Atkins so the film enjoyed very little success. In fact it was nominated for five "Razzie Awards", luckily "Hudson Hawk" came to the rescue that year picking up most of them. Thank you Bruce Willis.

Today, "The Blue Lagoon" is still a cult favourite. Many of its fans believe that the film has been unjustly criticized over the years. Yes, the cast looks great, the scenery is magnificent and its theme of young love is universal but somehow the film doesn't completely work. The performances are ordinary, the story is plodding and the ending is uninspiring. To top it off, Brooke Shields won the "Razzie Award" for the "Worst Actress in a motion picture that year. "The Blue Lagoon" had the potential of being a much better film. Considering its island setting, it all lacks a sense of real adventure and gets bogged down in its own romanticism. Nevertheless, "The Blue Lagoon" still has an innocent charm about it that still resonates with young audiences.

My Bodyguard *** ½

US Release Date: 11th July 1980
Running Time: 102 min
US Classification: PG
Director: Tony Bill
Starring: Chris Makepeace, Adam Baldwin, Matt Dillon, Paul Quandt, Hank Salas, Joan Cusack

Taglines:

* Terrorized in the toilets? Chased after school? Shaken down for your lunch money? Get A Bodyguard!
* Strength has nothing to do with size and together they are unbeatable!

Film Review:

"My Bodyguard" is the ultimate "bully" film. I don't think you will ever see another film like it. It's a "bully" film with heart. Chris Makepeace plays Clifford, the film's central character that comes from a dysfunctional family. He lives in the Ambassador East Hotel with his single father (Martin Mull) and alcoholic grandmother (Ruth Gordon). Clifford's father has just become the new resident manager of the hotel and his greatest pass-time with his son is to stand on their balcony and peak through their telescope on unsuspecting ladies in various states of undress. Now, Clifford is faced with the task of adjusting to life in a new school. He is a mild-mannered, easygoing kid who likes to keep out of trouble but bullying is prevalent at Lake View High so trouble is about to find Clifford. Trouble comes in the form of Melvin Moody, the school bully played with menace by a young Matt Dillon. Dillon's slicked backed Rudolph Valentino hair-do adds to his fear factor. Who wouldn't be frightened of a 1980s teenager sporting a hair-do straight out of the 1940s? Moody and his cronies are in the business of extorting lunch-money from students and they demand daily payments of $1 for protection. Clifford refuses to co-operate with them. School-life soon becomes so painful and unbearable that he is forced to recruit a bodyguard in the form of Ricky Linderman (Adam Baldwin). Linderman is bigger than most of the other teens and comes with a reputation to boot. He has supposedly raped a teacher, punched out a cop and killed his own brother. Everyone is frightened of Linderman including the adults. The truth, however, is that Linderman is really an unhappy young man who has suffered personal tragedy and is now struggling with his own internal conflicts. Yes, "My Bodyguard" does have a few serious overtones.

"My Bodyguard" is at its best in the confrontational scenes between the good guys (Clifford and Linderman) and the bad guys (Moody and Moody's bald-headed bodyguard). The scuffles are well acted, nicely choreographed and keep you on the edge. The friendship that develops between Clifford and Linderman is heart-warming and gives the film its special charm. However, one of the problems with "My Bodyguard" is that it gets too sidetracked with a sub-plot involving the wacky grandmother and her attempts to hook-up with a man. Maybe her inclusion in the film is for comedy relief? Her presence is a nuisance not only to the Hotel patrons but also to the audience. It's all out of place for this movie and just seems like padding to add extra minutes to the running time. The adults in this film are expendable and add very little to the enjoyment of the story, if anything they slow down the pace of the film. The film's quality is derived totally from the talented young cast and their delivery of the well-scripted situations that they are put in. "My Bodyguard" succeeds because it projects a message that people can connect with. Everyone has been to high school and has either been bullied or witnessed someone else getting bullied. For most people there is nothing better than seeing the bully get his comeuppance. The triumph of the underdog is a universal theme that touches everyone and makes you want to stand-up and cheer. "My Bodyguard" is a feel-good film that will make you do just that.

The Idolmaker *** ½

US Release Date: November 1980
Running Time: 117 min
US Classification: PG
Director: Taylor Hackford
Starring: Ray Sharkey, Peter Gallagher, Paul Land, Tovah Feldshuh, Joe Pantoliano.

Taglines:

* He's got the look... He's got the talent... He's got the Idolmaker... He's got it all!
* The gripping drama that lifts the lid off the pop music business!

Film Review:

Have you ever wondered what it would be like to become a pop star? Well, before "American Idol", there was the foot tapping musical "The Idolmaker", a rousing motion picture experience that takes audiences behind the scenes of the 1960s pop music industry. Today, thousands of hopeful young teens flood the audition venues for the reality TV show "American Idol". In the 1960s there was no such show but nevertheless searching for and turning young hopefuls into stars was something that was still happening. Ray Sharkey is electrifying in the role of Vinnie Vaccari, a songwriter-manager who turns two good-looking young teens into Rock "n" Roll mega-stars. Paul Land ("Spring Break") plays Tommy Dee & Peter Gallagher ("Summer Lovers") plays Caesare. Watching Sharkey turn these two nobodies into heartthrobs of the 1960's music world is riveting entertainment.

The film features a dynamic original music score and many standout musical performances. The scenes where Sharkey whips the youngsters into shape are powerful & lively. Gallagher actually sings two songs for the film, "Baby" and "However Dark The Night", while Land does an excellent job of miming his two songs, "Here Is My Love" and "Sweet Little Lover". The vocals for the Land tracks are actually performed by singer Jesse Frederick. Other catchy tunes include "Come And Get It" by Nino Tempo and "Ooo-Wee Baby" by Darlene Love that was used to good effect on the opening credits. Also, Sharkey performs the ballad "I Believe It Can Be Done", in the film's touching finale.

"The Idolmaker" is loosely based on the careers of 1950's pop idols Frankie Avalon & Fabian. The Ray Sharkey role is based on Rock "n" Roll producer Bob Marcucci who not only guided Avalon & Fabian in their careers, but also served as technical advisor on this movie. For authenticity nearly all the sets used were real locations such as concert venues, school halls, cafes and actual New York streets. Ray Sharkey deservedly won the Golden Globe Award for his mesmerizing performance but surprisingly wasn't nominated for the Oscar. Both, Peter Gallagher & Paul Land are amazing to watch as the two Italian street kids who become the teen idols. The producers checked out thousands of young hopefuls before casting their roles & they certainly didn't get it wrong, both Gallagher & Land turned out to be excellent choices. It is also interesting to note that future "Dirty Dancing" star Patrick Swayze auditioned for one of these roles.

"The Idolmaker" is captivating from start to finish; it has good 50's/60's period flavour with a nice 1980's groove. It is a mystery to some as to why it didn't do as well as it should have at the box office. Sadly, it ranked 99th in its year and grossed just $2,625,716 at the US box office, a dismal amount for a film of its quality. Given today's popularity of TV shows such as American Idol, I often wonder that if it was re-released in the cinemas today or re-made for that matter, would it have a bigger appeal? Whatever the answer to that question may be, "The Idolmaker" is still entertainment to the max and the music alone will have you tapping to the beat.

Chapter 2:

TEEN MOVIES OF 1981

Endless Love * ½

US Release Date: 17ᵗʰ July 1981
Running Time: 116 min
US Classification: R
Director: Franco Zeffirelli
Starring: Brooke Shields, Martin Hewitt, Shirley Knight, Don Murray, Richard Kiley, Beatrice Straight, James Spader, Ian Ziering, Tom Cruise

Tagline:
She is 15. He is 17. The love every parent fears.

Film Review:
When Director Franco Zeffirelli took on the task of making "Endless Love" he was no newcomer to romance drama having already directed the critically acclaimed 1968 version of Shakespeare's "Romeo and Juliet". With "Endless Love", Zeffirelli attempted to re-invent the love story for a 1980s audience but sadly this time round his new film proved to be a total misfire. "Endless Love" is based on the popular Scott Spencer romance novel but somehow the translation from page to screen doesn't quite work. In fact the general consensus among film historians is that Zeffirelli's film is a poor adaptation of the book. Roger Ebert from the Chicago Sun-Times describes the film as "a narrative and logical mess". Film critic Leonard Maltin states that the movie is "Rightfully regarded as one of the worst films of its time". Despite all the negative press the film still proved popular with filmgoers around the world, the draw-card of course being Brooke Shields. The film clocked up $31,184,024 at the US box office and ranked 22ⁿᵈ in the yearly box office.

"Endless Love" was a huge step forward for star Martin Hewitt who was selected from thousands of young hopefuls. It became his debut in a feature film with his only previous acting work being an appearance in the TV series "General Hospital". When viewed today Hewitt has an uncanny resemblance to actor Mark Ruffalo ("Just Like Heaven"), a rising talent in the new millennium. "Endless Love" also marked the film debuts of a number of other teen stars including, Tom Cruise ("Risky Business"), James Spader ("Tuff Turf"), Jami Gertz ("The Lost Boys") and Ian Ziering ("Beverly Hills 90210"). All these years later what do people remember of this film? They remember that Brooke Shields was in it, they remember that Tom Cruise made his film debut and of course they remember the title song by Lionel Richie and Diana Ross. The Oscar nominated love sung still stands today as one of the great love songs of all-time. For many years after the film, it was the number one song choice at weddings and today many still like to revisit the song but even this brilliant song couldn't save the film.

"Endless Love" plays out like a teen soap opera gone haywire. The teens fall in love, they are banned from seeing each other, the boyfriend burns down his girlfriend's house, the boyfriend gets put in an asylum, the girl's parents divorce, the boyfriend comes back looking for her and other unsettling events follow. The performances are inconsistent throughout and the story doesn't help as it unfolds in an unsettling and confusing manner. In an early scene we see the hippie mother eavesdropping on the young couple as they make love. She seems to be smiling about the whole thing. A strange scene if ever there was one. The film quickly moves from teen romance to constant scenes of unsettling distress. The boy's love for his girlfriend is so obsessive to the point of being scary for some viewers. It's an exhausting film experience for anyone with heartbreak and tragedy at almost every turn. The overall experience is depressing and there is not a bright moment in the entire film. Nevertheless, "Endless Love" still holds a special place for many, particularly the thousands of young girls who saw it on its original release and got caught up in this emotional roller coaster that goes off the rails. You have been warned, at 116 minutes "Endless Love" feels like "Endless Viewing". Today, it is best viewed with your finger on the fast forward button or if you don't have a remote control get your handkerchiefs ready.

Private Lessons * ½

US Release Date: 28ʰ August 1981
Running Time: 87 min
US Classification: R
Director: Alan Myerson
Starring: Sylvia Kristel, Eric Brown, Howard Hesseman, Patrick Piccininni, Ed Begley Jr., Meridith Baer, Dan Greenburg

Taglines:

* What happened to him should happen to you
* When Emmanuelle's Sylvia Kristel is your teacher, the bedroom is the classroom!

Film Review:

Many believe Porky's was the film that sparked the teen sex comedy craze of the 1980's but in fact "Private Lessons", shot in 1980 and released in 1981 jumped the que before it. This low-budget film costing less than $3 million to produce grossed over $26 million at the US Box Office alone and went on to make even more money worldwide. Dutch actress Sylvia Kristel, whose main claim to fame was the X-Rated adult film, "Emmanuelle" (1974) made the transition to Hollywood films in the late 70s with "Airport '79", "The Nude Bomb" (1980) and of course, "Private Lessons" the teen sexploitation flick which ruffled some feathers at the time and still continues to do

so today. It's controversial subject matter about an older woman seducing a teenage boy was always bound to generate some discussion.

Eric Brown plays Phillip Filmore, a shy, naive, 15-year-old boy whose favourite pastime is to spy on young females in various states of undress. He is often accompanied by his best friend Sherman (Patrick Piccininni) a chubby, know-it-all who serves as his mentor when it comes to advice about the opposite sex. When Philly's dad goes away on "business" he is left at home with the sexy, immigrant housekeeper (Silvia Kristel) and the shady chauffer (Howard Hesseman). The plot thickens when Eric develops a crush on the housemaid who surprisingly reciprocates by showing him more attention than he could ever have imagined. As it turns out the housekeeper and the chauffer are in cahoots with each other in a deadly plot to blackmail the boy and extort money from the family safe.

"Private Lessons" is a male teen fantasy film that lacks substance in the script department. Screenwriter Dan Greenburg who adapted the story from his own novel "Philly", even finds time to appear in the film briefly as a hotel desk clerk. The storyline is definitely flimsy and mainly serves as an excuse to show Kristel and the boy in intimate situations. What it lacks in production values, it certainly makes up for, with its use of popular soundtracks of the era. "I Need A Lover" by John Mellancamp, "Hot Legs" and "Tonight's The Night" by Rod Stewart and "Lost In Love" by Air Supply were used to great effect and help the film move along when not much is going on.

The performances in the film range from poor to mediocre at best; Ron Foster as Eric's father, Howard Hesseman as the unscrupulous chauffeur and Ed Begley Jr as the tennis instructor are all upstaged by the performances of the two teenage boys, Brown and Piccininni. Brown does well considering his age and the nature of the risqué material. Piccininni is the comedy relief of the film. He overacts at times but he nevertheless has some of the film's best lines and is on occasion hilarious. In a film riddled with questionable subject matter, Kristel does exactly what she was hired to do and her seduction of Brown is sweet to say the least. Other 80s teen films such as "My Tutor" (1983) and "Risky Business" (1983) adopted a similar theme but the young actors Matt Lattanzi and Tom Cruise were in their early 20s at the time. The star of "Private Lessons", Eric Brown was born in 1964 and was obviously about the same age as the character he portrayed in the movie. In a sense the experience for him must have been borderline reality. It is for this reason that the film can be unsettling to some viewers. "Private Lessons" is certainly a unique teen film that deserves its place in this book even if not for all the right reasons.

Taps ** ½

US Release Date: 9th December 1981
Running Time: 126 min
US Classification: PG
Director: Harold Becker
Starring: Timothy Hutton, Sean Penn, Tom Cruise, George C. Scott, Ronny Cox

Tagline:

This school is our home, we think it's worth defending.

Film Review:

George C. Scott, the Academy Award winning star of "Patton" and Timothy

Hutton the Academy Award winning star of "Ordinary People" headline this cast of young actors that include Tom Cruise and Sean Penn. George C. Scott plays General Harlan Bache, commander of Bunker Hill Military Academy, an institution that has a history dating back nearly 150-years. When it is announced that the Academy is going to be turned into a condominium complex, tensions rise and when a freak accident occurs involving General Bache, situations reach boiling point as the students take up arms against the authorities. Timothy Hutton plays Cadet Major Brian Moreland who leads the revolt with cadets Cruise and Penn by his side. Hutton's intense performance is outstanding and he was rewarded with a "Golden Globe" nomination for Best Actor. For both Tom Cruise and Sean Penn, Taps marked their first major appearances in a big screen feature film. Cruise had previously been seen briefly in "Endless Love" while Penn had previously worked off-Broadway and on TV. Both Cruise and Penn are solid in support with Cruise especially memorable as the gun-happy, loose cannon, pushed to breaking point in the films nail-biting and blazing finale. The real-life Valley Forge Military Academy became the stand-in for Bunker Hill Academy. Most of the cast spent a considerable amount of time at the facility during the pre-production period, undergoing some real training to acclimatise themselves with their roles. The end result shows with convincing performances from all concerned.

"TAPS" is a thought-provoking military drama that shifts gears constantly. Unfortunately, the pacing is inconsistent and the film suffers from an uneven tone, ranging from engaging situations with sudden bursts of energy, to long-stretches of plodding dialogue. Maybe at 126 minutes the film could have benefited from a swifter edit that would have given it a better overall balance. Ultimately, the film serves as a showcase for Oscar winner Timothy Hutton and a platform for promising new stars Tom Cruise and Sean Penn to strut their stuff in military garb. "TAPS" was a surprise hit at the US box office bringing in a neat $35,856,053 and clocking in at 16th in the yearly box office ranking. All these things aside "TAPS" is a compelling, well-produced, well-acted human drama highlighting the consequences of military discipline and ideals pushed to the edge and beyond.

Chapter 3:

TEEN MOVIES OF 1982

*Porky's *** ½*

US Release Date: 19ᵗʰ March 1982
Running Time: 94 min
US Classification: R
Director: Bob Cark
Starring: Dan Monahan, Mark Herrier, Wyatt Knight, Roger Wilson, Cyril O'Reilly, Tony Ganios, Chuck Mitchell, Kaki Hunter, Kim Cattrall, Nancy Parsons, Scott Colomby, Boyd Gaines, Doug McGrath, Susan Clark, Art Hindle, Wayne Maunder, Alex Karras, Eric Christmas, Bill Hindman, John Henry Redwood, Jack Mulcahy, Rod Ball, Pat Lee, Ilse Earl.

Taglines:

* The raunchiest movie about growing up ever made!
* Keep an eye open for it!
* One Fun Place, One Hip Movie!
* Keep an eye out for the funniest movie about growing up ever made!
* You'll be glad you came!

Film Review:

The original "Porky's" (1982) is the raunchy teen sex comedy that became the sleeper hit of its year. The two most successful teen comedies prior to "Porky's" were "American Graffiti" (1973) & "National Lampoon's Animal House" (1978), although the latter is often referred to as a college comedy rather than a teen comedy. All three films had a common denominator, they were set in a previous era ("Porky's" 1950's, "Graffiti" 1960's, "Animal House" 1960's) and featured an abundance of music, juvenile humour and sex-related gags, however, "Porky's" pushed these gags one-step further and set itself apart from the other two. The film came out of nowhere and established a new standard of raunchiness for a teen movie. Up to this point the term "Teen Sex Comedy" had not been widely used, but after "Porky's" the phrase became a common descriptor in movie vernacular. "Porky's" became a yardstick by which all other "Teen Sex Comedies" are measured. Filmmakers continued to use the same formula freely throughout the 1980's in lesser films such as "Screwballs" (1983), "Hardbodies" (1984) and "Fraternity Vacation" (1985) but none of these imitations reached the same level of success as "Porky's", until "American Pie" took the formula to another level again in 1999.

"Porky's" was a low budget (US $4 million), Canadian, teen-exploitation flick that was set and shot in Southern Florida in only 2 months. The time; 1954, the place; Angel Beach High School, the characters; six frustrated teenage boys, the plot; puberty, girls, sex and an Everglades strip joint called "Porky's". When the film was released in US cinemas in March 1982 it surprised everybody, especially critics, when it went on to gross over $105 million in the US alone. Why was it so successful? The movie is nostalgic; it tells a simple tale, is well paced and jam-packed with hysterical situations. Who can forget; the peep-show shower scene, the inflated condom, the school teacher with the lassie howl, the boys' initiation & humiliation at Porky's after being relieved of their money & then thrown into the murky croc-infested waters of the Florida Everglades and of course the sweet revenge as the boys take on Porky and destroy his waterfront brothel.

"Porky's" features a relatively unknown cast. The six highly charged teens in the film, or "The Dirty Half Dozen" as they are sometimes referred to are, Pee Wee (Dan Monahan), Tommy (Wyatt Knight), Meat (Tony Ganios), Mickey (Roger Wilson), Brian (Scott Colomby) & Tim (Cyril O'Reilly). Surprisingly, none of these young actors went on to become known for anything else other than their connection to the "Porky's" trilogy. The same can be said about Chuck "Porky" Mitchell, the redneck owner of the bordello of ill repute and Nancy "Miss Balbricker" Parsons, the behemoth gym teacher who is the brunt of many of the practical jokes. The only person from the cast to go on and achieve further fame was Kim Cattrall (Miss Honeywell) who would later go on to star in films such as "Police Academy" (1984), "Big Trouble In Little China" (1986) & "Mannequin" (1987) before winning critical acclaim and a Golden Globe Award for her work on the TV series "Sex And The City". When Porky's was first released the only familiar face was veteran actress Susan Clark, who was best remembered by cinema-goers for her work in films such as "Madigan"(1968) with Richard Widmark, "Coogan's Bluff" (1968) with Clint Eastwood, "Valdez Is Coming" with Burt Lancaster (1971) & "Skin Game" (1971) with James Garner. Although brief, Susan's role as hooker "Cherry Forever", who lines up the young boys in the cast for a preliminary inspection, is memorable to say the least. The boy's have turned up at Cherry's house expecting a good-time but as it turns out the boy's are victims of a prank and are forced to evacuate the house in a frenzy, dressed in nothing but their birthday suits. Comic relief, Pee Wee, is later picked up on the highway by police and asked to show his license. Also of note is the appearance of Susan Clark's husband, former football player, Alex Karras (Mongo from Blazing Saddles 1974) as Porky's ruthless brother, Sheriff Wallace.

Writer/Director Bob Clark who was a teenager during the 1950's already had a few mediocre successes to his credit including, "Breaking Point" (1976), "Murder By Decree" (1979) & "Tribute" (1980) before he struck box office gold with this nostalgic trip back to the pre-Elvis 1950's. Some of the scenes depicted in "Porky's" are supposedly a reflection of Clark's own youth. Amongst all the hi-jinks and mayhem the film contains some serious dramatic overtones, particularly those scenes involving anti-Semitic themes with the character of Tim. Tim's racist attitude is obviously the result of his upbringing by his overly abusive father, a subplot that is introduced & finally resolved in a tussle at the school dance. Although "Porky's" contains only a few brief moments of real drama, it's enough to give the film an added realism & quality. The drama, however, is always overshadowed by the comedic set pieces and practical jokes involving the boys.

It was inevitable that "Porky's" would spawn sequels, "Porky's II: The Next Day" (1983) and "Porky's Revenge" (1985) were churned out in quick succession, two years apart. The sequels, although not as successful as the original, still managed to satisfy most moviegoers and were certainly fun films for fans. What "Porky's II" lacked was the absence of Chuck "Porky" Mitchell, the cigar chomping fat-man with the cowboy hat and bad attitude. Chuck's large-than-life presence in the first film lifted it above the norm. In "Porky's II" the gang decides to stage "An Evening With Shakespeare" at their high school. When gym teacher, Miss Balbricker (Nancy Parsons, reprising her role from the original) views their stage play as obscene the boys get up to the usual hilarious hi-jinks which includes a snake in Miss Balbricker's toilet. The third installment of the trilogy, "Porky's Revenge" is considered by fans to be better than the second. It sees the return of Porky and the continuation of the conflict between Porky and the boys. After the demolition of Porky's nightclub, by the boys in the first film, Porky is back with a bigger and better set up, this time a lavish clubhouse on a river boat. For "Porky's Revenge", veteran TV director James Komack (Welcome Back Kotter, Get Smart, My Favourite Martian) took over direction from Bob

Clark (who directed the first two) and does an excellent job in generating laughs and maintaining the essence that made the original film so popular.

Although "Porky's" has offended some viewers because of its rude & crude tone, nudity included, it is often dismissed as a light-hearted "coming of age" tale of young boys learning about their ever-growing libidos as they approach manhood. It is interesting to note that when the "American Film Institute" was choosing its "100 Funniest US Comedies", "Porky's" failed to make the list. As a result, the American public conducted their-own poll to find out which film was the best comedy and yes, you guessed it, "Porky's" topped the list. Videos and DVD's have ensured the film's longevity and the flick seems to get re-discovered with each generation. Maybe it's because of the "infamous shower-scene"....every young boy's fantasy. Whatever the case, "Porky's" has certainly lasted the test of time and there has even been talk of a remake in the new millennium.

Paradise **

US Release Date: 7th May 1982
Running Time: 100 min
US Classification: R
Director: Stuart Gillard
Starring: Willie Aames, Phoebe Cates, Tuvia Tavi, Richard Curnock, Neil Vipond, Aviva Marks, Joseph Shiloach, Shoshana Duer, Jerry Rosen, Riki Halfon

Taglines:

* A World Where A Boy And A Girl Discover The Most Intimate Secret Of All.
* If Only It Could Have Been Forever...
* No Two People Have Ever Come So Close...
* Exotic Locations
* Exciting Action and Lyrical Love Scenes

Film Review:

"Paradise" is not your typical teen movie, there are no schools, no students, no teachers and no end of year prom, but the film does feature a sensual romance between two attractive teenagers. Instead of the usual high school settings we are treated to some beautifully filmed scenery on breath-taking Middle East locations. Willie Aames ("Charles in Charge" and "Zapped") and Phoebe Cates ("Private School" and "Gremlins") star as the two teenagers who embark on a journey from Baghdad to Damascus in the early 1800's. On their trek a ruthless Sheik and his band of warriors attack them. Everybody in their caravan is killed except the two youngsters who make their escape to a magnificent oasis, a place they can only call "Paradise". Here, they discover a new world of exquisite natural beauty including majestic beaches, rocky caverns and stunning waterfalls. They even find a couple of comedic sidekicks in the form of pet chimps to keep them company, but most of all the two teens are awakened to the love they have for each other. The two lovers overcome every obstacle that stands in their way, most notably the chase through the desert by "The Jackal" and his Arab slave traders. Yes, their story of survival and young love is far-fetched to say the least but what the film lacks in believability it makes up for with its stunning cinematography and of course the beautiful Phoebe Cates.

For Phoebe Cates, "Paradise" was her big break. It was not only her first feature film appearance but also her first starring role all rolled into one. On the other hand, Willie Aames was no newcomer to acting having already spent 10 years as a child star in various TV productions. Even so, the critics weren't so kind to his performance, nominating him for "Worst Actor" at the "Razzie Awards". Strangely enough, legendary actor Laurence Olivier piped Aames at the post for his work in the war drama "Inchon". Those "Razzie Awards" sure make you wonder sometimes? At least Aames can rest knowing that he was beaten by one of cinema's all-time greats. "Paradise" plays out like a teen version of "Tarzan and Jane" with the two leads looking great in their loincloths. The underwater photography is outstanding and the nude scenes are tastefully done. "Paradise" was made on a budget of $3.5 million and grossed $5.6 million in the US, not bad box office for an alternate version of the more famous Brooke Shields romance "The Blue Lagoon". "Paradise" is in fact, "The Blue Lagoon" with action and adventure but more importantly it is "The Blue Lagoon" with a happy ending. Thus, "Paradise" has taken two of the negative elements of "The Blue Lagoon" and turned them into positives. Like, Brooke Shields in its predecessor Phoebe Cates is the main draw-card in this one, particularly for teenage boys. Exotic locations, exciting action sequences and the film's sense of innocence are the other ingredients that make "Paradise", a romantic adventure tale that should satisfy most teen audiences.

Zapped! **

US Release Date: 23rd July 1982
Running Time: 98 min
US Classification: R
Director: Robert J. Rosenthal
Starring: Scott Baio, Willie Aames, Heather Thomas, Scatman Crothers

Taglines:

* The comedy that won't let you down!
* They're getting a little behind in their classwork

Film Review:

If you like "teenager gains superpowers" flicks, then "Zapped!" is the film for you. It is the 1980s answer to the popular Dexter Reilly Disney films that included, "The Computer Wore Tennis Shoes" (1969), "Now You See Him, Now You Don't (1972) and "The Strongest Man In The World" (1975). These films all had a common denominator, they were all teen fantasies, they all starred Kurt Russell and they were all family friendly. The difference with "Zapped!" is it's raunchier and it's not so family friendly. Scott Baio, Chachi from the "Happy Days" television series stars in this teen comedy that combines visual gags with boyhood fantasies. This time round Baio shakes off his cool TV image to play a teen science nerd called Barney Springboro. Barney spends most of his spare time working in the school chemistry lab and one day accidentally creates a substance that gives him telekinetic superpowers. This leads to Barney and his friends using this newfound ability to pop undone girls blouses and create general havoc wherever they go. Barney's friend, Peyton, is played by Willie Aames, who a few years later went on to star with Baio in the long running hit television series "Charles in Charge". The female cast in "Zapped" feature mainly in support roles and serve as window dressing for the boys to play their pranks on. Of note is Heather Thomas who plays Jane Mitchell, the hot chick at the school. In 1982, US Magazine readers voted Thomas as the "Favourite Female Newcomer" of the year. To date "Zapped!" still stands as her most memorable film role.

When you think of the teen movie "Zapped!" film awards don't exactly jump out at you but surprisingly "Zapped!" was nominated for "Best Fantasy Film" at the "Academy of Science Fiction, Fantasy and Horror

Films". It missed out to Jim Henson's "The Dark Crystal". No surprises there right? But on a different note Willie Aames was nominated for "Worst Actor" at the "Razzie Awards" for this film and also for "Paradise" (as stated in an earlier review). A double nomination in the one-year for Aames, wow, but when Laurence Olivier beats you, losing isn't so bad. "Zapped!" generated enough audience interest and box office revenue ($16.8 million) to spawn an inferior sequel "Zapped Again" (1990), this time, minus Baio and Aames. "Zapped!" may be strictly formula, standard 80's teen farce but it has a telekinetic wackiness that is enough to hook teenage boys and have them watching it repeatedly. Scott Baio's pin-up-boy status also helped the film win female fans. Baio has what it takes to be a big screen movie star and in "Zapped!" he does his best with the material on offer. The script and the special effects may be a bit cheesy by today's standards but nevertheless they did the job at the time. The film's tagline says it all "A comedy that won't let you down!" and for teen audiences of its day, "Zapped!" delivered exactly what it set out to do.

Tex *** ½

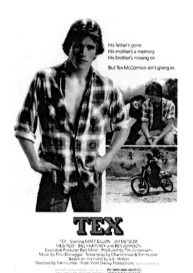

US Release Date: 30th July 1982
Running Time: 103 min
US Classification: PG
Director: Tim Hunter
Starring: Matt Dillon, Emilio Estevez, Meg Tilly, Jim Metzler, Ben Johnson

Tagline:

His father's gone. His mother's a memory. His brother's moving on. Tex McCormick isn't giving in.

Film Review:

"Tex" is a compelling coming-of-age tale set to the backdrop of small-town America. It marked Disney's contribution to the teen movie craze that was emerging steadily in the early 80s. With "Tex", Disney took their traditional family entertainment one step further by tackling some real teen issues. Sex, drugs and violence, the usual elements of teen films are all present here, only this time in rural Oklahoma. This thought provoking drama is as a window into the lives of two teenage brothers living alone without parental supervision. Their mother has passed away and their father spends most of the year on the rodeo circuit. For 15 year-old Tex (Matt Dillon), school is not very important and his main interests are his horse and his friends (Emilio Estevez and Meg Tilly). His older brother Mason wants to apply for a college basketball scholarship but this would see him leave home and would interfere with his responsibility of looking after Tex.

Growing up isn't easy for these two boys. On their way back from Tulsa, Tex and Mason pick up a hitchhiker who subsequently pulls a gun on them. In no time at all they are involved in a police chase that sees their vehicle veer off the road and into a ditch. Moments later bullets fly as the police gun-down the escapee. The boys survive the ordeal but the innocence and naivety of their TV interview that follows is a hoot. Dillon explains to the reporters that hitchhiker's aren't all bad, "I do it myself sometimes" he says.

By 1982, with "Little Darlings" and "My Bodyguard" under his belt, Matt Dillon was already hot property in Hollywood. When Disney signed him up for "Tex" they knew they had a star in the making. Dillon is perfectly cast in the title role and is a real natural as the young cowboy who discovers that life is full of unexpected twists and turns. "Tex", based on the best-selling novel by S.E. Hinton, became the first of Hinton's books adapted for the screen. Hinton, who also appears briefly as a teacher, was responsible for the teen angst classics "The Outsiders" and "Rumble Fish" with both film versions featuring Dillon. Tex was nominated for "Best Family Film" at the "Young Artist Awards" but was beaten to the punch by Stallone's "Rocky III". Matt Dillon also received a nomination for "Best Young Actor" but lost out to E.T.'s Henry Thomas. It is interesting to note that Jim Metzler who played Tex's older brother Mason, was born in 1951 and would have been around 30 years old when he played the 19 year-old teenager. Nevertheless he did a convincing job and was in fact nominated for "Best Supporting Actor" at the "Golden Globe Awards" but was beaten by Louis Gossett Jr. for "An Officer & a Gentleman".

The film, just like life, moves at a leisurely pace one minute and then suddenly shifts gears without warning. In the space of a few minutes Tex goes from being reprimanded at school from putting caps in his teacher's typewriter, to being offered a job at a horse ranch, to discovering that his father is not his "real" father, to joining his friend on a drug deal that goes wrong, to finding himself involved in a scuffle that has nothing to do with him, to getting himself shot and subsequently winding up in hospital fighting for his life. Life wasn't meant to be easy and it isn't for the characters in "Tex". How would you feel if your older brother sold your horse, the best friend you ever had, without telling you, just to scrape together a few bucks to put food on the table? That's right, you wouldn't be too happy about it, especially if your favourite book was "Smokey The Cow Horse". Well that's Tex. He's not happy about it, but he knows he has to accept it and move on. "Tex" is a fascinating character study of two teenage brothers, a superb drama that grabs you and never lets you go, the characters are so real that you can't help but feel for them. "Tex" is a film that has something to offer for everyone.

The Last American Virgin *** ½

US Release Date: 6th August 1982
Running Time: 92 min
US Classification: R
Director: Boaz Davidson
Starring: Lawrence Monoson, Diane Franklin, Steve Antin, Joe Rubbo, Louisa Moritz, Brian Peck, Kimmy Robertson, Tessa Richarde, Winifred Freedman, Gerri Idol, Sandy Sprung, Paul Keith, Phil Rubenstein, Roberto Rodriquez, Blanche Rubin, Michael Chieffo, Leslie Simms, Harry Bugin, Julianna McCarthy.

Taglines:

* A Very Funny Movie About The Very First Time!
* The Comedy That Puts Zip Into Being A Teen...
* See It Or Be It!
* There's Only One Thing Left To Lose.

Film Review:

In 1982 "Lemon Popsicle" came to Hollywood in the form of "The Last American Virgin". Four years earlier "The Last American Virgin's" Writer/Director, Boaz Davidson, hit the big-time when he unleashed the "Popsicle Boys" to an unsuspecting Israeli audience. The original "Lemon Popsicle" (1978), known in Israel as "Eskimo Limon", was also written and directed by Boaz. The film is set in 1950's Israel and focuses on the exploits of 3 teenage boys, Bobby, Benji & Huey. Bobby (Jonathan Segall) is the ladies man, Benji (Yftach Katzur) is the sensitive shy boy and Huey (Zachi Noy) is the mischievous fat boy who is the brunt of most of the films jokes. The film's superficial plot was secondary to the hilarious situations and the dynamic 50's & 60's Rock "n" Roll soundtrack that played in the background like an out of control jukebox. "Lemon Popsicle" hit a chord with Israeli audiences and the film was so popular that the "Popsicle Craze" spread to Europe, America and later the rest of the world. The film proved it wasn't just a flash-in-the pan, a one hit wonder, or a two-bit commercial success; it was also critically acclaimed. At the Berlin International Film Festival "Lemon Popsicle" was nominated for "The Golden Berlin Bear" and later at The Golden Globe Awards in the USA it was nominated for "The Best Foreign Film".

"Lemon Popsicle" had become big business and it was inevitable that numerous sequels would follow. The sequels played to packed houses in European cinemas and carried the popularity of the "Popsicle Boys" well into the 1980's. With the introduction of video, the films were able to reach an even greater audience and with the tapes flying off the rental shelves nearly everyone in the world now had the opportunity to experience the madness. With "Lemon Popsicle Fever" booming it was only a matter of time before Boaz would take his successful formula to Hollywood. In 1982 he remade "Lemon Popsicle" for American audiences and called it "The Last American Virgin". The film had a new look, a new sound, a new young cast of talented performers and most importantly it was successful in retaining the qualities and essence that made the original "Lemon Popsicle" a worldwide hit.

Like "Lemon Popsicle" before it, Cannon's Menahem Golan and Yoram Globus produced "The Last American Virgin". The main difference between the two films is that "Virgin" was made in the 1980's and set in the 1980's, whilst "Popsicle" was made in the late 1970's and set in the 1950's. Character parallels between the two films are evident. Lawrence Monoson (Gary) is the equivalent of Popsicle's Yftach Katzur (Benji); Steve Antin (Rick) is the equivalent of Popsicle's Jonathan Sagall (Bobby) while Joe Rubbo (David) is the equivalent of Popsicle's Zachi Noy (Huey). Both films feature an excellent selection of pulsating soundtracks of their eras. "The Last American Virgin" contains music by a number of popular 1980's artists including, Blondie, The Cars, The Commodores, Devo, Quincy Jones, Journey, The Police, Reo Speedwagon, Tommy Tutone and U2. Although not a huge success on its initial release ($5.8 million at the US box office), "The Last American Virgin" has nevertheless developed its own cult status worldwide.

"The Last American Virgin" begins with a long shot of the Hollywood sign and then quickly cuts to the central character, Gary, to reveal his line of work, pizza delivery boy for "The Pink Pizza" restaurant. As Gary drives off in his pizza mobile, a pink station wagon, complete with life-size model of an Italian chef on the roof, the credits begin to roll to the sound of Tommy Tutone's "Teen Angel Eyes". In a nice transition from day to night we next see Gary pull up in his pizza mobile at the local burger joint. As he walks in the diner he immediately catches sight of Karen. He doesn't say a word to her, he just stands there, mesmerized, in a semi-trance like state; Karen is his dream girl and he simply can't take his eyes off her. She orders some rocky road ice cream, while he continues to stare at her until she walks out of the shop. It is love at first-sight for Gary. He is infatuated with Karen. The emotional content of the story is beautifully set up with Gary firmly established as the sensitive nice guy and focal point of the film with Karen as his love interest.

Whilst still at the diner we are introduced to Gary's two-friends, the ladies man (Rick) and the fat guy (David). As the three boys begin to talk, their discussion quickly turns to the opposite sex and it soon becomes evident that the three teens have only one thing on their mind, losing their virginity. The tone for the early phase of the film is now set and it is not long before the hilarious sex-capades begin. Some of the film's notable moments include, the awkward party at Gary's house, the locker room measuring contest, the Hispanic nymphomaniac, the unhappy hooker, drowning their crabs at the pool and the subsequent purchasing of crabs medicine at the chemist. However, the key to the "The Last American Virgin's" popularity and longevity is not simply the lowbrow humour, it is the tender, heart-felt, story that looks closely at many real issues like, first love, first kiss, friendship, loyalty, teen pregnancy, responsibility, heartbreak and of course, growing up.

Unfortunately, right up until 2003, "The Last American Virgin" was not an easy film to get your hands on. It had never been re-released on video since its video rental debut, which took place not long after its cinema release in the early 1980's. Any copies that were available for purchase were usually old ex-rentals, many of which sold on Internet auction sites such as Ebay for prices in excess of US$80. We were fortunate enough to get our VHS copy at a video store's closing down sale. It was an old, well-worn tape with fading picture colour and deteriorating sound, but it was a valued addition to our video collection. Fortunately for fans, on August 5th 2003, MGM released this classic teen flick on DVD. It now comes complete with, original theatrical trailer, a clean, crisp, wide-screen transfer and a new case cover. Gone is the vintage artwork featuring the giant zipper with Gary and

Karen in a romantic cuddle and in its place we see the three boys in a swimming pool purveying on an unsuspecting girl. The bikini-glad girl with the curvaceous body is featured in the foreground and she is definitely not Karen. This sexy new cover suggests a marketing strategy aimed at teens of the new millennium.

"The Last American Virgin" may start off as your typical 1980's teen sex comedy with all the usual gags and hi-jinks but it slowly turns into a compelling emotional drama with an unforgettable surprise ending. The film succeeds on many levels, outstanding direction, convincing natural performances, realistic locations, and a soundtrack that beautifully compliments the time period and emotional content of the story. Teen's that saw "The Last American Virgin" on its original release in 1982 have never forgotten it and teens of today, that are fortunate enough to see it, can't help but join the growing fan base, the world over. "The Last American Virgin" is an excellent film with a powerful, emotionally charged ending. The story is a magnificent blend of comedy and drama that depicts teens and their problems in a realistic and sensitive way. The film has touched hearts and played an important part in the lives of many people. When the closing credits start to role and Gary drives off in his pizza mobile, the party is over for Gary and a new chapter in his life is about to begin. The ending has been known to bring a tear to many an eye. Today, "The Last American Virgin" remains one of the most insightful films about growing up ever made. It may not be a masterpiece of modern cinema but it is without doubt a true 1980's teen classic!

Fast Times At Ridgemont High ****

US Release Date: 13th August 1982
Running Time: 90 min
US Classification: R
Director: Amy Heckerling
Starring: Sean Penn, Jennifer Jason Leigh, Judge Reinhold, Robert Romanus, Brian Backer, Phoebe Cates, Ray Walston, Scott Thomson, Vincent Schiavelli, Amanda Wyss, D.W. Brown, Forest Whitaker, Zoe Kelli Simon, Tom Nolan.

Taglines:

* It's Awesome! Totally Awesome!
* At Ridgemont High Only the Rules get Busted!

Film Review:

In 1979, 22-year-old "Rolling Stone" magazine writer Cameron Crowe enrolled in a Californian High School with the intention of observing and writing about the activities of teenagers. After spending a year, undercover, as a high school senior, he was able to use his research to complete his book, "Fast Times At Ridgemont High – A True Story". Although the names of the students were changed, the incidents were true. Crowe later turned his eye-opening book into a screenplay that was sold to Universal and made into a feature film. "Fast Times At Ridgemont High" was released in cinemas one week after "The Last American Virgin". While "Virgin" struggled to scrape in a basic $5.8 million, "Fast Times" turned out to be a minor hit, bringing in over $27 million at the US box office.

Shot in less than two months, on a relatively small budget ($4.5 million), "Fast Times" boasted a flashy young cast, which included, Sean Penn, Jennifer Jason Leigh, Phoebe Cates, Judge Reinhold and veteran actor Ray Walston, as History teacher Mr. Hand. All is revealed in this realistic look into teenage life in a typical American High School. It's all there, first dates, virginity, sex, drugs, teen pregnancy, abortion and after-school-jobs. However, "Fast Times", was not released without its share of problems. The initial cut of the film was given an X rating due to its subject matter and some explicit sex scenes. Having a film about teens and making it available only to an adult audience was not a good idea. Some cuts had to be made to ensure a mainstream cinema release. Even the final cinema print of the film is often edited when shown on television.

"Fast Times" was shot predominately in real locations in and around Los Angeles. The multi-level "Sherman Oaks Galleria" shopping mall, with trendy see-thru lifts, was renamed "Ridgemont Mall" and served as the main backdrop for the film's characters. Shooting took place at night and finished before the mall opened in the morning. For exterior shots "Santa Monica Mall" was used. Two High Schools, Van Nuys High School and Conoga Park High School substituted for "Ridgemont High" and some of the school scenes were shot in real school time with real students as extras in the background. When the opening credits start to roll over scenes of the Galleria mall, complete with back to school banners, we begin to meet all the lead characters in their respective haunts (fast food hangouts, movie theatres and video game parlors), all set to the backdrop of the thumping soundtrack, "We Got The Beat" by The Go-Gos. Stacy (Jennifer Jason Leigh) and Linda (Phoebe Cates) work at Perry's Pizza, Mark (Brian Backer) is an usher at the cinema, Damone (Robert Romanus) is a ticket scalper, Brad (Judge Reinhold) flips burgers at the "All-American-Burger" joint while

Spicoli (Sean Penn) and his surfer buddies (Eric Stoltz and Anthony Edwards) hangout anywhere and everywhere.

"Fast Times" is an in-depth study of teens and their relationships with each other. The multiplicity of characters, played by the ensemble cast, all share the screen-time. All the characters ring true and are as real as real can be, right through, from the students to the teachers. Stacy is the central character around which the heavy drama revolves. Her life moves quickly, from losing her virginity to pregnancy and finally to an abortion. Her brother Brad is the after-school worker who goes from one fast food chain to the next. Stacy's best friend Linda is the worldly girl who knows it all and has done it all. Damone is the cool-dude conman who has advice for everybody and thinks he knows it all, but when real problems arise he has difficulty facing responsibility. Mark is the sensitive; insecure, shy-type who has trouble making it with the girl even when she makes the first move. Although having no more screen-time than any of the others, Sean Penn's Spicoli manages to emerge as the face of the film. His zonked-out surfer-dude character is there for one thing and that is for comedy relief. His classroom scenes with history teacher Walston, who believes everyone is on dope, are a standout. Who can forget their first meeting when Penn arrives late for class or the pizza delivery scene when Walston offers the pizza to the other students and then proceeds to take a slice for himself? And what about the scene when Penn answers Walston with the words, "I Don't Know", in which Walston then scribbles the words on the blackboard to humiliate him? The film is riddled with comedic moments; Reinhold's confrontation with the disgruntled breakfast customer, Damone's advice to Mark on girls, Mark and Stacy's first date at the restaurant, Spicoli's surf dream and of course Spicoli's destruction of the school jock's vehicle.

For New Yorker Amy Heckerling, "Fast Times At Ridgemont High" was to be her directorial debut and a springboard for other movie projects such as "Johnny Dangerously" (1984), "European Vacation" (1985) and "Look Who's Talking" (1989). In 1986 Amy returned to "Ridgemont High" to produce the short-lived, spin-off, TV series called "Fast Times", while writer Cameron Crowe served as creative consultant. The only original cast members returning to reprise their big screen roles were teachers, Ray Walston and Vincent Schiavelli. Thirteen-years after "Fast Times At Ridgemont High" Amy would go on to write and direct another teen classic, the Alicia Silverstone high school comedy, "Clueless" (1995). Also, making his feature film debut in "Fast Times At Ridgemont High", is Oscar winner Nicolas Cage, who is billed in the credits as Nicolas Coppola. He appears throughout the film in a number of "blink-and-you'll-miss-him" scenes. Two that come to mind are, as a spectator in the crowd at the football game and as one of the short-order cooks at the hamburger restaurant. It is also interesting to note that Nick was one of the original choices for the Judge Reinhold role but at only 17 years of age was considered maybe a little bit too young.

All teens have to grow up at some point in their lives. For some it happens gradually, they're the lucky ones. For others, growing up is forced upon them quickly. Some cope, some don't. Just like the title "Fast Times" suggests, the film is fast-paced and so are the lives of these teenagers. "Fast Times" was an honest representation of 1980's high school life but even today the film seems to hold up remarkably well. Fashions and music change with the times but teenage behavior and in particular human emotions stay the same. With a talented cast playing an assortment of memorable characters that most people can identify with, "Fast Times At Ridgemont High" remains an honest attempt, to tell it how it was, or maybe how it is.

Class of 1984 ** ½

US Release Date: 20th August 1982
Running Time: 98 min
US Classification: R
Director: Mark L. Lester
Starring: Perry King, Merrie Lynn Ross, Timothy Van Patten, Roddy McDowall, Stefan Arngrim, Michael J. Fox, Keith Knight, Lisa Langlois, Neil Clifford, Al Waxman, Erin Flannery.

Taglines:

* We are the future!... and nothing can stop us.
* The teachers at Lincoln High have a very dangerous problem... their students!

Film Review:

1982's "Class Of 1984" is "Blackboard Jungle (1955) taken to an extreme and then some. It could be even described as "Death Wish In A High School", as the teacher is pushed over the edge to the point of becoming a vigilante. This low-budget Canadian production, made 2 years ahead of its title time, is possibly the most violent classroom film ever made. Set in Abraham Lincoln High School, this gripping teen thriller is a brutal portrayal of a vicious gang of juvenile delinquents who will stop at nothing short of murder in their savage victimization of their music teacher Andrew Norris, played effectively by Perry King ("The Lord's Of Flatbush"). The schoolyard cronies are led by the crazy Peter Stegman (Timothy Van Patten) and will do anything and everything to protect their turf and their drug dealing business. For most of the terror stricken teachers at the high school survival has become the key issue. Discipline and actual teaching have had to take a back seat due to the teenage psychotics. Look out for a young Michael J. Fox in one of his first feature film roles as a victim of the school bullies. Unfortunately, Fox doesn't get out of this one unscathed and in the credit sequence he is even missing the famous "J" from his name.

"Class Of 1984" is a bleak look at what schools of the future might be like and the cheesy Alice Cooper title track, "I Am The Future", highlighted this perception. Although, only set two years into the future, it seemed to be pointing much further. The film is riddled with violent exchanges among students and teachers both in and out of the school environment and makes one feel a real concern about where things are headed in society. Apart from the Andrew Norris character, the only other teacher that tries to make a stand against the hoods is Terry Corrigan, an alcoholic biology teacher, played with conviction by veteran actor Roddy McDowell. In one of the film's many chilling scenes, an unhinged Corrigan takes a gun to school, points it at his students and tells them to pay attention and learn or else pay with your life. This depiction of a teacher driven to the ultimate is disturbing to say the least but in the context of the film, it may have been a simple warning sign of things to come.

At the "Academy Of Science Fiction and Horror films", "Class Of 1984" was nominated in two categories, "Best International Film" and "Best Supporting Actor", Roddy McDowall. Mel Gibson's "Mad Max 2" won "Best International Film" that year, while Richard Lynch for "The Sword And The Sorcerer" beat Roddy McDowall. "Class Of 1984" director Mark L. Lester, famous for action flicks such as "Commando" (1985) & "Showdown In Little Tokyo" (1991) later went on to make "Class Of 1999" (1990), a sci-fi sequel with a new look and a completely different cast. "Class Of 1984" is certainly the better of the two films and is the one that has maintained a cult status over the years. At the end of the day "Class Of 1984" is an engaging JD classroom drama that keeps you entertained for most of its running time but goes a little over-the-top in the final reel with its excessive violence and mayhem.

Liar's Moon ** ½

US Release Date: September 1982
Running Time: 106 min
US Classification: PG
Director: David Fisher
Starring: Matt Dillon, Cindy Fisher, Christopher Connelly, Hoyt Axton, Margaret Blye, Broderick Crawford, Molly McCarthy, Yvonne De Carlo, Susan Tyrrell, Richard Moll

Taglines:

* They were hopelessly in love...
* They chose the most forbidden love a boy & girl could know!
* His family worked the land... Her family owned it!

Film Review:

"Liar's Moon" is an emotionally charged teen melodrama with an underbelly of lies and deceit between two families spanning a couple of decades. It is not your typical 1980s teen movie. In fact it's a throwback to films of a much earlier era. It has all the elements of a Delmer Daves epic. Daves was the writer/director of a number of 1960s teen classics such as "A Summer Place" (1959), "Parrish" (1961), "Susan Slade" (1961) and "Rome Adventure" (1962). These films were all intense character driven dramas starring teen pin-up boy of the time Troy Donahue. By 1982 Matt Dillon had already become a pin-up boy of sorts for his generation having already carved out a string of outstanding film credits with "Little Darlings (1980)", "My Bodyguard" (1980) and "Tex" (1982). "Liar's Moon" may not have been as financially successful or as well known as Dillon's previous work but it nevertheless leaves a big impact on its target audience.

"Liar's Moon" begins with a brief scene set in the early 1930s involving a mother and her baby boy but without revealing very much, it quickly jumps forward to 1949 when the boy is roughly 18 years of age. Matt Dillon plays Jack Duncan, the boy in question. He comes from a poor but hardworking farming family in East Texas. Jack meets and falls in love with Ginny (Cindy Fisher), a rich girl from a nearby property. Ginny's father and Jack's mother are against the romance. Ginny is only 17 years old and by law cannot marry without her parent's permission so the two teens decide to elope to Louisiana were they can get married. The plot thickens when Ginny gets pregnant and her father hires a stop-at-nothing private detective to find her and bring her back.

Good performances all-round from a fine cast contribute to this absorbing teen drama about coming of age and first love. The simple love story starts off slowly but picks up pace when the romance begins to blossom at the fairground kissing booth. Partway through the film there is a phone call scene involving the parents that suggests that something isn't quite right. By the end of the film, family secrets are revealed, the romance reaches boiling point and everything comes to a head in the last 10 minutes for a gripping finale. The web of intrigue is unraveled with a flashback and all the loose ends are tied up nicely but not before a few twists and turns are thrown in for good measure.

For many "Liar's Moon" got its notice, not via its cinema release but during its cable TV run in the 1980s. The film is often remembered for its double ending and pops up in two different versions, one with a sad ending and one with a happy ending. Neither of which we will give away here. Internet information indicates that some fans who have revisited the film many years later have been stunned with the alternate ending. Not knowing that a second ending existed they start questioning their memory of the film. How you feel at the end of the film depends on which version you see, you could feel sad, happy or even enraged. Whichever ending you see, will leave a lasting impression and the film's two endings continue to generate discussion.

Chapter 4:

TEEN MOVIES OF 1983

My Tutor **

US Release Date: 4th March 1983
Running Time: 97 min
US Classification: R
Director: George Bowers
Starring: Caren Kaye, Matt Lattanzi, Kevin McCarthy, Clark Brandon, Bruce Bauer, Arlene Golonka, Crispin Glover, Amber Denyse Austin, John Vargas, Maria Melendez, Kitten Natividad

Taglines:

* School's out... but Bobby's education has just begun.
* Every schoolboy's fantasy, every woman's dream.

Film Review:

Matt Lattanzi, dancer turned actor and former husband of singer/actress Olivia Newton-John, makes his big screen-starring debut in this romantic teen sex comedy. Pretty boy Matt plays Bobby Chrystal a high school senior who is having trouble learning his French. It is crucial that Bobby passes a retest so that he can attend Yale. Concerned about his grades, his rich parents hire a French tutor to give him a few "lessons". However, the tutor just happens to be an extremely good-looking, sexy blonde (Caren Kaye). Bobby is pleasantly surprised with his parent's choice of tutor and his French may be remedial, but his romance soon becomes advanced. "My Tutor" is strictly routine stuff and so is Lattanzi's cardboard performance while Caren Kaye's presence is merely window dressing for the film. Kaye's not just a tutor she's also a part-time aerobics instructor so we get the occasional montage of women strutting their stuff in colourful leotards. Also, any excuse to throw in a topless babe is used with Lattanzi often shown spying on Kaye skinny-dipping in the pool. When Lattazni and Kaye get romantically involved they are shown in the pool, the bedroom and the hot tub. These scenes are all standard sexploitation and tend to get a bit tedious after a while so to add to the fun, Crispin Glover (George McFly from "Back To The Future") is brought into the film for comedy relief. Glover pops up throughout as Lattanzi's sexually frustrated buddy Jack and his hit and miss exploits add pacing to the storyline.

"My Tutor"starts out as your typical teen sex farce (visit to a brothel, confrontation with a biker gang after hitting on the gang-leaders girl, a scuffle with female mud wrestlers and of course sexy dream sequences) but soon develops into an interesting coming of age romance drama that connects well with its target audience, teenage boys. The film even comes with its own original song, "My Tutor", sung by Kathy Brown. This cheesy title track adds great early 80's period flavour to the production. "My Tutor" was made on a small budget but still managed to clock up a neat $22.6 million at the US box office. For those of you who are wondering what happened to Matt Lattanzi after this film, well for one, he married superstar Olivia-Newton John, had a daughter, divorced Olivia and apart from a handful of small roles in minor films he still managed to win a starring role in a short-lived Australian TV series titled "Paradise Beach" (1993 - 1994). Strangely enough, Matt may have started out as the drawcard for the TV series but in no time at all writers had his character go blind and eventually had him killed off before the series ended. At the time of writing, Matt hasn't resurfaced in the film or TV world with "Paradise Beach" remaining his last screen credit.

If you stumble upon "My Tutor" on the late night TV circuit, you could find that the first 25 minutes or so may give the impression that it is the teen sex comedy that it is billed as but surprisingly the film does have a little bit more to offer than other films in the genre. On the plus side, it features an attractive cast, a plodding but nevertheless engaging storyline, fair production values and a pupil teacher romance that has a touch of sensitivity about it. However, the performances and the outcomes in the storyline are not as convincing as they could be. Lattanzi scores a 91% in his final exam making it all a little implausible considering we see more of the teacher and student together in the bedroom, the pool and the spa than in the classroom. There is barely one learning scene that indicates that Lattanzi is making real progress with his French studies. Overall the film is passable at best and certainly doesn't score a 91% like his test result but if you can convince yourself, 24 year-old Matt Lattanzi, with his sweetie-pie voice is of schoolboy age then you should have a lot of fun with this 97minute recipe for teenybopper fluff.

The Outsiders *** ½

US Release Date: 25th March 1983
Running Time: 91 min
US Classification: PG
Director: Francis Ford Coppola
Starring: C. Thomas Howell, Matt Dillon, Ralph Macchio, Patrick Swayze, Rob Lowe, Emilio Estevez, Tom Cruise, Diane Lane, Leif Garrett.

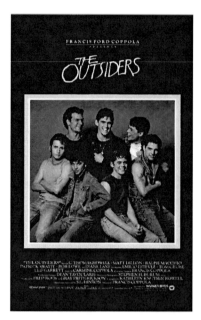

Tagline:

* They grew up on the outside of society. They weren't looking for a fight. They were looking to belong.

Film Review:

"The Outsiders" is based on S.E. Hinton's novel and tells the story of a group of young men growing up in Oklahoma. The following quote is taken from the closing credits of "The Outsiders", "This film is dedicated to the people who first suggested that it be made…Librarian Jo Ellen Misakian and the students of the Lone Star School in Fresno, California". This gritty teen drama may never have been made if it wasn't for the students of the Lone Star School and their suggestion in a letter to Francis Ford Coppola that he would be the ideal director to turn S.E. Hinton's novel about alienated youth into a big screen film. "The Outsiders" features a number of conflict situations between two rival gangs, "The Greasers" and "The Socs" who fight each other for control of their territories. Francis Ford Coppola managed to round-up a star-studded cast that combined so well that nearly all of them went on to become successful actors in later years, C. Thomas Howell ("Soul Man"), Ralph Macchio ("The Karate Kid"), Matt Dillon ("The Flamingo Kid"), Patrick Swayze ("Dirty Dancing"), Emilio Estevez ("Young Guns"), Rob Lowe ("Youngblood") and Tom Cruise ("Top Gun"). Shortly after "The Outsiders" and the teen high school flick "The Breakfast Club", a core group of these talented young actors became tagged, "The Brat Pack".

In the opening frames of the film C. Thomas Howell sits at a desk, pen in hand and deep in thought. Next we see a book, on the cover, the words, "Composition Book". The book is opened to reveal the first page, on the top line, the words, "Ponyboy Curtis English", on the next line the composition title, "The Outsiders". C. Thomas Howell begins to write, "When I stepped out into the bright sunlight from the darkness of the movie house..." As these words appear on the page we hear them spoken, as thoughts, just before the film's title "The Outsiders" slides across the screen from right to left in huge capital letters over a sunset that fades to reveal a railway track. Next, "The Greasers" and "The Socs" are listed on the screen like a team sheet, all to the sound of Stevie Wonder singing "Stay Gold". This opening sequence is a real mood setter, injecting both suspense and audience anticipation before any of the characters are officially introduced. As it turns out, "The Greasers" and "The Socs" are split by social backgrounds, each with their own territory and their own sense of importance. "The Greasers" wear jeans and jackets, have their hair slicked back and spend most of their time on foot, as they can't afford wheels. "The Socs" wear dress-up trousers with shirts and cardigans, while they drive around in their hotted up Mustangs.

When the credits fade, Dallas (Matt Dillon) stands on a street corner, in front of a beer lounge, leaning against a post while lighting up a cigarette. His two buddies, Ponyboy (C. Thomas Howell) and Johnny (Ralph Macchio) arrive, "What Do You Wanna Do?" asks Johnny. Dallas replies, "Nothing legal man, let's get outta here". As the three "Greasers" wander around their territory aimlessly, filing in time before the drive-in opens, they stumble across a gang scuffle that the cops bust up, they visit a couple of their buddies at a petrol station and Dallas even finds time to play tough-guy with a couple of little kids. When night falls the three punks sneak under a barbed wire fence and into the local drive-in theatre. Tonight's double feature is "Beach Blanket Bingo" and "Muscle Beach Party"; two fabricated teen films of the 1960's that have nothing in common with the lives that they live. Even at the drive-in, the boys can't sit still. Dallas makes a move on a couple of girls sitting nearby. Cherry (Diane Lane) tells Dallas, "Leave me alone or I'll call the cops...get lost hood". When Dallas leaves, Ponyboy moves in and begins a conversation with Cherry. She responds to Ponyboy, as he is less intimidating and much easier to talk to. After the movie, Ponyboy, Johnny and Two-Bit Matthews (Emilio Estevez) begin to walk Cherry home but tensions run hot when a car load of "Socs" turn up and demand that she leaves "The Greasers" and comes with them. The incident almost erupts into violence when Two-bit gets a little over-anxious and takes out his switchblade. The incident is diffused only after Cherry agrees to go with "The Socs" but not before telling Ponyboy that "If I see you in school and don't say hi, please don't take it personal, ok".

When Ponyboy returns home later that evening, his two older brothers Darrel (Patrick Swayze) and Sodapop (Rob Lowe) are waiting for him. Ponyboy's domineering brother Darrel is not happy because he has been out so late. After a heated exchange Ponyboy runs out of the house and meets up again with Johnny. As the two boys wander around in the night like lost sheep, they are set upon once again by a bunch of drunken "Socs". This time the "Socs" attempt to drown Ponyboy in a nearby fountain. To protect his friend, Johnny pulls out his switchblade and in the resulting scuffle one of "The Socs" is killed. The two distressed boys go to Dallas for advice. He hands them a gun and tells them to go and hide out in an abandon church. With a week's supply of food, a pack of cards and the book "Gone With The Wind", the two boys find time to give each other haircuts with a knife and talk about life. Ponyboy even dyes his hair blonde and reveals his love for poetry. About a week later Dallas turns up to check on the boys and as fate would have it, the three of them, end up at a burning school. They risk their lives to save some children and Johnny gets seriously burnt. Despite his injuries, Johnny feels no regret, as he has taken one life and has now been able to save other lives.

In a film about rival gangs it is inevitable that there will be a final showdown and in "The Outsiders", "The Greasers" and "The Socs" go head to head in vicious hand to hand combat on a rain-drenched muddy battlefield. The rumble looks so real that one would feel mistaken to think that it was staged. All the film's stars are involved in the battle, with the exception of Johnny, who later dies in hospital. When Dallas finds out about Johnny's death he loses control, takes a gun and robs a store. The film ends on a sad note and a second tragedy when police shoot down Dallas in a park. This ending leaves a small void with audiences wondering what will happen to the other characters. In 1990 fans were rewarded with a short-lived TV series, "The Outsiders, The Story Continues". The series begins where the film left off and stars an entirely new cast. It runs for 14 episodes and gives viewers further insight into the lives of the boys but more importantly it leaves viewers with a more optimistic conclusion.

"The Outsiders" is a JD film, reminiscent of the type that was made back in the 1950's and 60's. It's a tragic tale of lost young men, in a town with nowhere to go, not much to do and no one to guide them. All the players are bubbling with talent and bursting with energy but unfortunately a film such as this, can only center on a handful of leading men, in this case, C. Thomas Howell, Ralph Macchio and Matt Dillon were the lucky ones. Even in their bit parts, Patrick Swayze, Emilio Estevez, Rob Lowe and Tom Cruise find time to shine. For all of these actors "The Outsiders" was a turning point in their careers, the film is regarded as the first unofficial "Brat Pack" movie, made well before any of these young talents were labeled with the controversial tag. "Godfather" director, Francis Ford Coppola, shot "The Outsiders" back to back with "Rumble Fish" (1983), a lesser-known black and white flick that was also adapted from an S.E. Hinton novel. Matt Dillon and Diane Lane returned for "Rumble Fish" along with new faces Mickey Rourke and Nicolas Cage. "The Outsiders" is full of captivating images, from its poster artwork to its cinematography. The film is predominately photographed in close-up and the actors almost jump off the screen at you. It is successful in maintaining its suspense right through to the final showdown and the performances are so natural and engrossing that you can sympathize with the characters and their plight, in particular Ponyboy and Johnny.

In "The Outsiders" one image that lingers on long after the closing moments of the film is that of Ponyboy reading the letter written by Johnny before he died. As he reads, we see Johnny's image in the corner of the screen and hear his voice, "You're Gold when you are a kid...when you're a kid everything is new...like the way you dig sunsets, Pony, that's Gold...keep it that way, it's a good way to be...I want you to ask Dally to look at one, I don't think he has ever seen a sunset...there's still lots of good in the world, tell Dally, I don't think he knows.... your buddy Johnny". Johnny's letter is his beautiful explanation of "Stay Gold". Johnny's redemption is now complete and his message of goodwill to his friends is heartfelt. The letter brings forward the emotional core of the story and allows the two words "Stay Gold" to resonate with its audience. "The Outsiders" has depth and is more than just a gang film with famous faces. In 2005, "The Outsiders" was re-issued on DVD in a 2 Disc Special Edition, titled, "The Outsiders: The Complete Novel". The film has been re-stored, re-edited, contains 22 minutes of additional footage and comes complete with a new soundtrack, featuring six great Elvis Presley songs. Old audiences can now re-live it and enjoy the exciting changes, while new audiences can discover why this timeless teen classic has such wide appeal.

Spring Break **

US Release Date: 25th March 1983
Running Time: 102 min
US Classification: R
Director: Sean S. Cunningham
Starring: David Knell, Perry Lang, Paul Land, Steve Bassett, Jayne Modean, Corinne Alphen

Taglines:

* Like it's really, totally, the most fun a couple of bodies can have. You know?
* Spring Break… It's the reason kids go to college in the first place.

Film Review:

"Spring Break" is a return to the "Beach Party" formula that was made popular in the 1960s by Frankie Avalon and Annette Funicello. These films always featured good-looking teens, lots of sand and surf, hit music from the era and a throw away plot. "Spring Break" has all the same elements of its predecessors and more. While the earlier "Beach Party" films were Rated G or PG, "Spring Break" comes in with an R Rating due to its abundance of flesh, wet-shirts and teenagers with a much more racier vocabulary. Sadly, "Spring Break" focuses too much on the boys and their exploits. There are no Annette's in this one and the girls are strictly eye candy for the teenage males, Nelson, Adam, Stu and O.T.; played respectively by David Knell, Perry Lang, Paul Land and Steve Bassett. In 1960 there was a classic teen film called "Where The Boys Are" about a group of teenage girls going to Fort Lauderdale for spring break. This film is a complete role-reversal and could easily have been called "Where The Girls Are".

From the opening frame "Spring Break" is buzzing with energy. Set and shot in Fort Lauderdale Florida, 2 jocks and 2 nerds cross paths when they are forced to share a room and two single beds at the Breeze n' Seas Motel due to an overbooking in peak period. The opening credit sequence sets up the scene nicely, the atmosphere is one of hustle and bustle complete with hotels, cafes, nightspots and crowded beaches like you have never seen them before. There are literally people everywhere, of all shapes and sizes, the town in brimming with excitement and all kinds of activities. Teens in fancy cars, bodybuilders and bikini-clad girls jump out of the screen. As the camera follows the central characters you can't help but notice the masses of extras in the background of almost every shot. There are other places around the world, just like Fort Lauderdale, where this type of activity goes on. In Australia a similar event takes place when students finish their final school year. It is called "Schoolie's Week" and teens from around Australia converge to a place called Surfers Paradise on Queensland's Gold Coast. So a film like "Spring Break" inevitably connects with teens from around the globe.

For pacing the film bursts into a series of musical montages featuring belly-flop competitions, beer-guzzling challenges, wild party antics, male vs. female boxing bouts and of course, wet t-shirt contests for the girls and he-shirts for the boys. Popular 80s rock bands are featured on the soundtrack, most notably Cheap Trick with the film's title track. There's even an all-girl rock band fronted by former Penthouse Pet Corinne Alphen, popping up in the club scenes at Penrod's Volcano Nightspot. At Fort Lauderdale you never know what you are going to see next, one of the boy's even gets his trousers ripped off by a hungry crocodile. In between the teenage mayhem, the film cuts to the insignificant plotline involving adult authority figures wanting to take over the motel, one of them, being the stepfather of one of the boys. As with any teen film of this type, the adults are depicted as the idiots or villains of the piece and become the brunt of some of the jokes. In the finale, not surprisingly, the adults cop what's coming to them, in a free-for-all rumble complete with whipped cream and beer squirting brawl. As expected the teens come out of it as the victors.

Back in 1983, the idea of taking cinemagoers to Fort Lauderdale for "Spring Break" was still an exciting adventure and this was reflected at the yearly box office when the film ranked 29th and earned over $24 million. These days, viewers don't need to go to the cinema to see this type of thing; they can catch the mayhem that goes on at places like Ford Lauderdale any time of the week in TV shows such as "Wild On". "Spring Break" was and still is a straightforward teen-sexploitation flick with all the trappings. The acting, the script and the plotline have very little to offer, with the location being the film's star attraction. Today it serves as a slice of nostalgia, particularly for teenagers of the 80s who saw the film in cinemas when it was first released. Now as adults, they can reflect back on the fashions, the hairstyles, the music and the fun of a time gone by.

Bad Boys ***

US Release Date: 25th March 1983
Running Time: 123 min
US Classification: R
Director: Rick Rosenthal

Starring: Sean Penn, Reni Santoni, Jim Moody, Eric Gurry, Esai Morales, Ally Sheedy, Clancy Brown, Robert Lee Rush, John Zenda, Alan Ruck,Tony Mockus Jr., Erik Barefield, Dean Fortunato, Jorge Noa, Lawrence Mah

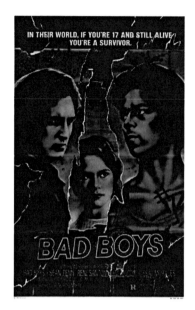

Taglines:

* There's Only One Person Left Who Believes Mick O'Brien Can Make It... Mick O'Brien
* Life Has Pushed Him Into A Corner... And He's Comin' Out Fighting.
* In their world, if you're 17 and still alive you're a survivor

Film Review:

"At the age of 9, they've joined a street gang; at 12, they're pushing drugs. At 16, they're part of a nightmare teenage underworld of rape, mugging, armed robbery and murder". If this statement that accompanies the video box cover grabs you, then "Bad Boys" is the film for you. 12 years before Will Smith and Martin Lawrence teamed up for the 1995 cops and robbers' blockbuster, "Bad Boys", Sean Penn led this cast of "Bad Boys" in a teen crime drama of the same name. The two films may share the same title but that is where the similarity ends. "Bad Boys" (1983) is a gritty, realistic portrayal of Chicago street gangs and is considered by many to be the film that first showcased Sean Penn's exceptional dramatic talent. "Bad Boys" was a complete change of pace and image for Penn who had just finished work the previous year on the teen comedy "Fast Times At Ridgemont High". Gone were the blonde surfer dude locks, the dumb voice and the spaced-out expressions of Spicoli and in with the tough, brooding, violent sensibilities of street hood Mick O'Brien. Rumour has it, that Kevin Bacon and Tom Cruise also auditioned for the role of O'Brien but when you see the finished product it's hard to imagine anybody else but Penn in the role.

The early part of the film is set on the tough streets of Chicago and then later shifts locations to a juvenile detention centre. The storyline sees street kid Mick O'Brien (Sean Penn) accidentally kill the brother of vicious gang leader Paco Moreno, played with menace by Easi Morales of "La Bamba" fame. Penn is sent to a detention centre for his crime and soon after, the film kicks into high gear when Morales joins Penn on the inside, when he is charged for raping Penn's girlfriend, played by a young Ally Sheedy. The film builds up to a vicious showdown between the two "Bad Boys" of the title in a finale that is both violent and disturbing. Aside from the subject matter, what sets "Bad Boys" apart from many other teen movies is the intensity of the performance of its young actors. From Sean Penn and Easi Morales right down to the supports, they all pack a wallop. "Bad Boys" may have struggled to make ends meet at the box office in 1983, but it has certainly become a real curiosity piece since, particularly for Sean Penn fans. Maybe the lackluster box office was because it did not depict the usual fun-side of teen life but instead it focused on the dark troubled existence of teenage youth. Whatever the case may be, Bad Boys" is violent, gritty and has a real edge about it with images that leave lasting impressions, who can forget the "Trojan Radio" well if you are wondering what that is; you will just have to see the film to find out. "Bad Boys" is tough, hard-hitting entertainment, an amazing teen prison film, like no other.

Losin' It ** ½

US Release Date: 8th April 1983
Running Time: 100 min
Classification: R
Director: Curtis Hanson
Starring: Tom Cruise, Shelley Long, Jackie Earle Haley, John Stockwell, John P. Navin Jr., Henry Darrow

Taglines:

* They were boozin' it, brusin' it and cruisin' it, but mostly they were . . .
* The last word about the first time

Film Review:

In the wake of teen sex comedies such as "Porky's" and "The Last American Virgin" comes "Losin' It", a fairly routine entry in this sub-genre, the difference this time being the Tijuana setting and of course the involvement of some famous faces including Tom Cruise ("Top Gun"), Shelley Long ("Outrageous Fortune") and Director Curtis Hanson ("L.A. Confidential"). The film begins with the statement "A Long Time Ago In A High School Not So Far Away..." not surprising when you discover that the film's cinematographer was none other than Gilbert Taylor, the guy who also worked on "Star Wars". With a talented cast and crew such as this, the film must have something going for it and although not a brilliant film, it does achieve exactly what it sets out to do, and that is, provide a bit of mindless entertainment for a teenage audience, particularly boys.

Most teenage boys at some stage in their lives have set out on a road trip with friends searching for adventure and girls…not necessarily in that order. In "Losin' It" the story sees four high school boys do just that so the connection of the film with its target audience is immediate. Woody (Tom Cruise), Dave (Jackie Earle Haley), Spider (John Stockwell) and Wendell (John P. Navin Jr.) are the four boys who set out looking for love in all the wrong places, in this case the sleazy brothels of Tijuana. All the characters are stereotypical from the teenage boys right down to the Mexican locals. The title makes it quite clear what the boys are trying to achieve but in going for their objective, anything and everything that you could imagine goes wrong. The boys steal from a convenience store, they get pursued by a crooked sheriff, they become involved in a barroom brawl with marines, they clash with junkyard hoods, one of them winds up in a dirty Tijuana jail and to top it all off they end up in a brothel with unattractive hookers. Throw into the mix some booze, an unhappily married woman, a carload of fireworks and what you get is an explosion of absolute mayhem at every turn.

"Losin' It" did not do well at the US box office, ranking 139th in is year and grossing a dismal $1,246,141. In fact most people that have seen it, viewed it well after Tom Cruise hit the big time in films such as "Risky Business", "Top Gun" and "Cocktail". It became a curiosity piece for audiences wanting to see a young Tom Cruise in an early role. "Losin' It" projects a fun-time for teenagers but can leave some viewers with mixed feelings about Tijuana. You're not sure whether you want to go there, let your hair down and have some fun or whether you should stay well and truly clear of the place for your own peace of mind and safety. It's not exactly a good travel advertisement for that part of the world and I highly doubt it will be shown as in-bus entertainment on the next coach ride down there. Having said all that, the modern viewer can see past all the mayhem and except the film for what it is, a south-of-the-border teen sex comedy.

Valley Girl ****

US Release Date: 29th April 1983
Running Time: 99 min
Classification: R
Director: Martha Coolidge

Starring: Nicolas Cage, Deborah Foreman, Michael Bowen, Elizabeth Daily, Cameron Dye, Heidi Holicker, Michelle Meyrink, Lee Purcell, Tina Theberge, Richard Sanders, Colleen Camp.

Taglines:

* She's cool. He's hot. She's from the Valley. He's not.
* Life in the Valley: Hair, clothes... and attitude!
* True Love Is Only A Zip Code Away!
* When punk meets prom the fun begins!

Film Review:

For documentary director Martha Coolidge, "Valley Girl" was to be her first big screen feature film, something that she describes as a "Rock n Roll, musical, love story". When Coolidge first read the script, which was supposedly written in 10 days and shot in 20, it reminded her of Shakespeare's "Romeo And Juliet". For the story to work Coolidge had to find the right cast. Deborah Foreman was an immediate choice. Her innocent charm and good looks deemed her the ideal lead for the female role of Julie, the girl from the Valley. Although Judd Nelson and Eric Stoltz were two of the young actors that were high on the list to play the two punks, it was Nicolas Cage and Cameron Dye who eventually won the roles. On the "Valley Girl" DVD commentary Coolidge explains how Cage won the lead role of Hollywood rebel, Randy. When discussing casting choices she picked up Cage's file from the top of the reject pile and stated, "Don't bring me any pretty boys, bring me somebody like this". In no time at all Cage was called in, and as it turned out, he was perfect for the role. Cage had only previously appeared briefly in "Fast Times At Ridgemont High" (1982). "Valley Girl" became his first opportunity to headline a film. Although not having the conventional leading man looks, Cage certainly displayed a unique screen presence that captivated audiences worldwide.

Cage's Randy is a funky new-wave guy from the city. He has punk hair, dresses like nobody else and sports a chest-hair logo that looks like a superhero's emblem. He knows everyone on Hollywood Boulevard and hangs out at the hippest nite-clubs. Foreman's Julie, however, is more conservative. She's a cute girl from the Valley whose pass-time involves fashion, music and hanging around the local shopping mall (the Sherman

Oaks Galleria, that was previous used in "Fast Times At Ridgemont High"). The city is a terrain that Julie likes to keep away from, that is, until she meets Randy. Their first meeting is brief and only via eye contact at the local beach. They next meet at a house party in the Valley, at which Randy turns up uninvited. The attraction between Randy and Julie is instant and is captured beautifully by the filmmakers. Randy is shown in the foreground (in focus) while Julie is in the background (out of focus). As Randy turns and looks in her direction everything is suddenly reversed. Julie is now in focus, while Randy, who is looking at her, is out of focus. They immediately make a connection and the on-screen chemistry between the two young stars is electric. It is this chemistry that holds the film together. It is not long after this romantic meeting that Randy is spotted, picked on and kicked out of the party by Julie's ex-boyfriend Tommy (Michael Bowen) and his cronies. However, the determined Randy is not about to be beaten. He returns to the party through a bathroom window and still manages to romance Julie into coming away with him.

Randy and Julie are from different worlds. Their differences are quickly revealed in a conversation that takes place on their first outing, a drive down Hollywood Boulevard, followed by a visit to one of Randy's favourite nite-club hangouts (a location that would later be owned by actor Johnny Depp and known as "The Viper Room"). Randy explains to Julie the importance of individuality, "It's the way we do things that makes the difference". "Yeah, I guess so", replies Julie. Randy answers, "You won't catch anything here it's the real world, not fresh and clean like a television show." The free-spirited Randy later says to Julie, "So when can I see you again". Julie answers, "Why don't you wait til the end of the evening to say these things". Randy replies, "It's the way I feel, it's what I want". Although their differences are evident, they are only superficial and as the film progresses their love becomes strong enough to cancel out any differences and survive any set back. Julie's love for Randy is so sincere that she even describes him to her friends as "The most awesome dude ever".

When Julie becomes conflicted about her relationships with Randy and Tommy, she goes to her father (Frederic Forrest) for advice. Her heart to heart conversation with her father, a former hippie and now health food shop owner, reveals that he would have to be one of the most understanding and easygoing fathers in screen history. The pot-smoking hippie from wayback seems to know more than anybody, what it is like, to look different, to act different and to be different. He understands his daughter's plight and his advice to her regarding Randy and Tommy is spot on. Julie's insecurities, however, escalate as she tries to juggle her love for Randy with her desire to be popular with her existing school friends. Tommy is jealous of Randy and makes every attempt to win Julie back, even to the extent of influencing her best friends to speak up against Randy. Every attempt is made to tear the two lovers apart and the drama heightens when Randy and Julie do eventually break up but this is only the scriptwriter's ploy to make their reuniting at the end of the film even more powerful.

When teenagers of 1983 saw the "Valley Girl" poster featuring a bare-chested Nicolas Cage, wearing a vest, a tie, tight black jeans, pointy toed boots and sporting a spiked multi-coloured hair-do, standing alongside a beautiful girl (which by the way does not resemble Deborah Foreman, in any way, shape, or form) wearing a sleeveless top, mini skirt, legwarmers and headband, it immediately caught their attention. To top it off the poster came with the hip tagline "She's cool. He's hot. She's from the Valley. He's not." and boasted a list of popular 80's music artists including Modern English, The Plimsouls, Josie Cotton, The Psychedelic Furs and Men At Work. Now if you were a teenager in that era wouldn't it reel you in hook line and sinker? Well in the 1980's "Valley Girl" did just that. Made on an extremely small budget, a reportedly low $350,000 (in many scenes cast members wore their own clothes), teenagers of the day warmed to the film and immediately set the cash registers at the US box office ringing to the tune of $17.3 million. "Valley Girl" became the surprise hit of 1983 and is now a time capsule of early 1980's Hollywood.

For some, "Valley Girl" is the definitive 1980's love story. It certainly has a lot to offer, a heart-warming tale of true love, complete with school prom and punch-up finale, a first-rate 80's soundtrack, two exciting young stars; the beautiful Deborah Foreman, the raw 17-year old Cage (in a loner role that almost reflected his real-life existence at that time) and for good measure, a "Graduate" type sub plot that is used for comedy relief. As a bonus the girls from the Valley introduce us to their way of speaking ("Like, Totally"), something that would become known as "Valley Talk", a vernacular that one could say was a predecessor of the teen talk used in "Clueless" (1995). For anyone who grew up in the 1980's "Valley Girl" should bring back pleasant memories of high school, dating, fashion and music. Today the "Valley Girl" soundtrack is one of the most sought after teen movie soundtracks ever. It proved to be so popular with fans that a 2nd CD was released titled, "More Music From Valley Girl". On August 5th 2003, to the delight of fans, a long-awaited special edition DVD was also released. "Valley Girl" has certainly achieved cult status and is considered by many to be new wave 80's cinema at its best.

WarGames ****

US Release Date: 3rd June 1983
Running Time: 114 min
US Classification: PG
Director: John Badham
Starring: Matthew Broderick, Dabney Coleman, Ally Sheedy, John Wood, Barry Corbin

Taglines:

* Is it a game, or is it real?
* ...Where the only winning move is NOT TO PLAY.

Film Review:

What if Ferris Bueller was a computer nerd? Well, that's the premise for WarGames, a first-rate teen thriller, so good, that it will have you glued to your seat from start to finish. Teenager David Lightman (Matthew Broderick) is a whiz kid when it comes to computers and arcade games. His advanced computer skills enable him to access the school's computer system with ease and thereby change his and his girlfriend's grades with the flick of a backspace key. Owning a home computer certainly has its benefits for David but his mischievous antics, while fun to begin with will not stay that way for long. Hacking into the school's computers is not enough to keep this computer-whiz entertained. In his search for further excitement, in the form of computer games, he accidentally taps into the US Defense Department's mainframe computer system "WOPR" (War Operation Planned Response) at the "NORAD" Combat Operations Center. After hacking through a number "WOPR" codes he stumbles onto a game list featuring one called "Global Thermonuclear War". For David "Global Thermonuclear War", was the most inviting choice. What he didn't know is that this game was for real and that absolute chaos was about to unfold. The primary objective of NORAD headquarters is to provide an early warning system in the event of a nuclear attack. Its mainframe computer "WOPR" spends all of its time, 365 days of the year, thinking about World War III. The computer has already fought World War III as a game and its purpose is to estimate Soviet responses to US responses and so on. At NORAD headquarters Defcon 5 means peace while Defcon 1 means World War III. As the game intensifies

WarGames moves briskly from Defcon 5 right through to 4,3,2 and finally to Defcon 1 when the world is on the brink of absolute disaster.

"WarGames" shares an appeal to both teenagers and adults; it is the thinking man's teen movie. You know that this could never happen but the filmmakers have managed to do it in such as way that you believe that maybe it could. The sets look real, the script is engaging, the acting is superb and the sound complements every aspect of the picture, no wonder the film was nominated for 3 Academy Awards, Best Cinematography, Best Sound and Best Writing. "WarGames" also proved to be a massive hit at the U.S. Box Office, grossing nearly $80 million and ranking 5th in its year, not bad for a film that was made on a budget of around $12 million. What makes "WarGames" special is that it plays all of its cards right from start to finish and the ingenious Tic Tac Toe ending puts an awesome cap on an already captivating film. For many fans WarGames is that gem of a film about a computer whiz kid that almost starts World War III while for some fans, "WarGames" is simply "Ferris Bueller Saves The World". Whatever the case may be, the film will make you think twice if your computer system ever challenges you to a game of "Global Thermonuclear War".

Class **½

US Release Date: 22nd July 1983
Running Time: 98 min
US Classification: R
Director: Lewis John Carlino
Starring: Rob Lowe, Jacqueline Bisset, Andrew McCarthy, Cliff Robertson, Stuart Margolin, John Cusack, Alan Ruck, Rodney Pearson, Remak Ramsay, Virginia Madsen, Deborah Thalberg, Fern Persons, Casey Siemaszko, Aaron Douglas, Anna Maria Horsford.

Taglines:

* The good news is Jonathan's having his first affair. The bad news is, she's his roommate's mother!
* Freshman English Was Never Like This!

Film Review:

After a couple of TV appearances and a small role in the teen drama "The Outsiders", Rob Lowe's career surged forward when he was given top billing in "Class", a teen film that was to become "The Graduate" of the 1980's. Like the Dustin Hoffman classic before it, the film focuses on a relationship between a young man and a married woman who is old enough to be his mother. Lowe however, was not given the central role of the naïve youngster who falls to the charms of the older woman, that part went to newcomer Andrew McCarthy, who with "Class" would make his feature film debut.

Andrew McCarthy plays Jonathon, a shy country boy who moves to a new prep school with the ambition of winning entry into Harvard University. Rob Lowe plays Jonathon's roommate Skip, a handsome, spoilt, rich-kid with an incessant desire to play practical jokes. Jonathon's induction into Vernon Academy turns out to be a nightmare when Skip cons him into dressing up in ladies underwear, telling him that it is a school tradition that helps teach humility. Skip leads him out of the school building and then locks the door on him leaving him stranded outside to the bemusement of the other students. Jonathon is humiliated all right, as he scrambles up the side of the building and through an open window, while Skip laughs hysterically at the prank. For Jonathon the humiliation continues in the lunchroom with snide remarks thrown at him from all angles. In retaliation Jonathon decides to play a prank on Skip, by having him believe that he has hung himself in his room. Skip falls for it and in a panic calls in the principal and the students only to discover that Jonathon is just kidding. After this the two boys become good friends and in a late-night drinking session, Jonathon confides in Skip that his whole life depends on getting into Harvard, so much so, that he even cheated in his SAT exam by purchasing a stolen paper with the answers. Jonathon's naivety and clumsiness with the opposite sex becomes apparent when he ruins a double date through a fit of vomiting and later accidentally destroys a tea party held at their sister school. Jonathon is now banned from attending any social function between the two-schools and when the night of the Halloween school dance comes around, Skip hands Jonathon $100 and encourages him to go to Chicago to visit the "Free & Easy" club.

At the club Jonathon succeeds once again in making an absolute fool of himself. When trying to look cool while chatting up a girl he puts his foot through a chair and later becomes the brunt of a practical joke, when a girl cons him into running a coin from the top of his forehead to his chin and then across his face from ear to ear. Unbeknown to him the coin leaves marks on his face, much to the amusement of Ellen (Jacqueline Bisset) who watches from afar. Although feeling somewhat sorry for him Ellen is nevertheless charmed by his inexperience and vulnerability. She immediately goes over to him and begins to wipe the marks off his face. Jonathon leaves the club feeling dejected and heads straight for the nearest taxi. Much to his astonishment, Ellen opens the door of his taxi and invites herself in. It is not long before their physical attraction gets the better of them and Ellen seduces Jonathon in a glass elevator. This is when the fun starts and continues, well for a while anyway, until the relationship ends abruptly when Ellen discovers that Jonathan attends the same school as her son. The emotional drama begins to kick in however, when Skip invites Jonathon to his family home for Christmas and Jonathon then discovers that Ellen is in fact Skip's mother. Jonathon is now torn between his affections for Ellen and his friendship with Skip. Whilst at the home, it becomes apparent that Skip's father (Cliff Robertson) has a major problem with his wife. Their rocky relationship is summed up when Skip says to Jonathon "He tells her exactly what to do and she ignores him". Knowing that Ellen is his friend's mother, Jonathon decides to end the affair but Ellen is persistent for it to continue. She refuses to take no for an answer and repeatedly calls him on the phone until Jonathon agrees to meet her in a hotel room. At this point "Class" looks like it could have headed in the direction of films such as "Play Misty For Me" (1971) or "Fatal Attraction" (1987) but instead it chooses to resolve the matter by having Skip and his mates follow Jonathon to the Hotel room, only to discover Ellen in Jonathon's bed. After Ellen is humiliated the implication is that she suffers a breakdown and ends up in hospital to undergo psychiatric help. The film then shifts focus to the stolen exam papers and the relationship between the two boys that leads to a climatic fistfight.

When "Class" opened to cinema audiences in July 1983, with a taking of $4.6 million on its opening weekend, it ranked 4th at the US box office behind, "Jaws 3-D", "Staying Alive" and "Return Of The Jedi". By the end of its US run "Class" managed to clock up a gross of $21.7 million. The film's main appeal being its popular stars, 70's pin-up girl Jacqueline Bisset, Academy Award winner Cliff Robertson (Best Actor for Charly 1969) and the two future brat-packers Rob Lowe and Andrew McCarthy. Also, adding to the film's attraction was its "Graduate" like plotline and of course its outstanding movie poster that featured the beautiful Bisset seated on a sofa between the two young stars. "Class" is also remembered for featuring the first on-screen appearances of future teen stars John Cusack (The Sure Thing 1985) and Virginia Madsen (Fire With Fire 1986). Cusack plays a mischievous school student who knows how to flip a smoke in his mouth to conceal it, while Madsen's brief appearance at the tea party is somewhat revealing.

"Class" is fairly straightforward 80's teen fodder that promised more but delivered a little less. The film's brilliant poster and catchy tagline leaves one with high expectations and it is inevitable that some viewers will be left unfulfilled. Its mix of comedy, drama and romance is a little too disjointed as the film takes on "Animal House" style hi-jinks while trying to combine a sensitive story of friendship with a sensual love story between a young man and an older woman. Not an easy task for director Lewis John Carlino, who only has a few films to his credit. In some scenes the comedic potential is untapped and for this, the film lacks a little flair. Although the younger actors put in fine performances, the older actors are somewhat underused. Cliff Robertson who is no newcomer to teen movies, having appeared as a teenager in the original "Gidget" (1959) opposite 60's teen queen Sandra Dee and of course later as grandfather of new teen superhero "Spider-Man" (2002) is given very little to do while Jacqueline Bisset's role is also restrictive and ended rather abruptly. That's not to say that "Class" is a bad film, in fact, it is quite entertaining and so it should be with its talented cast of veterans and newcomers along with its fitting Elmer Bernstein music score. "Class" is mostly remembered today, as being the breeding ground for its predominately young cast and for that alone is worthy of attention.

Private School * ½

US Release Date: 29th July 1983
Running Time: 89 min
US Classification: R
Director: Noel Black
Starring: Phoebe Cates, Betsy Russell, Matthew Modine, Michael Zorek, Fran Ryan, Kathleen Wilhoite, Ray Walston, Sylvia Kristel, Jonathan Prince, Kari Lizer, Richard Stahl, Julie Payne.

Taglines:

* You won't believe what goes on and what comes off in ... Private School
* Private School is where kids leave parents behind, and learn what growing up is really all about.

Film Review:

You have seen it all before and now you get to see it again. "Private School" is not unlike any of the other teen sex comedies that came before it, such as "Animal House", "Porky's", "Losin' It" and "Private Lessons". The film revolves around the happenings at two schools, Cherryvale Academy for Women and Freemount Academy for Men. The boys spend most of the time trying to score with the girls, while the girls, particularly Betsy Russell wander around the film scantily clad. "Private School" is completely devoid of plot, except for a minor romance between Phoebe Cates and Matthew Modine, which is thrown in for pacing amongst the endless barrage of sex jokes and mindless nudity. That's right, "Private School" is one sex comedy sketch after another and it doesn't let up for the entire duration of the film. All the hi-jinks you expect to see are here and more, shower scenes, topless horseback riding, boys dressing up as girls to get into a dormitory, boys spying through bedroom windows, attempts to buy condoms from a chemist, sex education in the classroom.... and the list goes on and on and on.

"Private School" tries to and does outdo some of its predecessors in the genre, particularly in the nudity department. The film's shower scene certainly tries to outdo Porky's by making it one of the most extensive shower scenes in film history and it goes on and on and on... to the point of becoming voyeuristic. Luckily, one thing that does keep the film moving along is its catchy 80s pop soundtrack which features artists such as, Rick Springfield, Vanity Six, Stray Cats and Bow-Wow-Wow just to name a few. Production values are okay but what "Private School" hasn't got is a good plotline or script to back it up. The jokes are hit and miss and the performances of stars Phoebe Cates and Matthew Modine are only adequate but I suppose how much more can one expect with the material on offer. Betsy Russell is strictly reduced to eye-candy in a series of scantily clad scenes, she must have been a good sport or well paid to play along with the mayhem. Sylvia Kristel ("Private Lessons") pops up as a sex education teacher in a fairly lackluster classroom scene while veteran actor Ray Walston ("My Favorite Martian") is wasted in a minor role as a randy chauffer. If you are looking for a film with substance, then you may have to visit another school. The end result is "Private School" is a male fantasy piece, simply an excuse to show girls in bikinis and girls in various states of undress, a film recipe that mostly appeals to teenage boys.

Risky Business *** ½

US Release Date: 5th August 1983
Running Time: 98 min
US Classification: R
Director: Paul Brickman
Starring: Tom Cruise, Rebecca De Mornay, Joe Pantoliano, Richard Masur, Bronson Pinchot, Curtis Armstrong, Nicholas Pryor, Janet Carroll, Shera Danese, Raphael Sbarge, Bruce A. Young, Kevin Anderson, Sarah Partridge, Nathan Davis, Scott Harlan.

Taglines:

* Meet the model son who's been good too long.
* There's a time for playing it safe and a time for Risky Business.

Film Review:

When "Risky Business" hit cinema screens in 1983 it proved to be a teenage comedy with a difference. It is a stylish study of American youth and in particular it looks at the misadventures of a responsible rich-kid caught between his desires to discover the wild side of life, before reaching adulthood, while at the same time trying to live up to his parent's high expectations. "Risky Business" saw a dynamic new teen star, light up the screen with his winning smile and charming good looks, that new star was Tom Cruise. Tom had already appeared in "Endless Love" (1981), "Taps" (1981), "The Outsiders", (1983) and "Losin' It (1983)" but it was "Risky Business" that catapulted him from actor to superstar. The film's poster featuring Cruise peering through dark "Ray-Ban" sunglasses is now an image recognized the world over. After the film was released the sale of "Ray-Ban" sunglasses went through the roof and "Time Magazine" described Cruise as a "baby faced Christopher Reeve".

In "Risky Business", Tom plays Joel Goodsen an ambitious 17-year-old Chicago high school student, of model parents, who will do anything to gain acceptance into Princeton College. His character initially comes across as a mature responsible young adult, who would never think of breaking family rules, that is, until his parents go on holidays, entrusting him with the family home, expensive Porsche and money. The moment Joel's parents leave the house he pumps up the volume on his stereo and prances around in his underwear to the beat of Bob Seger's "Old Time Rock 'n' Roll". This would have to be the signature scene of "Risky Business" and it is often replayed on talk shows whenever the film is discussed. For Tom Cruise this scene may well go down in his career as the one he will be most remembered for. Even Tom's ex-wife Nicole Kidman did a hilarious parody of it on "Saturday Night Live" many years later.

The situations in "Risky Business" are at times outrageous and even unbelievable. The film however should not be taken too seriously; it is predominately a comedy or teenage fantasy that will undoubtedly have special appeal to male high school students. For Joel, the trouble starts when his fast-talking buddy Miles (Curtis Armstrong who later went on to play Booger in "Revenge of The Nerds") attempts to persuade him to call a hooker. Joel refuses, but Miles calls anyway. This is when Joel's life spins wildly out of control. Enter the sexy call girl Lana (played by the beautiful Rebecca De Mornay) who after one night of passion with Joel, forcefully moves in with him, to avoid her psychotic pimp, Guido (played menacingly by Joe Pantoliano). Joel's life becomes a nightmare as a series of madcap events unfold, his father's Porsche ends up in Lake Michigan, he uses his "Future Enterpriser" school skills to raise money (he turns the family home into a brothel) to get the car fixed and his mother's expensive crystal egg lands in the hands of Guido "the killer pimp", all while trying to prepare for his college exams and a pressure-cooker interview with a Princeton admissions teacher. Joel's life becomes a hilarious race against time as he struggles to restore the house; the furniture and his life back to normal before his parents return home.

"Risky Business" proved to be a financial success bringing in $63.5 million at the US box office. Teens loved it and so did the critics. At the "Golden Globe" awards Tom Cruise was nominated for "Best Performance by an Actor in a Motion Picture - Comedy/Musical" and at the "Writers Guild Of America" awards Paul Brickman was nominated for "Best Comedy Written Directly for the Screen". Writer/director Paul Brickman unfortunately never capitalized on the film's huge success and after a 7 year absence would go on to direct only one other film of note "Men Don't Leave" (1990), a comedy-drama starring Jessica Lange, Joan Cusack and a very young Chris O'Donnell. "Risky Business" has a lot of qualities; it is witty, slick and inventive. Its stylish cinematography is probably some of the best ever seen in a teen movie. The film begins with a fantastic night shot of Chicago, the camera slowly pans across the Chicago skyline to the combine sound of synthesizer music and a moving train. You almost feel like you are in the train looking out of the window. Before you know it the camera cuts to a close up of Tom Cruise's eye-ball as seen through his Black "Ray Ban" sunglasses, as the camera opens wide Tom is shown staring at the camera with a smoke hanging from his mouth. He begins to speak "the dream is always the same…" and as the narration continues the dream sequence goes from a bathroom fantasy to a school exam room, thus setting up the two facets of Joel's existence, the opposite sex and the pressures of school. Tom Cruise and Rebecca De Mornay are outstanding in their roles and have the star chemistry to make the well-written script soar. Both stars are young, energetic and raw. The film's atmosphere is complemented by its creative soundtrack which features a strong synthesizer music score by German group "Tangerine Dream" and who can forget the moody Phil Collins number "In The Air Tonight" during the steamy train sequence. "Risky Business" is well paced, entertaining and a good mix of comedy and drama, it's a coming-of-age story that will keep your attention right through to the final scene. The ending is not predictable, some would say that's good, but in reality, would Joel have really got away with all this? I don't think so.

All The Right Moves **

US Release Date: 21st October 1983
Running Time: 91 min
US Classification: R
Director: Michael Chapman
Starring: Tom Cruise, Lea Thompson, Craig T. Nelson, Charles Cioffi, Gary Graham, Paul Carafotes, Chris Penn, Sandy Faison

Taglines:

* He had a dream but the dream had begun to sour...busting to break out he had to make...
* He has everything at stake. He can't afford to lose. He's got to make all the right moves.
* He plays to win.

Film Review:

By the time "All The Right Moves" hit cinemas in October 1983 Tom Cruise was already an established teen star of the decade, having appeared in five teen movies, "Endless Love" (1981), "Taps" (1981), "The Outsiders" (1983),

"Losin' It" (1983) and "Risky Business" (1983). "All The Right Moves" did not receive the same critical notice, box office or fanfare of "Risky Business" but it was nevertheless a neat entry to his growing filmography and certainly helped cement his teen star status. "All The Right Moves" is set in a steel-mill town in Western Pennsylvania. Cruise plays high school footballer Stefen Djordjevic whose ambition is to escape his mundane small-town existence by winning a football scholarship to a prominent university in order to study engineering. Stefen's coach (Craig T. Nelson) also wants out, but when the two clash heads at a major school football match, the conflict between them puts both their dreams and aspirations at risk. To add to the mix, Lea Thompson ("Back To The Future") is thrown in as Stef's girlfriend, Lisa Litski. Their relationship is merely padding to the story and adds a little emotional weight to Cruise's plight but ultimately plays second fiddle to the central football theme.

The film has generated discussion over the years not for "All The Right Moves" but for "All The Wrong Reasons". There is one love scene in the film between Cruise and Thompson that involved nudity. Some believe that it reveals more of Cruise's "private part" than he would have liked. There are only a few frames in it and if you blink you will surely miss it. Other reports suggest that a body double was used for this scene. Only Cruise, Thompson or the filmmakers would know the answer to this one. "All The Right" grossed $17,233,166 at the US box office, the success of Risky Business a couple of months earlier would surely have helped generate these figures. Whatever, the case may be "All The Right Moves" has left an impression on its target audience and according to one internet fan, a video rental stall called "All The Right Movies" was set up in Johnstown Pennsylvania where the film was made. "All The Right Moves" may share a place in the hearts of football fans or Tom Cruise fans for that matter but the bottom line is, the film is a strictly-by the numbers, high school football drama, nothing more, nothing less.

Chapter 5:

TEEN MOVIES OF 1984

Reckless ***

US Release Date: 3rd February 1984
Running Time: 90 min
US Classification: R
Director: James Foley
Starring: Aidan Quinn, Daryl Hannah, Kenneth McMillan, Cliff De Young, Lois Smith, Adam Baldwin, Dan Hedaya, Billy Jacoby, Toni Kalem, Jennifer Grey, Haviland Morris, Pamela Springsteen, Susan Kingsley, Adam LeFevre, Ellen Mirojnick.

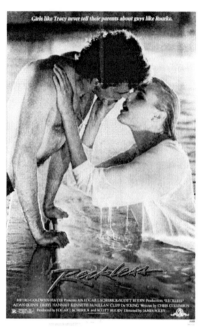

Tagline:

Girls like Tracy never tell their parents about guys like Rourke.

Film Review:

For James Foley, the teen drama "Reckless" was to be his directorial debut. Foley has carefully crafted a love story set in a smoggy little steel town, with characters that are a throwback to the days of the 50's and 60's JD films. Like Brando and Dean before him, star, Aidan Quinn straps on the leathers and burns rubber, to play Johnny Rourke, a rebellious bike-riding footballer. In this, his first film, Quinn became the 1980's version of the stereotypical loner. Blonde-haired Daryl Hannah plays Tracey Prescott, the rich girl with the "perfect" life. She has a boyfriend, is attractive, very athletic, and is a popular school cheerleader who can do a mean summersault on the parallel bars.

When the film begins there are no credits, just the title "Reckless". Within minutes you realize the significance of the title. We are immediately introduced to Johnny as he places a can of "Iron City Beer" on the edge of a platform at the town lookout. He revs his bike and heads for the can at high speed, a fraction of a second before he reaches the can he spins his bike around and flicks the can over the edge with his back wheel. Johnny is clearly a boy, who lives life on the edge. In the next scene Johnny rides his motorcycle down the highway towards an oncoming vehicle. The chicken run duel turns out to be against Tracey and her boyfriend Randy (Adam Baldwin). A collision is avoided only because Randy grabs the steering wheel and diverts the car seconds before impact. It is obvious that life means very little to Johnny, he has a death wish mentality and at this point you also begin to wonder about Tracey's outlook on life.

Johnny's rebellious character is clearly established, he is the bad boy from the wrong side of the tracks. His mother has left him, he lives with his alcoholic father and he has no friends. He is a brooding, angry young man with a very short fuse. He demonstrates this behaviour at the bowling alley when a drink is accidentally spilt on him. He immediately erupts like a volcano, grabs the person responsible and is just about to pound him, before being told to leave by a security guard. Johnny's life seems to be heading nowhere, he has a negative attitude towards society and there are very few people that he respects. At a high school career day, he is asked to fill in a questionnaire. When asked to state his "Career Goal", his answer is, "To Get Out Of Here". When asked, "What do you hope to get out of life", Johnny's answer is "More".

Johnny and Tracey's paths cross once again, when five football players and five cheerleaders are drawn out of a lottery and matched at random to enjoy free tickets to the school dance. Johnny is matched with Tracey to the disapproval of her boyfriend Randy. At the dance their attraction is not immediate. Johnny's first remark is, "Don't expect me to stick around here all-night". Nevertheless things take a turn for the better when he asks her to dance. Johnny even takes it upon himself to walk over and change the record that is playing. The two ignite in a vibrant dance routine to an up-tempo new-wave 80's track. The sequence is alive, featuring some interesting cinematography that has the dancers and the camera spinning around to the beat of the music, creating a sense of dizziness that makes you feel like you are on the dance floor. Jealous Randy, watching from afar, can't take it any longer. He muscles in, splits them apart and attempts to take Tracey away from Johnny. In the scuffle Johnny is asked to leave the dance. Tracey feels sorry for him and runs after him, only to get the reply "What do you want". She feels insulted and turns away but Johnny calls her back and asks her "Do you wanna go for a ride". Tracey accepts and her tumultuous love/hate relationship with Johnny begins. Johnny and Tracey are exact opposites so a relationship is not going to be easy. Johnny is a rebel from a dysfunctional family and Tracey is looking for something different but not quite sure what it is.

Johnny's problems are never ending. After an argument with his father, he is kicked out of the house. In a fit of anger his father destroys his stereo equipment and in retaliation Johnny puts his fist through the window. In the meantime Tracey has an altercation with her mother regarding her so-called "perfect" life. As the two flee their respective homes in anger, their paths cross once again. In the film's standout scene, the two lovers, in a fit of animal attraction, break into the school and wreak havoc. They scatter files, release animals from science labs, run wild through the corridors and belt each with padded clubs in the school gym before stripping down to their underwear for a dip in the school's indoor pool. All this to the sound of Kim Wilde's "Kid's In America".

Despite the physical attraction, Tracey is unsure and confused about her feelings for Johnny. After their romantic encounter at the school, she leaves him there asleep. When he comes to the house looking for her she refuses to let him in, but when he produces a pair of her underwear she is taken by his charm. When they meet at the lookout and Johnny becomes aggressive towards her, she decides to leave him and go back to her boyfriend. At this point Johnny learns an important lesson, you can't mistreat people, particularly those that you love and care about and expect that there will be no consequences. Filled with rage and emotion after his father's death, Johnny turns up at the school on his bike. He rides up the stairs and down the corridors until he finds Tracey in the school assembly. In one last-ditch effort to win her back, Johnny takes her aside and tells her, "I need you to come with me and do everything with me and feel everything with me, it's just not good alone".

With these winning words we think it's all over, until Randy bursts in and a fight breaks out. As the school watches the drama unfold, Johnny has no alternative but to hop on his bike and leave, but will Tracey go will him? No, not until Johnny utters the magic words, "Tracey, I Love You". In the film's touching finale, Tracey, all teary eyed, jumps on the back of Johnny's bike and the two lovers ride off, through the school corridor and down the highway. As the wind blows through their hair and they ride into a new life together, their happy faces light up the screen to the pulsating beat of Bob Segar's "Roll Me Away". Thus, another chapter of teen-angst has come to an end.

Written by Chris Columbus (director of "Adventures In Babysitting" and "Home Alone"), "Reckless" is a fairly typical teenage love story that makes use of all-the usual cliques to tell its simplistic story. Without a complicated plot, misunderstood poor boy falls in love with spoilt-little rich-girl; the success of "Reckless" relies strongly on the chemistry between its two stars. Aidan Quinn and Daryl Hannah, although a little old to be playing teenagers (both in their 20's), are excellent as the two young lovers. Blue-eyed Quinn and blue-eyed Hannah, together, generate an attractive screen presence that harks back to the teenage movies of yesteryear. After "Reckless", oddball roles and off-kilter characters continued for Quinn in films such as, "Desperately Seeking Susan" (1985), "Stakeout" (1987), "Crusoe" (1988) and "The Assignment" (1997), in which Quinn played the dual role of terrorist and naval officer. In 1986 Quinn was even listed in "Screen World" as one of twelve "Promising New Actors". Statuesque Daryl Hannah was no newcomer to the big screen when she signed on to do "Reckless", she had already appeared in "Blade Runner" (1982) with Harrison Ford and "Summer Lovers" (1982) with Peter Gallagher. After "Reckless" her career continued to flourish, in films such as "Splash" (1984) with Tom Hanks, "Legal Eagles" (1986) with Robert Redford and "Roxanne" (1987) with Steve Martin. Quinn and Hannah were not the only stars to rise from this film, Jennifer Grey who only appears in a few small scenes as a school student would quickly move from "Reckless" to "Red Dawn" (1985) to "Ferris Bueller's Day Off" (1986) and then to the blockbuster dance flick "Dirty Dancing" (1987) where she and Patrick Swayze achieved temporary super-stardom. "Reckless" grossed only $8.3 million at the US box office. Its use of profanity, nudity and sex scenes earned it an R certificate in the US and deemed it unsuitable for younger audiences. With a little bit more left to the imagination, "Reckless" may have been a bigger hit for MGM.

Footloose *** ½*

US Release Date: 17th February 1984
Running Time: 107 min
US Classification: PG
Director: Herbert Ross
Starring: Kevin Bacon, Lori Singer, John Lithgow, Christopher Penn, Jim Youngs, Sarah Jessica Parker

Taglines:

* The music is on his side
* He's a big-city kid in a small town. They said he'd never win. He knew he had to.

Film Review:

"Footloose" is an energetic dance musical that was the surprise hit of 1984. The film did not feature any household names but it did come with a title track that was enough to blow you away. On release, word of mouth was positive and rapid fire. Teen audiences took to it like candy bars, the effect was simple, it made them want to get up and dance. Almost overnight, the movie and its soundtrack album became phenomenal successes across the globe. "Footloose" is set in a mid-western town that condemns Rock "n" Roll music and dancing. This is the catalyst that drives the film and its characters. Kevin Bacon plays the new boy in town who has a hard time coming to terms with the strict bans. John Lithgow plays the town minister and influential authority figure. It is gradually revealed that the reason for the music ban revolves around Lithgow's loss of a child in a car accident a few years earlier. His rebellious daughter Lori Singer falls in love with Bacon much to the annoyance of her father and her hotheaded boyfriend played by Jim Youngs. Situations reach boiling point and sparks fly between all characters before the dust settles for the show-stopping finale.

"Footloose" may get a little heavy-handed and plot driven at times but luckily it emerges from the confines of the emotional drama thanks to its frequent injection of music and dance numbers. The film has a splendid soundtrack and opens with a dynamic credit sequence featuring the hit title track played over a variety of different dancing feet, all-jump cut MTV style. Another memorable music number is "Let's Hear It For The Boy" played over scenes of Kevin Bacon teaching a young Christopher Penn how to dance. Both songs; the Kenny Loggin's title track "Footloose" and the Deniece Williams track "Let's Hear It For The Boy" were nominated for Academy Awards in 1985 but lost out to Stevie Wonder's "I Just Called To Say I Love You", from the hit film "The Woman In Red" (1984). "Footloose" also features a number of nail biting stunt sequences. Lori Singer's death wish scenes with the truck and train are a standout, not to mention unsettling and of course who can forget the Kevin Bacon/Jim Youngs dueling tractor confrontation, that owes more than a little to the James Dean chicken run sequence from "Rebel Without A Cause" (1955).

"Footloose" is the movie that sparked Kevin Bacon's film career but it could easily have gone another way as three higher profile actors, Christopher Atkins, Tom Cruise and Rob Lowe were all considered for the lead role. Bacon was the lucky one and he has never looked back since. The film also marked a good warm up for "Sex In The City" star Sarah Jessica Parker who appears in a small role as Chris Penn's girlfriend, the two get to strut their stuff briefly in a bar scene to the fantastic beat of John Cougar

Mellancamp's "Hurt So Good". The following year Parker would go on to star in her own teen dance musical "Girls Just Want To Have Fun" (1985), a low-budget production in comparison to "Footloose" but nevertheless just as entertaining.

"Footloose" had a production budget of around $8 million. It went on to gross over $80 million at the US Box office alone and ranked an overall 7th in its year. It was a major financial hit for Paramount Studios proving once and for all that teen dance musicals, if done right, were a very marketable commodity. No wonder the film was remade in 2011, it certainly has the goods. The bottom line is "Footloose" is an appealing cinematic delight, fun for all the right reasons; great music, well choreographed dance numbers, strong performances and of course a good message. That's right, Lithgow roars and Bacon's cool-factor soars while the soundtrack and theatrics are a match made in heaven.

*Where The Boys Are '84 ***

US Release Date: 6th April 1984
Running Time: 94 min
US Classification: R
Director: Hy Averback
Starring: Lisa Hartman, Lorna Luft, Wendy Schaal, Lynn-Holly Johnson, Russell Todd, Howard McGillin, Christopher McDonald, Daniel McDonald, Alana Stewart, Louise Sorel, Danny B. Harvey, Michael K. Osborn.

Taglines:

* When girls want a vacation filled with fun sun and romance, they go to Fort Lauderdale... Where The Boys Are '84
* Where all your dreams come true

Film Review:

"Where The Boys Are '84" is the flipside of "Spring Break", a girl's Fort Lauderdale movie as opposed to a boys Fort Lauderdale movie. In fact "Where The Boys Are '84" often ran on a double-bill with "Spring Break" on the drive-in circuit. "Where The Boys Are '84" marked producer Allan Carrs' attempt to update the 1960's classic for 1980's audiences – mixed results and opinions definitely ensued. The result was raunchier than its predecessor but lacked real substance. The 1960 version was a real gem in the genre with a great cast, good performances and an engaging script to back it up, while the 1984 remake is so paper-thin that the producers haven't even bothered to release it on DVD at the time of writing. The story of the '84 version is straightforward, 4 college girls go to Fort Lauderdale for Spring Break hoping to find their Mr. Right. All the usual hi-jinks you would expect in a film of its type are present, sex, drugs, alcohol, rock n roll music and a few topless babes, it's all here, but the film just goes nowhere pretty fast. Even the 80s soundtrack can't save it. The 1960 version came with a memorable love song title track sung by Connie Francis, this '84 version also comes with its own rendition of the same song, this time performed by lead actress Lisa Hartman but unfortunately, like everything else, it falls short of the original.

It's hard to figure out what producer Alan Carr was trying to do with this one. The idea or concept was fine, it certainly needed to be revisited for a 1980s audience but somehow the film just lost its way. The innocence and charm of the 1960s version is missing and everything about this one feels exploitative. The script is smutty, the jokes are mindless and the cast are all too old to be college students. Unfortunately, "Where The Boys Are '84" has an unbelieve-ability factor that is hard to shake. Lisa Hartman was about 28 years old, Lorna Luft (Judy Garland's daughter) was 32 years old, Wendy Schaal was 30 years old and Lyn-Holly Johnson, fresh from her stint as a Bond chick in "For Your Eyes Only" was the baby of the group, clocking in at 26 years of age. Also, the film's male star, Russell Todd (who was apparently discovered by Carr after Carr saw Todd's photo on his barber's wall) clocked in at around 26 years. Despite all its short-comings, the film's failures were not due to any lack of trying by the cast who all seemed to be giving it their all.

At the Razzie Awards in 1985 the film was up for 5 Awards including, Worst Picture, Worst Screenplay, Worst Musical Score, Worst New Star and Worst Supporting Actress and yes it did come out a winner with one award, Lyn-Holly Johnson was voted Worst Supporting Actress. "Where The Boys Are '84" might not have anything substantial to offer in the way of plot or performances but the Florida scenery and Fort Lauderdale backdrop are enough to keep some viewers interested... anyway, I am sure that there are some fans out there that still fondly remember something about this film.....the Hot-Bod Contest......maybe?

Footnote: In August 2011, "Where The Boys Are '84" was finally released on DVD in the United States by Scorpion Entertainment. Special features include original Theatrical Trailer and on camera interviews with stars Wendy Schaal and Russell Todd, who by the sound of things had an absolute ball making this picture.

Breakin' ***

US Release Date: 4th May 1984
Running Time: 90 min
US Classification: PG
Director: Joel Silberg
Starring: Lucinda Dickey, Adolfo Quinones, Michael Chambers, Ben Lokey, Christopher McDonald, Phineas Newborn III, Bruno Falcon, Timothy Solomon, Ana Sánchez, Ice-T, Peter Bromilow, Eleanor Zee, Scott Cooper, Ed Lottimer, Teresa Kelly

Taglines:

* The dance explosion of the 80s
* For the break of your life! Push it to pop it! Rock it to lock it! Break it to make it!
* Here The Beat... It's On The Street! Breakin' & Poppin' Everywhere!
* The beat of *the st*reets is...

Film Review:

"Breakin'" (aka "Breakdance The Movie) became the first big screen feature film to bring worldwide audience attention to the art of "Breakdancing", a phenomenon that was sweeping the U.S. in the early 1980s. At the time, Golan Globus or Cannon Films tapped into anything and everything that was a fad or a craze. They were the exploitation kings of the decade and churned out novelty films like they were hotcakes. Some of their films even featured big name stars like Chuck Norris, Charles Bronson, Sylvester Stallone and Christopher Reeve. They are remembered today for launching some of the most popular movie franchises of the decade including the "Missing In Action" film series, the "American Ninja" film series, the "Death Wish" sequels and of course the "Breakdance" movies. "Breakin'" may not have featured any big name stars but it did tap into the new dance craze of the moment and it did showcase an assortment of talented young dancers.

We missed "Breakin'" on its cinema release but we were fortunate enough to catch up with it at a local club, that' right, in the early 80s when film's finished their cinema run they popped up on big-screens in clubs around town, sometimes a matter of a few weeks or a few months later. It cost us nothing to see the film but the price of a few drinks and a packet of potato chips. What an absolute bargain and what a great experience. It was school holidays and the club hall was jam-packed with young teens. The atmosphere was electrifying or should I say, electric boogaloo...but that's the sequel. Everybody enjoyed it and I am sure a lot of the teens in attendance would have gone home, found a piece of cardboard, fired up their ghetto-blaster and busted a few moves in their neighbourhood streets, the big concern for parents being their kids trying to do the head-spins.

"Breakin'" features spectacular dance sequences, a catchy hip-hop soundtrack and energetic performances from the three leads, Lucinda Dickey, Adolfo Quinones & Michael Chambers. Trying to turn actors into dancers doesn't always pay off, so the filmmakers went for the reverse and all three leads were chosen because of their exceptional dance skills. In this case, choosing dancers with some acting ability was the right decision and it paid off. Acting wise, the three leads brought a raw freshness to the production (including their own wardrobe) while their show-stopping dance moves shine in every frame of the film. Lucinda Dickey especially, was a stand-out as Kelly (aka Special K). Her drop-dead gorgeous looks added a signature dimension to the film. Lucinda had only previously appeared in a small blink-&-you'll-miss-her role as a girl greaser in "Grease 2" (1982).

An interesting dynamic of "Breakin" is that is takes conflicting situations (that would normally turn in to fights) and allows them to be settled by dance-offs instead of fight-offs. Dance-offs may be a bit of a throwback to "West Side Story" but these well staged "combat" dance sequences are some of the most unique dance moments put on the big screen. It is easy to see why this low-budget film became a surprise hit grossing over $36 million at the US box office and ranking 18th in its year. Its success paved the way for the sequel "Breakin 2: Electric Booglaoo", that was released about 6 months later, just before the year was out. Many fans believe the sequel is as good if not better than the original. "Breakin'" also inspired a number of other films of its type including, "Beat Street" (1984), "Body Rock" (1984), "Rappin'" (1985) and "Krush Groove" (1985) all entertaining in their own way, but certainly inferior to "Breakin'".

Dance and teen movie fans aside, "Breakin'" still has another drawcard. Over the years it has become a curiosity piece for martial arts fans wanting to get a glimpse of the pre-stardom "Muscles From Brussels". Yes, that's right; look out for kung fu superstar Jean-Claude Van Damme in an early scene of the film. He is clearly visible as a background dancer in the exhilarating Venice Beach dance sequence. You can't miss him, he's the one wearing the signature black tights and trying to muscle in on all the action. Van Damme is hilariously super-charged, fighting for every frame of screen time and clearly demonstrating his desire to become a movie star. Also, look-out for rapper Ice-T in a small appearance - doing what he does best, you guessed it? Rappin.

Although the 1980s are well and truly behind us, "Breakin'" has still retained a strong- fan base worldwide due to the on-going interest in the art of dance. Turbo's unique broom dance is still a talking point today amongst dance aficionados. Is it because of the incredible skill of the dance? Or is it because of the clearly visible magic string that brings the broom to life? I'm not sure, but the bottom line is, the real stars of "Breakin'" are the dance numbers and there are plenty to boot so if you like dance films they don't come much better than this. With songs such as "There's No Stopping Us" by Ollie and Jerry and "Ain't Nobody" by Chaka Khan on the soundtrack, the gang will have you poppin' and lockin' long before the end credits roll. Now, if the dancing doesn't grab you, then some of the names might, Ozone, Turbo, Special K, Shabba-Doo and Boogaloo Shrimp, not names you hear every-day but certainly colourful just like the film.

Sixteen Candles ****

US Release Date: 4th May 1984
Running Time: 93 min
US Classification: PG
Director: John Hughes
Starring: Molly Ringwald, Anthony Michael Hall, Michael Schoeffling, John Cusack, Paul Dooley, Gedde Watanabe, Joan Cusack

Taglines:
* It's the time of your life that may last a lifetime.
* When you're just sixteen anything can happen!
* This is Samantha Baker and today is her 16th birthday. The problem is, nobody remembers.

Film Review:

For Writer/Director John Hughes this is where it all began. "Sixteen Candles" marked his first venture into the director's chair and the film set a benchmark for other teen movies of the decade. While many of the teen movies of the early 80s revolved primarily around raunch and sex, John Hughes gave his characters a beating heart, with sensitivity and charm. Apart from the script one of the key factors for the film's quality was the casting of rising star Molly Ringwald. Molly's previous work included some TV roles and film appearances in "Tempest" (1982) and "Spacehunter: Adventures In The Forbidden Zone" (1983). "Sixteen Candles" was Molly's first major starring role, it proved to be her breakout performance and everything looked bright from here on for both Ringwald and Hughes. "Sixteen Candles" may have been the first collaboration between Hughes and Ringwald but it certainly wasn't the last. The director and the star struck up a fruitful partnership during the decade that continued on for two more successful projects, "The Breakfast Club" (1985) and "Pretty In Pink" (1986) which established the brilliantly talented redhead as a marquee name and earned her the label of "Teen Queen of the 1980's". Molly even made the front cover of "Time" magazine during this decade.

Molly Ringwald is likeable and sympathetic in her portrayal of Samantha Baker, the high school student who is dumbfounded when her family forgets her 16th birthday. Her birthday is the day before her sister's wedding. Her family and relatives are so preoccupied with the wedding plans that they simply forget her special day. It is this that triggers off a series of hilarious and unforgettable situations. Molly feels that her family just doesn't care anymore and to add to her disappointment the school geek, Farmer Ted, played delightfully off-the wall by Anthony Michael Hall is desperately in love with her and spends most of the film chasing her around. Molly has other ideas; she has her eyes focused on the boy of her dreams, Jake Ryan, played by Michael Schoeffling, a Matt Dillon look-alike. To add insult to injury two sets of grandparents come to stay at her house for the wedding, not to mention Chinese exchange student Long Duk Dong who is also brought into the picture to add comedy relief. Party animal, Long Duk Dong, played to a tee by Gedde Watanabe rivals "the Geek" for some of the film's funnier moments. Also, watch out for future teen star John Cusack and his sister Joan Cusack in fun supporting roles as geeks

"Sixteen Candles" has a goofy, way-out, but sweet sense of humour that seems outrageously original. The film has a number of stand-out moments including, the introduction of the geek on the school bus, the grandmothers cringe-worthy dialogue about Molly's breast size, the awkward moments at the school dance, the geek charging for peaks at Molly's panties in the locker room and of course the film's signature frame featuring the cake and the two lovers looking dreamily into each other's eyes as the end credits roll. "Sixteen Candles" has it all and more, even a party scene in which the house gets trashed, Jake's girlfriend gets drunk, the geek gets trapped inside a glass table and Long Duk Dong makes an absolute fool of himself as he comes crashing through the floor on an exercise bike. "Sixteen Candles" grossed over $23 million at the US box office and ranked 44th in its year. The film left a mark with cinemagoers and critics alike, with both Molly Ringwald and Anthony Michael Hall winning "Best Young Actress" and "Best Young Actor" at the Young Artists Awards. All of this, together with Molly Ringwald's exceptional charm, Hughes' superb direction and the outstanding performances from the entire supporting cast is why "Sixteen Candles" will forever remain an essential, must-see, teen comedy classic. A trip back to the awesome 80s doesn't get much better than is.

Making The Grade ** ½

US Release Date: 18th May 1984
Running Time: 105 min
US Classification: R
Director: Dorian Walker
Starring: Judd Nelson, Jonna Lee, Gordon Jump, Walter Olkewicz, Ronald Lacey, Dana Olsen, Carey Scott, Scott McGinnis, Andrew Dice Clay, John Dye, John Stevens

Taglines:

* If you can't make it fake it!
* Palmer Woodrow III earned his diploma the old-fashioned way. He hired Eddie Keaton to graduate for him.
* His major was attitude.
* The comedy that hits higher education below the belt! (From the Trailer)
* A couple of guy's run a con on the snootiest prep school in America. (From the Trailer)
* He is going to lose his inheritance if he doesn't graduate from Hoover prep. (From the Trailer)

Film Review:

In 1984 Judd Nelson was a virtual unknown when Golan-Globus took a chance on casting the 25- year-old newcomer as a college student in the teen comedy "Making The Grade". Internet sources suggest that funny-man Jim Carrey was also up for the role. Nevertheless, despite Nelson's excessive age for playing a college student and lack of previous film work, he impressed producers enough to score the lead role and mark his feature film debut. In the previous year the screwball comedy "Trading Places" starring Dan Aykroyd and Eddie Murphy grossed over $90 million at the US Box office making it one of the highest grossing comedies of the decade. "Making The Grade" became the teen movie's answer to "Trading Places". Although, "Making The Grade" could not replicate the same success at the US box office of its predecessor, it is nevertheless an adequate entry in the role reversal sub-genre. The storyline of "Making The Grade" is a slight variant on the rich guy trades places with the poor guy scenario. In "Trading Places", a wealthy stockbroker (Aykroyd) trades places with a down-and-out street hustler (Murphy), literally. In "Making The Grade", a lazy millionaire playboy (Palmer Woodrow III played by Dana Olsen) hires a dropout street-wise kid (Eddie Keaton played by Judd Nelson) to take his place in college while he goes on vacation in Europe. Palmer is on the verge of losing his inheritance unless he graduates while Eddie is in debt and on the run from a ruthless bookie (The Dice Man played by Andrew Dice Clay). If Eddie can graduate for Palmer there is a huge bonus in it for him, enough to solve all his money problems and enough laughs to be had for the audience.

"Making The Grade" also known as, "The Last American Preppie" is ultimately a routine college farce and as the trailer so wittingly states, it is the story of "Two guys and one great scam that could ruin the rep of Hoover prep". The film sets up the premise well and introduces the two characters and their class differences effectively. The message from Palmer's father is "If you don't go to school and graduate you will be cut off, no trust fund, no allowance and you will actually have to get a job". On the other hand the message from Eddie's Bookie, The Dice Man is "break his legs, then get me a pizza". Both Palmer and Eddie are in a predicament and both need each other to get out of it. While on the run from the Dice man, Eddie ends up in Palmer's locker and before you know it the switch is made. When Eddie hits the college campus, he arrives in a beat-up-taxi, complete with red polyester suit, a stereo held high, the volume on full throttle, a smoke in his mouth and a strut to match his "Saturday Night Fever" attitude. Along the way Eddie falls in love with Tracey (Joanna Lee) thereby unsettling the jealous college bully Biff (Scott McGinnis). "Making The Grade" features some absurd situations which include, a maid wearing a Michael Jackson surgical mask upon entry into Palmer's bedroom, a blindfolded violinist playing music in an Elvis Presley hotel room while Palmer and his girlfriend make-out and of course who can forget Eddie trying to impress Tracey at the school dance by bursting into an impromptu breakdancing number that is absolutely wild to say the least. The dance is clearly performed by Judd Nelson's stand-in or stunt dancer, although Nelson does some of the robotics in close up.

Nelson and Olsen are well cast in the central roles but it's the supports that steal some of the film's best moments with Coach Wordman (Walter Olkewicz) and The Dice Man (Andrew Dice Clay) both standouts. Overweight coach Wordman is a hoot, he spends time watching nudie movies with the boys in the dormitory and when sprung tells the principal that they were watching National Geographic documentaries. At the school dance, the boys assemble in a football huddle as the Coach advises them on the dos and don'ts about the opposite sex, his one-liners in this pep talk being some of the best in the film. The Dice Man is outstanding as the heavy and it's fun watching his on-screen persona in its infancy. Dice has a hilarious Travolta moment; complete with headband, in the "Staying Alive" party sequence and his Al Pacino impersonation in the film's closing moments is also treat.

"Making The Grades" end credits indicate that "Palmer and Eddie will be back in Tourista" but unfortunately the sequel never materialised. Poor US box office receipts may have been the reason, with the film bringing in just over $4.5 million that year. Judd Nelson's next film was the hugely popular hit, "The Breakfast Club" and his star was certainly on the rise so I suspect it would have been impossible for Golan-Globus to snag him again for the sequel "Tourista". Whatever the case may be teen movie fans that missed it in its cinema release certainly caught up with it on the video circuit and loved every minute of it. Many critics have also been very kind to it; Variety described, "Making The Grade" as "Genuinely funny...splendidly played" while Los Angeles Times, says it is "Well cast and likeable" with "real-out-loud laughs". Although a little plodding in the middle third and maybe a-tad-too-long overall "Making The Grade" is still a good film of its type, the cast connect with the material, the college hi-jinks raise a smile and the film stands as a raw representation of Judd Nelson's 80s work. All up the film earns a passing grade for its target audience.

The Karate Kid **** ½

US Release Date: 22nd June 1984
Running Time: 126 min
US Classification: PG
Director: John G. Avildsen
Starring: Ralph Macchio, Pat Morita, Elisabeth Shue, Martin Kove, Randee Heller, William Zabka Chad McQueen

Taglines:

* Only the 'Old One' could teach him the secrets of the masters.
* He taught him the secret to Karate lies in the mind and heart. Not in the hands.
* The Moment Of Truth…

Film Review:

"The Karate Kid", the teen version of "Rocky" was the surprise box-office hit of 1984. It was shot in about 6 weeks and grossed over $90 million at the US Box Office alone. The film features a heart-warming story about a fatherless New Jersey kid, Daniel LaRusso (Ralph Macchio) and the problems he encounters when he moves to L.A. with his mother (Randee Heller). Being the new kid in town, Daniel is bullied by Johnny (William Zabka) and his gang of tough students from the local karate school. Sadistic karate instructor John Kreese (Martin Kove) and his warped "show no mercy" philosophy provides the fuel that pushes Johnny's delinquent behavior into hyper-drive. When Daniel falls for pretty Californian girl Ali, (Elisabeth Shue) his problems escalate when he discovers that she is in fact the former girlfriend of karate champion, Johnny. Daniel soon befriends a Japanese handyman, Mr. Miyagi (Pat Morita who played Arnold on "Happy Days") who is the janitor at his apartment block. Daniel is later trained by him and taught the ancient art of Kung Fu and more importantly the wisdom of eastern philosophy which he uses to overcome the bullies.

"The Karate Kid" is not your standard run-of-the-mill teen film. It is a sensitive story of friendship between an old man who has lost his son and a young teen that has lost his father. Mr. Miyagi's karate teachings are unusual to say the least. When Daniel is asked to wash cars and paint fences, he is at first confused but eventually realizes that there is method in Mr. Miyagi's system of training. The terms "Wax on / Wax Off" used in Daniels training regime have now become a part of cinema folklore. As for, the 1950s Chevrolet convertible that Daniel waxes and drives, actor Macchio has proudly owned it ever since completion of the film and claims that it is now one of his most prized possessions. The appeal of "The Karate Kid" is in its feel-good story and the positive message that is found in the philosophies it projects, winning is not important and kung fu fighting should only be used in self-defense. As Mr. Miyagi points out to Daniel, we learn martial arts not so we can fight, but rather, so we won't have to fight.

"The Karate Kid" is irresistible from start to finish with outstanding performances from the entire cast. One's hat would have to go off to the casting agents who selected such an impeccable blend of personalities that have been able to bring Robert Mark Kamen's emotionally charged script to life. Comedian, Pat Morita got his dream-role, playing against-type, as the wise Mr. Miyagi. The filmmakers were hesitant at first in casting a comedian in this pivotal role but were convinced otherwise after his brilliant audition. Pat went on to be nominated for an Academy Award for his exceptional portrayal and as Director Avildsen believes, Pat got the nomination for his mesmerizing "drunk scene" that was almost left on the cutting room floor. Pretty, Elisabeth Shue with the girl-next-door looks, who took time off from Harvard University to make her film debut, is wonderful as Macchio's love interest. Elisabeth even snagged a "Best Young Supporting Actress Award" at the 1985 Young Artist Awards. Cute, dark-haired, Ralph Macchio, with his boyish looks, is charismatic in the title role and proved beyond doubt that he was the ideal choice, despite being almost 23 years old at the time. Athletic, blonde-haired, William Zabka, although 4-years-younger, was the perfect contrast to Macchio, while Martin Kove's intense portrayal of the ultimate bad-guy instructor is the perfect antagonist to Pat Morita's portrayal of the mystic, quietly spoken and wise sensei who could handle any situation with fine precision if required.

I was fortunate to see "The Karate Kid" on the big screen in 1984 and have since watched it a number of times on video and DVD. I was recently surfing the cable T.V. channels and it just happened to be on. After watching only 2 minutes, it had me hooked. "The Karate Kid" is one of those uplifting films that you can watch over and over again and it is just as entertaining every-time. Apart from performance and story, one of the film's qualities that contribute to its re-watch-ability factor is its exciting soundtrack. "The Karate Kid" soundtrack is a nice blend of 80s pop tunes ("Young Hearts" by Commuter and "Feel The Night" by Baster Robertson), powerful rock ballads ("The Moment Of Truth" by Survivor and "You're The Best" by Joe Eposito) and of-course, beautiful mood music by master musician Bill Conti. The film's gripping climatic karate tournament is complemented immensely by Conti's dynamic music score which highlights the emotion and propels the on-screen action superbly. It is easy to see why this remarkable motion picture has gained an international fan-base and why it has become one of the most loved film franchises of all-time.

It's no surprise then, that the world-wide box office success of "The Karate Kid" spawned three sequels, "The Karate Kid Part II" (1986), "The Karate Kid Part III" (1989) and "The Next Karate Kid" (1994), with Oscar winner Hilary Swank replacing Ralph Macchio in the final installment. Viewers just couldn't get enough of the wonderful characters and the interesting confrontations that they engage in, so much so, that in 2011 a remake starring Jackie Chan and Will Smith's son Jaden Smith, hit the multi-plexes to the tune of more box office dollars. The bottom–line is "The Kartate Kid" is old-school entertainment at its best. It was not only one of the best motion pictures of 1984 but is considered by many to be also one of most inspirational. Literally thousands of young kids, the world-over, have taken up some form of self-defense training since the release of this film, while some have even tried to catch flies with chopsticks, all to varying degrees of success. More importantly, the message the film leaves is a positive one; Karate is to be used for self-defense only. With "The Karate Kid", John G. Avildsen (director of the original "Rocky") has triumphantly brought to the screen another crowd-pleasing classic.

The Last Starfighter ***

US Release Date: 13th July 1984
Running Time: 101 min
US Classification: PG
Director: Nick Castle
Starring: Lance Guest, Robert Preston, Dan O'Herlihy, Catherine Mary Stuart, Barbara Bosson

Taglines:

* In his wildest dreams Alex never suspected that tonight he would become...The Last Starfighter
* He didn't find his dreams... his dreams found him.
* Alex Rogan is a small town teenager with big time dreams. Dreams of college... of

success... of marrying his girlfriend, Maggie. He's just like everybody else, except Alex has a very special talent... that no one on Earth can appreciate. But, tonight, a mysterious stranger has called on Alex. He's come from a galaxy that's under attack from an alien force. And Alex's unique ability is their last hope.

* He's got one extraordinary chance at the dream of a lifetime.

Film Review:

When "The Last Starfighter" hit the scene in 1984, computer generated visual effects were still in their infancy. The film was amongst the first to use extensive computer graphics to show real objects in place of models. The popularity of video games, however, had reached a peak and anyone under 21 years-of-age loved to spend their spare time and spare change playing their favourite video games in the local arcade parlours. The time was just right for this film to make its mark; Computer graphics had moved forward, Sci-Fi was popular, teen movies were reaching a peak and arcade games were thriving. A teen, Sci-Fi flick with a video game angel, how could they go wrong? It was inevitable that "The Last Starfighter" would be a hit with the teenage crowd. The film was every video gamers dream come true and still stands today as a nostalgic piece of 1980s pop culture.

Teenager, Alex Rogan (Lance Guest) lives in the Starlite Starbright trailer park with his mother (Barbara Bosson). He spends all of his spare-time playing a video game called The Starfighter. Alex's video game skills approach genius level when he reaches the final stage of the Starfighter game and wins to the applause of his friends and family. The win is the beginning of a new chapter in his life. In no time at all Alex is visited by Centauri (Robert Preston in his last screen role), an alien from another world. Centauri's purpose is to recruit Alex as a Starfighter to help his people save the universe from destruction by rebel invaders. To fine-tune Alex's skills he is teamed up with fellow Starfighter, Grig (Dan O'Herlihy), a lizard-like-alien who will serve as Alex's navigator when the inter-galactic battle begins. So that family and friends do not miss Alex, Centauri replaces Alex with a beta-unit, a look-alike-android that will take his place on earth until he finishes his mission in space. This adds some fun to the proceedings, particularly in the sequences between Alex's android replica and his girlfriend Maggie (Catherine Mary Stewart). Unfortunately, the android has a tendency to short circuit when Maggie gets intimate.

Ultimately, "The Last Starfighter" is a fun, science-fiction fantasy that can be enjoyed by all ages. The cast is a nice blend of Hollywood veterans (Robert Preston, Dan O'Herlihy) and rising young talent (Lance Guest, Catherine Mary Stewart). The film was released at a time when arcade games were all the rage and the "Star Wars" movies were big box office. "The Last Starfighter" capitalized on both markets, becoming a successful film not only with Sci-Fi fans but also with most critics. The special effects and alien creatures were outstanding for their time and the movie has developed a cult status over the years. If the visual effects don't transport you into this fantasy world of Starfighters and space battles, Craig Safan's powerful main title theme certainly will. This grand soundtrack is almost bigger than the film itself. Trumpets, trombones, you name it, this one has it all and everything comes together brilliantly to create a trademark title track that is nothing short of epic. Pump up the volume on your home theatre system for this one and watch Alex as he is whisked away into space to take part in an inter-galactic war to protect a civilization from destruction…where he will become "The Last Starfighter".

Revenge Of The Nerds ***

US Release Date: 20th July 1984
Running Time: 90 min
US Classification: R
Director: Jeff Kanew
Starring: Robert Carradine, Anthony Edwards, Timothy Busfield, Andrew Cassese, Curtis Armstrong, Larry B. Scott, Brian Tochi, Julia Montgomery, Michelle Meyrink, Ted McGinley, Donald Gibb, James Cromwell, David Wohl, John Goodman.

Taglines:

* They've been laughed at, picked on and put down. But now it's time for the odd to get even! Their time has come!
 * The time has come for REVENGE OF THE NERDS
* Let the battle begin!

Film Review:

"Revenge Of The Nerds" is a madcap teen comedy that could be best described as a cross between "Animal House" and "Porky's". The film takes the Frat House elements from "Animal House", the raunchiness of "Porky's" and then adds flavor to the mix by pitting Nerds against jocks in a battle for supremacy on a college campus that has gone insane. Over the years the film has developed a cult status and is considered by many to be one of the better teen sex comedies that were unleashed to cinema audiences of the 1980's. Coarse-language, nudity and crude humor are part and parcel of this type of film but the key to this film's success is its likeable underdogs, the downtrodden, the bullied outcasts, the guys we came to know as the "Nerds", who grouped together to fight back against the jocks and sportos who picked on them, put them down and made their every existence a living hell. Yes, there is a moral to the story amongst all this absurdity and it's the film's final reel, a speech by Nerd, Louis Skolnick that brings all the elements together and gives the film its heart.

The filmmakers have done a great job creating an assortment of rag-tag characters to populate the two fraternities, The Tri-Lambas (The Nerds) and their archenemies, The Alpha Betas (The Jocks). Louis Skolnick (Robert Carradine) and Gilbert Lowell (Anthony Edwards) are the head-nerds complete with pocket-pens, calculators, glasses and daggy clothes, while Stan Gable (Ted McGinley) and Danny Burke (Matt Salinger) head the gang of muscular pretty-boy-jocks with their trendy sports jackets and cheerleader girlfriends led by Betty Childs (Julia Montgomery). The supporting characters, however, are the ones that add real color to the proceedings and at times steal the show. There's Poindexter (Timothy Busfield); the absolute geek, Wormser (Andrew Cassese); the child-like goon, Booger (Curtis Armstrong); the grotty nose-picker with the powerful burp, Lamar (Larry B. Scott); the gay Negro, Takashi (Brian Tochi); the fruity Asian and who can forget the biggest brute of them all, Fred "The Ogre" Palowakski from the Alpha-Beta fraternity. Relatively unknown actors played all of these characters at the time and each actor has done an excellent job of bringing his or her character to life in one hilarious situation after the next.

"Revenge Of The Nerds" was the surprise success of 1984. Made on a small budget of $8 million the film surprised everybody when it went on to gross over $40 million at the US box office. The film soon became a franchise and spawned the popular big screen sequel "Revenge of The Nerds II: Nerds In Paradise" (1987) and in the 1990's two made for TV sequels "Revenge of The Nerds III: The Next Generation" (1992) and "Revenge of The Nerds IV: Nerds In Love" (1994). "Revenge Of The Nerds", although made in the 1980's has not dated very much. The weak rising up against the strong is a universal theme and today's teenagers should still enjoy the exploits of these lovable characters just as much as previous generations of teenagers did. If you haven't seen "Revenge Of The Nerds" you won't know who Dudley "Booger" Dawson is and if you don't know who Dudley "Booger" Dawson " is, then you are missing out on knowing one of the most off-beat characters of 1980's teen movie folklore. For the Nerd out there, "Revenge Of The Nerds" would have to be the most uplifting movie of the century.

No Small Affair ***

US Release Date: 9th November 1984
Running Time: 102 min
US Classification: R
Director: Jerry Schatzberg
Starring: Jon Cryer, Demi Moore, George Wendt, Peter Frechette, Elizabeth Daily, Ann Wedgeworth, Jeffrey Tambor, Tim Robbins, Hamilton Camp, Scott Getlin, Judith Baldwin, Jennifer Tilly, Kene Holliday, Thomas Adams, Myles Berkowitz

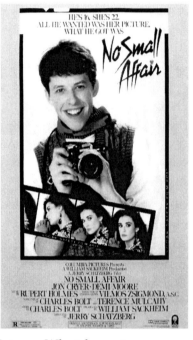

Taglines:

* From a face in a photograph she became the focus of his fantasies and then the woman in his arms.
* It won't be the last time she'll rock a younger man's world.
* He's 16. She's 22. All he wanted was her picture. What he got was... no small affair.

Film Review:

"No Small Affair" is a cute romantic comedy featuring Jon Cryer in his first big screen-starring role. His co-star is a youthful Demi Moore who looks her stunning best as Cryer's object of affection. When cast, Demi was fresh from a stint on the TV series "General Hospital" and she had also recently appeared as Michael Caine's daughter in the raunchy comedy "Blame It Rio" (1984). Cryer on the other hand was a relative unknown and this film proved to be a showcase for his talents. "No Small Affair" has an intriguing plot which sees a 16 year-old-photographer, Charles Cummings (Jon Cryer), accidentally snap a photo of 23 year-old rock singer Laura Victor (Demi Moore). Cummings begins to fall in love with her image before ever meeting her in the flesh. He later discovers that she works as a singer in a downtown bar only to find out that her career is on the slide. Cummings' infatuation with the struggling singer leads him to shell-out most of his life savings to promote her career by having her image placed on top of a fleet of San Francisco Taxi cabs. His efforts pay off, he wins her affection and the film soon moves into love-story territory. Two of the film's highlights include, Cryer's intimate moment with a call girl and the scene where Cryer and Moore gatecrash a wedding reception.

"No Small Affair" makes good use of San Francisco locations such as the Golden Gate bridge, Pier 39, Fisherman's Wharf, the steep streets, the trams, the Victorian houses and of course the nite-club district. The film is an enjoyable way to spend 100 minutes or so watching future stars Cryer and Moore developing their craft in an early performance. No Small Affair" is also notable for marking the film debuts of Tim Robbins and Jennifer Tilly. Demi Moore fans remember this movie as the one in which Demi gets to sing some songs, however, Demi doesn't actually sing in the film at all, her songs are performed and dubbed over by singer Chrissy Faith. If you didn't read the end credits you probably would never know, as the huskiness of Demi's voice is a good match for Faith's vocals. Cryer and Moore put in great performances and together make an appealing on-screen couple but if the film had of been made in 1981 when it was first scheduled for production the partnership could have gone a different way. The 1981 film was originally cast with Matthew Broderick and Sally Field in the two lead roles, if it went this way, the age difference between the two stars would have being much greater and the subtext of the story somewhat different. Whatever the case, the new cast with their age differences, work in this film. Some say "life imitates art" and for Demi Moore maybe this film was a dress rehearsal. Her highly publicised real-life romance with the "much younger" Ashton Kutcher adds a new dynamic to the film when viewed today. The end result is "No Small Affair" is an amiable charmer, Cryer shines as the naïve romantic who scoots around the city on his bike, while Moore has fun lip-synching the music numbers and dolling it up in exuberant 80s fashion. The film may not have set the box office alight on its initial release but it's definitely the ideal entertainment for the romantic at heart.

Chapter 6:

TEEN MOVIES OF 1985

*Tuff Turf ** ½*

US Release Date: January 1985
Running Time: 112 min
US Classification: R
Director: Fritz Kiersch
Starring: James Spader, Kim Richards, Paul Mones, Robert Downey, Matt Clark, Claudette Nevins

Taglines:

* Meet Morgan Hiller. He's always been a rebel. Now he's about to become a hero.
* Tuff Turf ... Where reputations are earned.
* Where enemies are made, reputations are earned and love is the most risky affair of all.
* Meet Morgan Hiller. He's a rebel about to become a hero.

Film Review:

"Tuff Turf" is a teen action flick that is a cross between "West Side Story" and "The Karate Kid". The street gangs are there but they don't break into song and dance like they do in "West Side Story" yet music is still a key factor in "Tuff Turf" with a number of sequences featuring bands and dance routines. Lookout for lively performances by The Jim Carroll Band and Jack Mack & The Heart Attack, plus a cheesy rendition of The Beatles song, "Twist and Shout" sung at an upmarket Beverly Hills golf club by Dale Gonyea with J.R. & the Z-Man. The kung fu fighting of "The Karate Kid" has been replaced by scuffles, brawls and street-fights, often involving weapons such as knives, clubs, guns and spray-cans. The action sequences are well choreographed and the confrontations come thick and fast.

The central character, teenager Morgan Hiller (James Spader) is tuff, he's cocky and he's been in trouble before, "Ever shot anybody with that thing?" he says to the security guard when he arrives at his new school. He is obviously an angry young man and being a smart-alecky rebel is his way of dealing with it, but underneath all that he's also somewhat of a loner and a sensitive good guy. In his opening scene he enters on his pushbike, armed with a spray-can and comes to the aid of a man being mugged by a bunch of hoods. Sure enough, at school the next-day, the hoods are all there. They humiliate Hiller and destroy his bike in a gripping showdown. Hiller doesn't have a mentor to discuss his problems with and finds it difficult communicating with his family. There is no Mr. Miyagi in this one to talk to like Ralph Macchio had in "The Karate Kid". He is left to his own devices and has to fight his own battles. In a rare scene with his father (Matt Clark), he is told, "Life isn't a problem to be solved. It's a mystery to be lived". This advice is enough to bamboozle anybody let alone a troubled teenager. Dr. Phil where are you?

Being a new student in a new school is tough for any teenager, but when you have a run-in with the school gang-leader (Paul Mones) and fall in love with his girl (Kim Richards) survival becomes your only option. Morgan Hiller is a man of action, he shoots cockroaches crawling on his bedroom wall with a splatter gun and he doesn't think twice about rescuing people in distress. He is fearless in his approach to most things, wears his sunglasses into the principal's office, dances with the gang-leaders girlfriend right under his nose and steals a car that has the keys left in it. He even sneaks into an exclusive country club, of which he is not a member, just to impress his friends and when the band goes for a break, he makes his way to the piano and sings his girl a love song. Yes, Spader sings in this one… you have been warned! However, his fearlessness is put to the ultimate test when he comes head-to-head with the local gang. He gets more than what he bargained for including a towel whip lashing that will make you wince. The ongoing feud between Spader and Mones is the catalyst that propels the story culminating in a violent finale that takes place in a rundown warehouse. At the "Stuntman Awards" in 1986, "Tuff Turf" won "Best Fight Sequence In A Feature Film", not bad for a high school flick.

For James Spader, "Tuff Turf" was his first major starring role. He played the good guy with attitude, in a film that had a lot of potential. It could have been his breakthrough role but it wasn't. Somehow it just didn't work for him or the other actors for that matter. There are no standout performances. Most of the acting is mediocre, often hit and miss and a little bit uninspired. Spader looks at times to be just going through the motions of the story. When he visits his dying father in hospital, who has just been shot, his emotional contribution to the scene is lacking. After "Tuff Turf", Spader spent the rest of the 80s in support roles playing bad guys in films such as "The New Kids" (1985), "Pretty In Pink" (1986), "Mannequin" (1987) and "Less Than Zero" (1987). Spader's love interest, Kim Richards is memorable for having the longest head of hair on a teenager you are ever going to see, a real attention getter if ever there was one. It is also interesting to see a young Robert Downey Jr. in an early performance displaying some raw energy as a shirtless drummer in a punk band sequence. Paul Mones looks the part as the gang-leader while Spader's parents are given very little to do in thankless roles. JD films always have something to offer and as far as "Tuff Turf" goes, this gritty teen gang drama about angry youths; may be a tad over-long but is nevertheless an amiable time pleaser; thankfully the music and the action sequences kick it up a gear when the dramatics are a little dull.

Mischief ***

US Release Date: 8th February 1985
Running Time: 92 min
US Classification: R
Director: Mel Damski
Starring: Doug McKeon, Catherine Mary Stewart, Kelly Preston, Chris Nash, D.W. Brown, Jami Gertz, Margaret Blyem, Graham Jarvis, Terry O'Quinn, Darren Ewing, Dennis L. O'Connell, Bob McGuire, Bryce Kasson, Andrew Ream, Julie Noble.

Taglines:

* The first time seems like the worst time but it's the one time you'll never forget.
* Young Love and Wild Doings

Film Review:

When "Mischief" begins with the title screen "A long time ago in a galaxy far, far away…" you start to wonder whether you have put the correct tape in the VCR. Seconds later you realize that everything is ok when the words "…. Ohio, 1956" pop up on the next screen. From this moment onwards the comical nod to "Star Wars" ends, as we hear a radio announcer say, "Let's rock n roll right now with the fat man, here comes Fats". The credits begin to roll over the picturesque countryside of Nelsonville, Ohio, to the tune of Fat's Domino's classic 1950's hit Blueberry Hill.

"Mischief" wastes no time in setting up its locations and main characters. Doug McKeon (who has an uncanny resemblance to British pop star Tommy Steele) plays Jonathon, a shy, insecure, teenager, who isn't a big hit with the ladies, but would like to be. Jonathon is madly in love with the beautiful blonde-haired Marilyn (Kelly Preston) but he can't even work up enough courage to talk to her, let alone ask her on a date. Jonathon's infatuation with Marilyn is quickly established, when he is shown running his vehicle off the road and crashing it into a fire hydrant, whilst gawking at her through the car window. With water spurting out of the hydrant, Jonathon stumbles out of his father's banged-up vehicle, while Marilyn walks over and begins to cool her legs in the gushing water. As Marilyn and her friend giggle away Jonathon stands there speechless with a dumfounded look on his face. Jonathon is Mr. Average, he's not the school geek, nor is he Mr. Cool, he lifts weights to improve his self-image and secretly likes to check out his "Sunshine and Heath", nudie magazines that he keeps hidden under his birdcage. When he's pumping iron, we're treated to the tune of his old 45's, and the sound of Tab Hunter singing "Young Love".

The plot kicks in when Jonathon's new neighbour Gene arrives in town from Chicago. Gene (Chris Nash) is a leather-clad "Wild One" who makes a big entrance by riding his motorcycle straight out of the back of a removal truck. He tears up the quiet suburban street, to the disapproval of his father and other onlookers, before being knocked off his bike by a car driven by the town bully Kenny (D.W. Brown) and his girlfriend Bunny (Catherine Mary Stewart). Immediately there is a connection between Bunny and Gene and as the film progresses their relationship develops and Kenny's jealously starts to fire up. After witnessing Gene's motorcycle antics from his bedroom window, Jonathon befriends his new neighbour and it is not long before the more-worldly Gene takes Jonathon under his wing and offers him tips and advice about the opposite sex, in particular how to win over the town beauty, Marilyn. On the surface Gene appears to be a slick, Mr. Cool, but underneath it all he's a troubled youth that has suffered. Gene was expelled from his old school, his mother has died and his father beats him up. In one of the film's touching moments Gene says to Jonathon, "You may not be the world's greatest stud Jonathon but at least you've got a family". Jonathon's "girly problems" are obviously superficial compared to Gene's problems that are deeper and much more serious. The relationship between the awkward Jonathon and the rebel Gene is not unlike that of Richie Cunningham (Ron Howard) and Arthur Fonzarelli (Henry Winkler) from the television series "Happy Days". While "Mischief" and "Happy Days" may have their similarities, "Mischief" is certainly the raunchier of the two, with a few instances of coarse language, nudity and one sex scene thrown in.

At the town fair Gene is successful in making an impression on both Marilyn and Bunny. When Gene finally chooses Bunny over Marilyn, Jonathon now gets the opportunity to date his dream girl, only to realize later that beauty is only skin deep and that he and Marilyn are not suited for each other. In an emotionally charged confrontation over the affections of Bunny; Gene and Kenny go head to head in a vicious fistfight that sees Jerry's Diner reduced to ruins. As a result Gene gets kicked out of town by his father but later returns to the school prom in a last ditch effort to win back the love of Bunny. When Gene is told to leave the prom it is his true friend Jonathon that saves the day, by convincing Bunny to come with him to see Gene. All ends well when Gene and Bunny sort out their feelings for one another to the sound of Elvis' hit song "Don't Be Cruel", before leaving town on Gene's motorcycle. Just when you think it's all over it isn't, in the exciting finale Jonathon returns to town only to be bullied once again by Kenny. Jonathon now realizes that he has to make a stand, once and for all. He reverses his car into Kenny's and what ensues is an action-packed smash and crash car rally in the town square. The film is book-ended with a car crashing into a fire hydrant but this time it is not Jonathon, but Kenny.

What makes "Mischief" work is its excellent period flavour. Set to the backdrop of jukebox hits from the era, it comes complete with diners, drive-ins, fistfights; dollar kisses at the town fair and a chicken-run sequence reminiscent of "Rebel Without A Cause" (the difference being that the cars go head to head, rather than towards a cliff). The awesome 50's soundtrack includes artists such as, Fats Domino, Chuck Berry, Buddy Holly, The Platters, The Cleftones, Little Richard and Elvis Presley.

"Mischief" features a likeable young cast of talented performers. Doug McKeon had a handful of TV appearances, a supporting role in "On Golden Pond" (1981) and a starring role as boxer Ray Mancini in "Heart Of A Champion" (1985) to his credit before being cast as Jonathon. On the other hand, for Chris Nash, the role of biker Gene was to be his film debut. The girls, Catherine Mary Stewart and Kelly Preston were certainly no newcomers to films. Catherine's previous films included, "The Apple" (1980), "The Last Starfighter" (1984) and "Night of The Comet" (1984), while Kelly (Mrs. John Travolta), had already appeared in "10 To Midnight" (1983), "Christine" (1983) and "Metalstorm" (1983).

"Mischief" is a sweet little film that grossed only $8.7 million at the US box office. At the time it may have got lost in the shuffle and hype of some of the bigger and more famous films of the mid 80's but it's certainly worth one's attention. It is a fairly realistic and at the same time very funny coming of age film. Who can forget moments like; the pencil drop in the classroom, the handkerchief in the pants, Jonathon and Marilyn in the Studebaker, Gene and Jonathon singing "Ain't that a Shame" while doubling on the motorbike and of course Jonathon's hilarious escape from Marilyn's house when the parents arrive. "Mischief" is a well directed and wonderfully acted teen comedy, with more charm than most. It is a 1950's time capsule of clothes, hairstyles, cars, drive-ins, diners, rock n roll music and growing up. Although "Mischief" should appeal to most teenagers, it will certainly have special appeal to anyone who lived through the era.

The Breakfast Club ****

US Release Date: 15th February 1985
Running Time: 97 min
US Classification: R
Director: John Hughes
Starring: Molly Ringwald, Emilio Estevez, Judd Nelson, Anthony Michael Hall, Ally Sheedy, Paul Gleason, John Kapelos

Taglines:

* They only met once, but it changed their lives forever.
* They were five total strangers, with nothing in common, meeting for the first time. A brain, a beauty, a jock, a rebel and a recluse. Before the day was over, they broke the rules. Bared their souls. And touched each other in a way they never dreamed possible.
* Five strangers with nothing in common, except each other.

Film Review:

"The Breakfast Club", written and directed by teen movie entrepreneur John Hughes is a thought provoking character study about 5 high school students on Saturday detention in the school library. It is considered by many of its fans to be the greatest teen film of the 1980's mainly because the feelings and emotions of its characters ring true. The five students come from different backgrounds, each with their own unique personality. The talented young cast is successful in making their amazing characters come to life, John Bender the criminal (Judd Nelson), Alison the weirdo (Ally Sheedy), Brian the brain (Anthony Michael Hall), Andrew the athlete (Emilio Estevez) and Claire the popular prom queen (Molly Ringwald). All the actors in the film turn their characters into something more than thinly guised caricatures, the characters become three dimensional, their feelings and emotions come to the fore as their conversations intensify while the hours, the minutes and the seconds tick away on this arduous detention day. Judd Nelson, with an underbelly of anger, stands out in the meatier role of troubled teen John Bender. His state of mind is summed up in this quote to one of the other students, "What do you care what I think anyway? I don't even count... Right? I could disappear forever and it wouldn't make any difference. I might as well not even exist at this school". His portrayal is compelling to say the least and arguably his best work.

"The Breakfast Club" features an interesting soundtrack with some appropriate mood setters. The film kicks off with the theme tune, "Don't You Forget About Me" sung over the opening credits by Simple Minds. This is shortly followed by an unexpected written quote by musician David Bowie, an extract from his song "Changes". The theme song, "Don't You Forget About Me" was recorded in London and reached number 1 on the US charts after the success of the movie. The song has since become somewhat of an anthem for 1980s teenagers and very rarely does an 80s retro show omit this one from its track list. Other notable songs include, "Fire in the Twilight" by Wang Chung and "We Are Not Alone" by Karla DeVito, played feverously over the film's cheesy dance sequence with signature moves from the era brought to life by the cast. Fans often imitate these dance moves that have now become synonymous with all that is 80s.

"The Breakfast Club" is an insightful peak into the teenage psyche that continues to intrigue audiences from one generation to the next. In the opening scenes of the film the students are asked to write an essay for the principal during their detention stint. The completed essay is featured as a strong narrative in the film's powerful ending: "Dear Mr. Vernon, We accept the fact that we had to sacrifice a whole Saturday for whatever it was you thought we did wrong, but we think you're crazy to make us write an essay on who we think we are. You see us, as you want to see us, in the simplest terms and the most convenient definitions. But what we found out is that each one of us is a brain and an athlete, a basket case, a princess and a criminal. Does that answer your question? Sincerely yours, The Breakfast Club". The film ends with the John Bender character (Judd Nelson) triumphantly punching the air, symbolizing a positive progression of his character.

"The Breakfast Club" is unforgettable teen entertainment from start to finish; it is a unique experience due to its engaging script and confined setting. It is brilliantly directed by John Hughes and wonderfully acted by the electrifying young cast. Both critics and fans fell in love with it and the film has become a point of reference in 1980s pop culture. It wasn't long after the film's release that New York magazine writer David Blum labeled the young stars "The Brat Pack" in his infamous cover story, circa June 1985. The term "Brat Pack" was obviously a play on the 1960s "Rat Pack", a group of Las Vegas crooners that included Frank Sinatra, Dean Martin, Sammy Davis Jr, Peter Lawford, Joey Bishop and others. While the "Rat Pack" was a bunch of middle-aged entertainers, the "Brat Pack" was Hollywood's new breed of emerging young sparks with talent and money to burn. "The Breakfast Club" went on to gross over $45 million at the US Box Office, not bad for a film that was written by John Hughes in just two days and shot over a 2 months period, predominately in a school gymnasium, posing as a school library. When teen films are mentioned "The Breakfast Club" usually ranks in most people's "Top 10 List". In 2006, the film confirmed its status when it was ranked #1 in "Entertainment Weekly's 50 Best High School Movies". "The Breakfast Club" is definitely the quintessential 1980's teen classic. If you haven't seen it, rent it or buy it today and witness for yourself, the power of the film that spoke to the teen generation of the 1980's.

The Sure Thing *** ½

US Release Date: 1st March 1985
Running Time: 100 min
US Classification: PG-13
Director: Rob Reiner
Starring: John Cusack, Daphne Zuniga, Anthony Edwards, Boyd Gaines, Tim Robbins, Lisa Jane Persky, Nicolette Sheridan

Taglines:

* A Romantic Comedy From Rob Reiner
* A sure thing comes once in a lifetime... but the real thing lasts forever.

Film Review:

"The Sure Thing" is a coming of age story on a road trip. It has more in common with the 1930s Clark Gable /

Claudette Colbert comedy "It Happened One Night" than it does with the raunchiness of a "Porky's" or a "Private School". That is not to say that "The Sure Thing" doesn't have a crude moment or two along the way. Heck, the film title suggests it but clearly avoids the excessiveness of it. Not unlike Blake Edward's "10", Rob Reiner's "The Sure Thing" centres indirectly on the ultimate fantasy girl. In "10" we have Bo Derek, in "The Sure Thing" we have Nicollette Sheridan ("Desperate Housewives") in her first ever screen role. Executive produced by Henry Winkler (The Fonz) and Directed with a sure-hand by Rob Reiner ("When Harry...Met Sally"), "The Sure Thing" plays out like an old-fashioned romantic comedy but with teenagers.

At the start of the film Walter Gibson (John Cusack) and his buddy Lance (Anthony Edwards) discuss the probabilities of them attending different colleges. As it turns out Walt goes to New England while Lance moves to California. As the school year kicks in Cusack's character quickly becomes frustrated with College life. He finds it difficult to develop a real connection with a female but he does have his eye on one, the attractive and intelligent Alison Bradbury (Daphne Zuniga). To pass the time, Walt exchanges letters with his buddy Lance, who seems to be enjoying his Californian party lifestyle much more than Walt's mundane New England existence. Lance sends him a postcard of a bikini-clad girl with the statement "This is the ugliest girl in California" written on the back of it. The girl on the card is a perfect 10 and this immediately captures Walt's attention. In the meantime Walt snags a date with Alison, albeit brief, but Walt's irresponsible, child-like behaviour collides with Alison's more mature demeanour. Alison rejects Walt's advances by pushing him away when he tries to kiss her. Walt's timing is way-out-of-whack and his relationship with Alison is now doomed.

Later, Lance contacts Walt on the phone and asks him to come to "Sunny California" for Christmas. To persuade Walt, Lance brings the girl on the postcard into the conversation by telling him, "I told her all about you and she's dying to meet you". Lance goes on to promise him... "She loves sex"... "She's a Sure Thing"..."No questions asked, no strings attached, no guilt involved'. Walt is ecstatic and can't wait to get there. He decides to take the plunge and immediately checks the Ride-board notice at the College. Walt books himself a car ride to California with a couple of show-tune singing lovebirds (Tim Robbins & Lisa Jane Persky) but wouldn't you know it, Alison also happens to be taking that same car ride. Reluctantly, the two now have to share the back seat. Alison's trip to LA, however, is not just about sexual gratification; she plans on visiting her finance to finalize "real plans" for her future. Anything and everything you can imagine goes wrong on the road trip and it is how they overcome these obstacles that give the film its sense of fun. Walt and Alison are ditched by their ride and are forced to hitchhike to California. They are low on funds and along the way, they have to eat together, share a bed in a hotel room, put up with bad weather and accept rides from unsavoury truck drivers but more annoyingly they have to put up with each other's bickering and bad habits. During this fateful road trip both Walt and Alison learn things about themselves that they would never have anticipated.

After brief appearances in "Class" (1983), "Sixteen Candles" (1984) and "Grandview USA" (1985), "The Sure Thing" marked John Cusack's first starring role. Daphne Zuniga was also somewhat of a newcomer. Prior to this, Daphne's screen credits consisted of small appearances in the TV teen movie "Quarterback Princess" (1983), a couple of episodes of the TV series "Family Ties" (1984) and the teen wrestling movie "Vision Quest" (aka "Crazy For You" 1985). "The Sure Thing" may not have done huge numbers at the box office ($18,136,000 US) but it certainly raised the profiles of its stars and has since gone on to be affectionately remembered as a teen movie with heart, something many strive for but struggle to achieve.

The essence and charm of "The Sure Thing" is Cusack's "coming of age" during this eventful road trip. He doesn't follow through with "The Sure Thing" because of this romantic awakening and journey he has gone on with Zuniga. For the first time in his life Cusack's character truly falls in love. He is no longer just a young man with a sexual urge. Cusack's character has grown, the audience has seen his progression and believes it. That's why "The Sure Thing" stands tall when it comes to teen romance flicks, somehow the feeling and emotions of its characters ring true because the script is a "Sure Thing" and the young actors masterfully pull it off.

Girls Just Want To Have Fun *** ½

US Release Date: 12th April 1985
Running Time: 90 min
US Classification: PG
Director: Alan Metter
Starring: Sarah Jessica Parker, Lee Montgomery, Helen Hunt, Shannen Doherty, Jonathan Silverman, Morgan Woodward, Ed Lauter, Holly Gagnier, Margaret Howell

Taglines:

* Getting into trouble is easy but getting out of it is all the fun!
* That's all they really want!
* Life will be serious soon enough. But for now...

Film Review:

"Girls Just Want To Have Fun" breezed in and out of cinemas very fast, receiving minimal box office gross and very little notice, however the film is not without merit. I (Tony) first caught up with this low-budget gem when it became a new release video rental in 1986. I was very young at the time and I loved the movie. Although it left a lasting impression, I did not get to see the film again until about 10 years later, once again on video. It was almost like watching a new movie all over again. It was even better on the 2nd viewing. When I first saw it in 1986, I didn't have a clue who Sarah Jessica Parker was or Helen Hunt for that matter. Just before my second viewing I had just watched Helen Hunt's Academy Award Winning performance in "As Good As It Gets", it was a pleasant surprise to see her pop up as a youngster in "Girls Just Want To Have Fun". It is always great to see stars "before they were stars". I now own the movie on DVD and have watched it several times since. I still enjoy it every time. "Girls Just Want To Have Fun" has a simple plot, predictable but nevertheless very effective and what's most important is that it makes you feel good. You may even want to get up and start dancing after you've seen it. That's the effect it has on me.

Sarah Jessica Parker plays Janey Glenn, a catholic schoolgirl and daughter of a strict military man (Ed Lauter) who dreams of one day becoming a DTV dancer. Her best friend, Lynne Stone (Helen Hunt) shares the same passion. When the two girls attend the DTV auditions Lynne gets injured while Janey is accepted to appear on the TV show. Janey is an impressive dancer with gymnast qualities and is quickly partnered with Jeff Malene (Lee Montgomery), the motorcycle-riding rebel who she eventually falls in love with. The two go through a rigorous training program for the eventual DTV dance off which takes place in the films spectacular finale. "Girls Just Want To Have Fun" features a vibrant title song backed up by a bouncy pop soundtrack that sums up the true spirit of the 1980's. Surprisingly, the film's catchy title track is not the original Cyndi Lauper hit that was on the charts around the same time, instead it is an alternate version performed by Deborah Galli, Tammi Holbrook and Meredith Marshall. Nevertheless the song does the job well and features prominently in a fun montage sequence involving flyers being passed around town. Other track highlights include "Come on Shout" by Alex Brown; used effectively in the opening credits, "Dancing In The Street" by Animotion; is a high-energy fix for the DTV auditions, and "Dancing In Heaven" by Q-Feel complements the uplifting finale.

Dancing and soundtrack aside, one of the film's main assets is its solid cast. Sarah Jessica Parker of "Sex in the City" fame, Academy Award winner Helen Hunt, Shannon Doherty of the popular TV series "Charmed" & "Beverly Hills 90210", 1970s child actor Lee Montgomery and not to mention Jonathan Silverman of "Weekend At Bernie's" fame in support. The male star of the film, Lee Montgomery was the only one of the leads that did not go on to fame and fortune after this film. Montgomery was the child star of the Walt Disney classic "The Million Dollar Duck" (1971) and the rat film "Ben" (1972) which was a sequel of sorts to "Willard" (1971). "Girls Just Want To Have Fun" should have been Montgomery's breakthrough film but his career stagnated after this one. He hasn't been heard of or seen much these days. He made a few appearances after "Girls Just Want To Have Fun" and was last seen on screen in the 1988 film "Into The Fire". Montgomery has a good screen presence, particularly in his scenes with Jessica Parker. Female fans of "Girls Just Want To Have Fun" have certainly not forgotten him. His athleticism and build is showcased prominently throughout the film and his character of Jeff Malene will linger on in their memories.

Director, Alan Metter, made his directorial debut with "Girls Just Want To Have Fun". A year later he went on to make the successful "Back To School" with Rodney Dangerfield. "Back to School" grossed more than $100 million on its initial US release. Alan's clever casting of Sarah Jessica Parker & Helen Hunt in their first lead roles helped make "Girls Just Want To Have Fun" the cult classic that it is today. "Girls Just Want To Have Fun" is simply a fun-filled teen flick especially for fans of dance films like "Footloose", "Dirty Dancing", "Flashdance" and "Breakin". Good dancing, great music and fun energetic performances by a talented young cast are just some of the ingredients that keep this 1980's feel-good entertainment rollicking from start to finish. The title may suggest that it is primarily a girl's film but I am sure that boys will have a lot of fun watching it as well. "Girls Just Want To Have Fun" is an absolute treat; it has that special something, a likeability factor, a unique quality that makes teen audiences want to revisit it again and again.

Just One Of The Guys ***

US Release Date: 26th April 1985
Running Time: 90 min
US Classification: PG-13
Director: Lisa Gottlieb
Starring: Joyce Hyser, Clayton Rohner, Billy Jayne, Toni Hudson, William Zabka, Leigh McCloskey, Sherilyn Fenn, Deborah Goodrich, Arye Gross, Robert Fieldsteel, Stuart Charno, John Apicella, Kenneth Tigar, Steven Basil, J. Williams

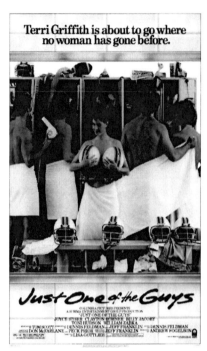

Taglines:

* Terry Griffith is about to go where no woman has gone before
* Oh boy! He's a girl! Or is she…Just One Of The Guys

Film Review:

"Just One Of The Guys" is "Tootsie" in reverse for the teen crowd. Joyce Hyser plays Terry, an ambitious journalism student at Edwina Pearl High School. Terry has got it all, she's bright, she's attractive, she's very popular and she's got a handsome boyfriend. All she needs now is for her story to be entered into the Sun Tribune journalism competition that could see her win a summer job. When her article is knocked back, she begins to believe that her teachers are sexist. She tells her friend, "I write an excellent article, but just because I'm cute nobody takes me seriously". Terry is prepared to go to all lengths to win entry into the competition, with her parents away for two weeks, she decides to change schools and disguise herself as a boy in order to give herself a second chance. After a humorous-induction into manhood by her moronic, sex-starved younger brother Buddy (Billy Jacoby), who gives her lessons in how to walk, talk, where to scratch and where to put the sock, Terry, or should I say Terence, is ready to attend her new school, Sturgis-Wilder High. Billy Jacoby (sometimes credited as Billy Jayne) almost steals the film with some of the best lines ("Who do you think you are, Tootsie") and some of the funniest moments (who can forget his method of dishwashing). He is the ultimate sex-maniac, a randy young man with a sharp tongue. He plays the sleaze-ball role to perfection and is a total embarrassment to his sister. He could easily be described as the long lost cousin of Bud Bundy from TV's "Married with Children". He wears sleeveless shirts, likes to act tough, decorates his room with pin-up girls from Playboy magazine and tries to hit on any girl and every girl that he sees, including his study dates and Terry's girlfriends.

Joyce Hyser is excellent in both roles and especially convincing in the male role. She is stunning as the girl and has an uncanny resemblance to Sandra Bullock. She is believable as the guy and with her hair cut short, her look and mannerisms remind you of a young Ralph Macchio ("The Karate Kid"). Even the girl's at her new school think so, when Sandy (Sherilyn Fenn) sees Terry and takes a liking to him (her), she says to her friend, "He dresses like Elvis Costello and looks like the Karate Kid, I'm going to get him". At her new school Terry befriends, sensitive nice guy Rick (Clayton Rohner), who is a bit of a loner, likes James Brown music and has a crush on the most popular girl in school. Rick's dream girl however, is dating tough guy and school bully Greg (William Zabka the blonde-haired creep of "Karate Kid" fame), who in one amusing scene Terry describes as being, "Strong as an ox and almost as smart", before being picked up and thrown into the thorn bushes.

One of Greg's daily rituals is to terrorize the inhabitants of the lunchroom by picking up tables and spilling food over anyone that is an easy target, his favourite line to his victims being "No pain, no gain". In one of the film's standout scenes Greg meets his match when Rick decides to stand up to him. Rick humiliates Greg with a speech in front of his peers, which renders him and his idiotic behaviour foolish (Rick describes Greg as a person who spends his time at the gym lifting weights just so he becomes "strong enough to lift tables and spill food"), thus setting up another confrontation in the final act. Greg's embarrassment works in Rick's favour, when Greg's girl asks Rick to the prom. In the film's finale anyone and everyone turns up at the school's Hawaiian-themed prom night that takes place at an entertainment venue right on the beach. By now Terry has fallen in love with Rick but Rick of course doesn't know that Terry is really a girl. Jealousies run hot at the dance as Terry can't bear to see Rick dancing with another girl and Greg is nearly boiling over with anger as he watches Rick dancing with his former girlfriend. To add to the fun Terry's boyfriend Kevin (Leigh McCloskey) and her brother turn up looking for her. Fisticuffs break out between Greg and Rick. When Terry tries to help Rick, Greg picks her up and throws her into the surf. When Terry's brother sees this, he attacks Greg and so on. Eventually the fight comes to a conclusion, but not before Rick sends Greg crashing into the tropical buffet. When Terry's boyfriend pledges his love for her, Rick begins to suspect that maybe Terry is gay. In the film's most revealing scene Terry is forced to convince Rick, that she's not, "Just One Of The Guys".

Lisa Gottlieb, in her directorial debut has succeeded in creating an entertaining teen comedy with one romantic twist after another. "Just One of The Guys" is well paced and features many comedic situations, as Terry discovers that life, as a boy, is more complicated than she bargained for. Who can forget Terry's first time in the boys toilet and locker-room, Terry's survival of the "shirts and skins" gym class, Terry's double date at the cave, Terry and Rick dancing with each other instead of their dates at the prom and of course Terry's Clark Kent/Superman routine as she changes from "boy to girl" and vice versa to accommodate her two dates. "Just One Of The Guys" opened in April 1985 in 2nd position behind Burt Reynolds' action comedy "Stick". It received good reviews and went on to gross $11.5 million at the US box office. At the "Young Artist Awards", "Just One Of The Guys" was nominated for "Best Family Motion Picture – Comedy or Musical", "Best Actress", Joyce Hyser and "Best Young Actor", Billy Jacoby. Two of the movie posters used in the marketing campaign show Hyser in the boy's locker-room holding football helmets in one and soccer balls in the other. It is interesting to note that no such scene appears in the film and in fact there is no football game or soccer match either. "Just One of The Guys" is not your average role reversal comedy. There is no reliance on a magic potion, a special formula or gimmick, for the switch to take place, just a change of clothes, a haircut and an actress talented enough to make the whole thing believable. Joyce Hyser is wonderful in the role and it is surprising that "Just One Of The Guys" did not lead to bigger and better things in her career.

Private Resort ** ½

US Release Date: 3rd May 1985
Running Time: 82 min
US Classification: R
Director: George Bowers
Starring: Rob Morrow, Johnny Depp, Hector Elizondo, Dody Goodman, Leslie Easterbrook, Andrew Dice Clay

Taglines:

* They're looking for hot times. And they came to the right place...
* Spend a weekend with no reservations!
* Where every room has a great view!

Film Review:

Long before "Pirates Of The Caribbean" set sail, Johnny Depp hit the waters in a different way when he starred alongside Rob Morrow in "Private Resort", a low-budget teen sexploitation flick that is easy on the eyes and melodic to the ears. Now, to make things extremely clear from the get-go, "Private Resort" is not a film to be taken too seriously, it has

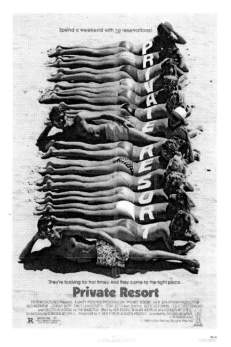

nothing really important to say and if viewed in this light there is plenty of mindless fun to be had. If it's logic, drama or an engrossing plotline that you are looking for it is best to look elsewhere. On the other hand, if it's good-looking babes, hilarious situations and campy Caribbean melodies that wet your appetite, then check into this "Private Resort" for the vacation of a lifetime. Why "Private Resort" made absolutely no money at the box office on its initial cinema release is anybody's guess, but one thing is for sure it has since become a curiosity piece for Johnny Depp fans. With Depp now being one of the hottest box office earners in the world, things must be really paying off for producers in the long haul who have remarketed the film for DVD sales in the new millennium.

Johnny Depp and Rob Morrow play Jack and Ben, two teenage boys who spend their spring break weekend at a posh Florida resort looking for love and excitement. Their adventure takes a turn for the worst when the boys try to seduce Bobbie Sue (Leslie Easterbrook of "Police Academy" fame), the wife of a maniacal jewel thief known as The Maestro (Hector Elizondo from "Pretty Woman). The Maestro specializes in charming wealthy widows and then robbing them of their valuables, one of which is clueless Mrs. Rawlings, played here by veteran actress Dody Goodman (Blanche from "Grease"). Outrageous moments are a plenty in "Private Resort" and in one of the film's standout scenes Depp tries to make-out with The Maestro's wife while Morrow unwillingly poses as the hotel barber and gives The Maestro a haircut to kill for... to kill Morrow and Depp that is. An ensuing chase begins and machine gun bullets fly as the weird and wonderful characters pile up in hilarious slapstick situations. The pace is so rapid fire that the film's 82 minute running time is over before you know it, just like that pina-colada you ordered at the bar.

To top it off "Private Resort's" lively soundtrack is a winner, with catchy beats and tunes by Bill Wray that will be buzzing around your head for days long after the end credits roll. "Private Resort" is definitely one of the better spring break sex comedies of the 80's, Deep looks his best and the Key Largo location scenery is a treat. The film even has a scene-stealer in the form of a young boy who uses his fishing line to remove the bikini tops from some of the poolside babes. Yes, "Private Resort" has everything you would expect to find in a raunchy teen sex flick, including topless bimbos for the boys and even a brief butt shot from Depp for the ladies. Now to add even more punch to the proceedings, comedian Andrew Dice Clay (Ford Fairlane) drops in and hams it up as a cool dude lothario with an abundance of body hair but ultimately it is Johnny Depp fans that will get the most out of this underrated carefree romp.

The Goonies ****

US Release Date: 7th June 1985
Running Time: 114 min
US Classification: PG
Director: Richard Donner
Starring: Sean Astin, Josh Brolin, Ke Huy Quan, Jeff Cohen, Corey Feldman, Martha Plimpton, Kerri Green

Taglines:

* They call themselves "The Goonies." The secret caves. The old lighthouse. The lost map. The treacherous traps. The hidden treasure. And Sloth... Join the adventure.
* The pirates map, The villainous crooks, The underground caverns, The booby traps, the skeletons, The monster, the lost treasure, and the magic that is... THE GOONIES

* It's excitement all the way as Steven Spielberg and Richard Donner, the makers of 'Indiana Jones', 'Gremlins' and 'Superman', combine forces to create the Family Adventure of the year!

Film Review:

"The Goonies", although aimed at young teens, is an old-fashioned, matinee-type adventure film that can be enjoyed by people of all ages. It is fast-paced and action-packed in true "Indiana Jones" style, only this time the heroes of the movie are a bunch of young teenagers from a seaside town on the west coast of America. After a couple of minor TV appearances Sean Astin, son of 1960s teen actress Patty Duke, was called in to lead the cast of talented youngsters. Making his feature film debut as Astin's older brother is Josh Brolin, son of actor James Brolin. The plot kicks in when this bunch of kids, who call themselves "The Goonies", uncover a treasure map showing the whereabouts of "One-Eyed Willy's" hidden treasure. They take on the search in the hope that the treasure will save them and their families from being evicted from their homes by greedy land developers. However, the kids are not the only ones who know about the treasure. In hot pursuit are the villainous Fratelli family who will stop at nothing to get the loot. Mama Fratelli, an obnoxious, loud-mouthed old woman, who rules with an iron-fist, leads the Fratelli family. Anne Ramsey ("Throw Momma From The Train") plays Mama Fratelli in over-the-top fashion while her misfit sons Jake and Francis Fratelli (Robert Davi and Joe Pantoliano) cater to her every whim.

I saw "The Goonies" on the big-screen in 1985 when it first hit cinemas and I was simply blown away by it. I have watched it a few times since and it is just as entertaining now as it was on my original viewing. "The Goonies" is the type of adventure story young teenagers can only dream about. The film provides them with the opportunity to live-out their fantasies as our young heroes trek through underground caves, escape treacherous booby traps, slide down steep waterfalls, jump aboard a gigantic pirate ship and take part in hand to hand combat with the villains. The child-stars and the villainous supports are all excellent in their roles thanks to the brilliant direction of Richard Donner, best known for his work on the classic comic-book fantasy "Superman The Movie" and of course the "Lethal Weapon" film series. Standout characters include, Data (Ke Huy Quan better known as Short Round from "Indiana Jones & The Temple of Doom") as the young gadget inventor, Clark 'Mouth' Devereaux (Corey Feldman) as the motor mouth who can't keep out of trouble and Chunk (Jeff Cohen) the loveable fat kid who supplies most of the film's comedy relief. For supporting actor Robert Davi playing Mama Fratelli's right-hand man and henchman was a good warm-up role for his subsequent bad guy portrayals in films such as "Raw Deal" with Arnold Schwarzenegger, "Action Jackson" with Carl Weathers and of course the 007 thriller, "License To Kill" with Timothy Dalton where he plays super-villain Frank Sanchez. Also, a great visual presence in the film is the other Fratelli, the 6" 7' gentle giant with the deformed face known as Sloth, played sympathetically by ex-football player John Matuszak.

"The Goonies" was popular with both critics and audiences alike proving to be a huge financial hit for Warner Bros. It set cash registers ringing to the tune of $61.3 million at the US box office and ranked 9th in its year. At the "Young Artist Awards" in 1986, "The Goonies" was nominated for "Best Family Motion Picture – Adventure" missing out to "Back To The Future". Also, stars, Sean Astin, Jeff Cohen, Corey Feldman and Martha Plimpton were all nominated for "Best Young Actor Awards", with Sean Astin taking out the prize for "Best Starring Performance by a Young Actor". Performances aside, the film is also complemented with a strong music score, a highlight being the Cyndi Lauper hit, "Good Enough". With "The Goonies" director Richard Donnor has created the ultimate adventure for young teens. Donner even finds time to get himself involved in the on-screen happenings, with a small, blink-and-you'll miss him cameo, as a sheriff in the background, when the kids exit the cave in the films finale. Also, in the film's closing moments, Donner plays homage to his previous success by having Sloth rip open his shirt, revealing a "Superman" emblem all to the sound of the Superman theme that audiences know and love so well. For writer/producer Steven Spielberg, "The Goonies" is another success story, the film is a thrill a minute adrenaline rush of non-stop cliffhanging chills and gasps, that any young teenager would not want to miss. The posters and artwork for the film were enough to make anyone want to see it, they were eye-catching to say the least and audience expectations were set at a high level but more importantly this teen adventure tale lived up to its hype in style and then some.

*Secret Admirer ***

US Release Date: 14th June 1985
Running Time: 90 min
US Classification: R
Director: David Greenwalt
Starring: C. Thomas Howell, Lori Loughlin, Kelly Preston, Dee Wallace-Stone, Cliff De Young, Leigh Taylor-Young, Fred Ward, Casey Siemaszko,

Geoffrey Blake, Rodney Pearson, Courtney Gains, J.J. Cohen, Scott McGinnis, Corey Haim, Michael Menzies.

Taglines:

* He never knew what hit him
* Sometimes What You're Looking For... Is Right Beside You.
* Toni gave Michael a letter, so he could give Debbie one...

Film Review:

When two anonymous and very passionate love letters are written and delivered, they set off a chain of events when they fall into the wrong hands, causing confusion and turmoil in the lives of two families until it is revealed who wrote which letter and to whom. This is the premise for "Secret Admirer" a romantic teen comedy about a young girl's secret love for a young man that happens to be her best friend. The young man is also in love with her, but unfortunately he doesn't know it yet because he thinks he's in love with somebody else. Lori Loughlin plays Toni, the "Secret Admirer" of the title. C. Thomas Howell plays Michael the boy Toni is madly in love with, while Kelly Preston plays Debbie the object of Michael's desire. Does this sound familiar? Well it's not unlike the Joey/Dawson relationship from TV's "Dawson's Creek". That's right, sometimes the girl you are looking for is so close that you can't see for looking. In "Secret Admirer", the universal theme of secret love is allowed to unfold beautifully and in comedic style with the film's passionate love letter being the perfect catalyst to keep the story moving.

The film begins with a sheet of blank paper on which the title appears followed by a hand that begins writing the love letter. "I don't know how to tell you what I want to tell you, so I'm writing it down. I'll never find the nerve to give you this letter anyway......I love you more than words can say....XXXOOOXXX". The letter is unsigned, placed in an envelope and then put inside a book titled "The Pageant of World History". In the next scene we see the book, in close up, being carried through the school campus and down a corridor towards a locker. The letter is slipped into the locker through the ventilation grill, setting up the film's premise and the hilarious chain of events that are to follow. It is the last day of summer vacation and

Michael can't get out of school quick enough. He opens his locker grabs the contents and heads straight for the garbage bin, everything goes into the bin, except a magazine and the letter. He's so anxious to make a quick exit that he doesn't bother to open the letter. He puts it in the magazine and takes off like a rocket, all to the sound of the film's theme song "No Secrets" performed by Van Stephenson and all this before the final director's credit.

Michael and Toni are good friends, so much so, that Michael confides in her about his feelings for Debbie. Unfortunately for Michael, Debbie already has a boyfriend, Steve (Scott McGinnis who has an uncanny resemblance to a young Gary Busey), but Michael is still convinced that he can win her affections. "Do you think she'll go out with me if I grow a moustache?" he says to Toni. "Well I don't know! Can you?" answers Toni. As Michael and his buddies prepare for a big night out they discover the letter. After teasing him about it, his friends convince him that Debbie may have written the letter. When they turn up at a party, Michael's friend Roger (Casey Siemaszko) creates a diversion allowing Michael an opportunity to make a move on Debbie but things get out of hand when Steve catches on and prepares to bash Michael. When Toni comes to the rescue Michael and his buddies flee the party in a panel van with Steve and his goons in hot pursuit. No one gets hurt but the van gets destroyed after crashing into a gate.

Michael eventually tells Toni about his letter. Toni advises him to write Debbie an anonymous letter in return but when Michael asks Toni to pass the letter on to Debbie, Toni can't help her-self and opens it. Michael's letter is so badly written that Toni decides to write a new one before giving it to Debbie. With two letters now in circulation and a chain reaction sparked by Michael's light-fingered little brother Jeff (Corey Haim), the first letter finds its way in to Michael's father's textbook. When Michael's mum (Dee Wallace-Stone) finds the letter she begins to believe that her husband (Cliff De Young) is having an affair with his night school teacher who turns out to be Debbie's mum (Leigh Taylor-Young). The chain reaction continues when Debbie hides her letter in her mother's handbag after her boyfriend turns up unexpectedly. When Debbie's Dad (Fred Ward) discovers the letter in his wife's handbag he begins to believe that she is having an affair with Michael's father. After a strange twist of fate, the two letters end up into the hands of Debbie's mother and Michael's father who really begin to fall in love, believing that they wrote the letters to each other. Does all this sound confusing, well it is, but not if you watch the film.

When Michael realizes that both letters were written by Toni, the film's touching finale becomes an emotionally charged race against time, as Michael has to "borrow" Steve's vehicle in order to get to the dockyard in time to stop Toni from going on the "school afloat" for a year. As Michael runs down the dock he can see that the boat has just left, so he climbs on top of a cargo shipment and begins to call out, "I know you wrote the letters, I love you, do you love me?" When Toni replies, "Yes", Michael dives into the water and begins to swim towards the boat. On seeing him jump, Toni follows suit and the two swim frantically towards each other. When they meet, they embrace passionately and the credits roll.

David Greenwalt, who made his directorial debut with "Secret Admirer", also co-wrote the film with Jim Kouf. David is successful in keeping the film well paced and moving from one comedic moment to another. All scenes are carefully constructed, well timed and superbly executed by the outstanding cast. Who can forget moments like, C. Thomas Howell's progressive food order at the diner, Corey Haim's nutritious breakfast of fruit loops with chocolate syrup, Lori Loughlin's destruction of the van with the baseball bat, Scott McGinnis's heartfelt speech outside the bathroom door, Kelly Preston's over-reaction when food is spilt on her, Fred Ward and Cliff De Young's punch-up at the bridge game, and of course the antics at the lover's lane lookout when anybody and everybody shows up. It is Fred Ward (of Remo fame) however, who wins many of the film's laughs. He is hilarious as the jealous husband, overprotective father and vice squad detective. He is definitely a standout and almost steals the show in every scene that he appears in. Who can forget Fred, patting his gun, as he tells his daughter's boyfriend what he will do to him if he gets her pregnant and what about Fred's pulsating vein, ticking like a time bomb at the side of his head, when he first discovers the letter. It is not surprising to see Fred show up in later years playing a parent in a number of teen-orientated movies like "Road Trip" (2000), "Summer Catch" (2001) and "Sweet Home Alabama" (2002), he just seems to be able to play the hyper-active parent so well.

"Secret Admirer" was only moderately successful at the US box office, grossing only $8.6 million on its initial release, but the film has gained a whole new legion of fans on VHS and DVD. It's sweet-natured storyline of mistaken deliveries and misunderstandings, together with its cute teens and bumbling adults make it a romantic comedy that appeals to both teens and their parents. Teens like it because their parents are made to look like bigger idiots than them. Parents like it because it gives them the opportunity to laugh at themselves. When you have won over both audiences how can you go wrong?

Back To The Future **** ½

US Release Date: 3rd July 1985
Running Time: 116 min
US Classification: PG
Director: Robert Zemeckis
Starring: Michael J. Fox, Christopher Lloyd, Lea Thompson, Crispin Glover, Thomas F. Wilson, Claudia Wells, Marc McClure, Wendie Jo Sperber, George DiCenzo, Frances Lee McCain, James Tolkan, J.J. Cohen, Casey Siemaszko, Billy Zane, Harry Waters Jr.

Taglines:

* 17 year old Marty McFly got home early last night. 30 years early.
* He was never in time for his classes... He wasn't in time for his dinner... Then one day... he wasn't in his time at all.
* Marty McFly's having the time of his life. The only question is -- what time is it?
* Meet Marty McFly. He's broken the time barrier. Busted his parents' first date. And, maybe, botched his chances of ever being born.
* Marty McFly just broke the time barrier. He's only got one week to get it fixed.
* He's the only kid ever to get into trouble before he was born.

Film Review:

Would you like to meet your parents when they were teenagers? Through the concept of time travel, "Back To The Future" gave teenagers of the 1980s a unique peak into the lives of their parents as teenagers in the 1950s. Yes, the time travel scenario may be a bit far-fetched but it is the way that the concept is executed in the brilliant script that makes the whole experience extremely enjoyable. Fresh from his success with the action-adventure "Romancing The Stone", Director Robert Zemeckis hits the bulls-eye once again. With the support of producer Steven Spielberg, Zemeckis has carefully crafted an intelligent teen fantasy film that will have you believing that time travel is possible and that skateboards were invented in 1955.

Set in 1985, high school student Marty McFly (Michael J. Fox), with the help of his whacko inventor friend Doc Brown (Christopher Lloyd complete with Albert Einstein hair-do), is accidentally transported back to 1955 via a plutonium-powered De Lorean car that has a time travel facility. A lot of the film's humour is derived from the fish out of water scenario that Marty is placed in. It may be his town, but not his time. The town-folk think his jacket is a life preserver, at a diner he asks for a "Pepsi Free" and is told he will have to pay for his drink and when he watches TV he knows all the jokes because he's already seen the re-runs. Marty's entrance into the 1950s certainly puts a spanner in the works when his mother (Lea Thompson) begins to fall for him. During his stay Marty must ensure that his Father (Crispin Glover), a bumbling nerd, meets and falls in love with his mother so that when he returns to the 1980s he does in fact still exist.

Michael J. Fox does such a great job as Marty McFly that it is hard to imagine that somebody else was in the role when shooting began. 24-year-old Eric Stoltz ("Some Kind Of Wonderful") was original cast as Marty but after a number of weeks work filmmakers felt that Stoltz was "too intense" for the role so they recruited Fox to take over. Fox at the time was hot property due to his popularity in the TV series "Family Ties". Also of interest is the fact that a refrigerator was almost used as the time machine, fortunately for audiences, the filmmakers changed their mind and decided to use the De Lorean. Producers felt that the refrigerator idea may have had a negative effect on children. It's difficult now to imagine the film without the De Lorean. Soon after the film's release the car made guest appearances in shopping malls around the world. The De Lorean was such a hit that everyone wanted one and fans loved to have their picture taken with it. The icebox could never have been that cool.

"Back To The Future" was a huge critical and financial success for Universal. It was the highest grossing film of 1985 bringing in over $210 million at the US box office alone. It won an Oscar for "Best Sound Effects Editing" and was nominated at the Golden Globe Awards for Best Film, Best Song, Best Screenplay and Best Actor (Michael. J Fox). It spawned two popular sequels, "Back To The Future II" (1989), where Marty and Doc move forward in time to the year 2015 to resolve further family problems and "Back To The Future III" (1990) that sees Marty go back in time again, on this occasion to the wild west cowboy days of 1885 to rescue the Doc. In the 1990s Universal Studios created an entire area of their theme park devoted to the film, including an exciting 3-D ride, a souvenir store with t-shirts, books, DVDs and other memorabilia (dubbed the Time Travel Depot), Doc Brown's famous fried chicken dinners were on sale nearby and of course the De Lorean was there for a photo opportunity. Sadly, in 2007 the rides closed in Universal Studios Florida and California but the ride continues to operate in Universal Studios Japan.

"Back To The Future is not a film riddled with special effects but it has just enough to keep everything on track, the most famous being the final shot of the De Lorean, lifting from the ground, it's wheels folding under and then jetting off into the sky like a spaceship. In this sequence the Doc delivers his final and certainly most memorable line to Marty, "Roads? Where we're going, we don't need roads". This signature quote leaves the viewer gasping for more. "Back To The Future" is the teen movie to end all teen movies, it has it all, comedy, romance, action and fantasy. Add to this mix a likeable cast (Michael J. Fox, Christopher Lloyd), a powerful pop ballad ("The Power Of Love" by Huey Lewis & The News), an engaging music score (Alan Silvestri) and the result is a highly entertaining motion picture experience that you will want to revisit again and again. "Back To The Future" is not just a great teen film of the 1980s but it is one of the great films of all-time.

The Heavenly Kid ***

US Release Date: 26th July 1985
Running Time: 90 min
US Classification: PG-13
Director: Cary Medoway
Starring: Lewis Smith, Jason Gedrick, Jane Kaczmarek, Richard Mulligan, Mark Metcalf

Taglines:

* Thou Shalt Be Cool! * In Life And Love We're All Just Winging It!
* For Bobby to go Uptown, he must look into his heart.
* Street smart. Heaven sent.
* You never know who's looking out for you.
* 1962 was a bad year for Bobby. First he drove 300ft over a cliff, then they wouldn't let him into heaven...

* Back in the 60's, on a dark deserted highway, Bobby and his '57 Chevy bought it at 90 miles an hour. Today he's making a comeback.

Film Review:

The 1980s was a boom decade for teen fantasy films and "The Heavenly Kid" proved to be one of the coolest and most inventive of the era. Shot predominately in North Miami Florida in 1984 under the working title of "Teen Angel", the film is a throwback to films of an earlier era, most notably, "Rebel Without A Cause" due to its chicken-run-inspired opening and finale. Although, "The Heavenly Kid" was released in 1985, smack-bang in the middle of the decade, it wasn't until the late 1980s that I first attempted to view the film. It was the 8:30pm TV movie of the week but unfortunately I was only able to see about half the film because my parents sent me to bed. It wasn't until the late 90s that I came across the film again and was able to watch the entire movie. So as it turned out I had to wait about 10 years until I was able to finish watching the film and discover the fantastic father-son twist ending that puts a neat cap on a great film. Since then, I have watched the movie on a few occasions and have enjoyed it every-time.

"The Heavenly Kid" is one of those feel-good films that you can revisit from time to time. It has that universal fish-out-of-water appeal, this time in the form of an ultra-cool "Guardian Angel" who has come from the 60s to the 80s on an assignment to befriend and help an insecure teenage nerd who has been bullied by some of the local school thugs. Lewis Smith plays "Guardian Angel" Bobby Fantana, a cross-between Fonzi from "Happy Days" and Danny Zucko from "Grease" with a snippet of James Dean thrown in for period flavor. Jason Gedrick plays Lenny Barnes, the wimpy nerd that is guided and shaped by the Angel into a cool kid that can stand up for himself but more importantly the Angel helps him come to the realization that popularity isn't the answer to all of life's problems. The plot thickens when the Angel discovers that his former girlfriend is Lenny's mother and that she is married to the guy that he was drag racing when he lost his life in the 1960s. Although forbidden-to-be-seen by anyone other than Lenny, the Angel now allows himself to be seen by the mother for one last time. This jeopardizes his position in the afterlife and his ability to prevent his son from suffering the same fate as him.

"The Heavenly Kid" is full of cheesy-low-budget special effects that add a-certain-innocence to the proceedings and do not take away at all from the enjoyment of the film. Cornball invisible man sequences such as bikes and cars moving without drivers always raise a chuckle. Add to that some neat levitation tricks involving cars and people, together with some good-old-fashioned walking through-walls-effects and you have a recipe for loads of fun. An interesting facet to "The Heavenly Kid" and I am sure one of the reasons for the film's appeal is that it creates a father and son situation between the Angel and the nerd where both are about the same age. That's right, what teenage boy wouldn't like to hang out with his teenage Dad and discover what it would be like to enjoy each other's company as best friends. Well this film does just that and does it well, with comedic fun and lots of charm. It is no surprise that the film was the winner of the "Best Family Motion Picture Comedy or Musical" at the 1986 Young Artist Awards, the accolade is well deserved and really what more could you want from a teen movie such as this, "The Heavenly Kid" has it all; good performances, an engaging story, a cool theme song and more importantly an uplifting finale.

Weird Science ***

US Release Date: 2nd August 1985
Running Time: 94 min
US Classification: PG-13
Director: John Hughes
Starring: Anthony Michael Hall, Kelly LeBrock, Ilan Mitchell-Smith, Bill Paxton, Robert Downey Jr., Vernon Wells.

Taglines:

* It's all in the name of science. Weird Science.
* It's purely sexual
* If you can't get a date, make one!
* They went from zeroes to heroes in one fantastic weekend.

Film Review:

Written & Directed by specialist teen filmmaker John Hughes, "Weird Science" marked the final chapter in the John Hughes / Anthony Michael Hall trilogy of films. Their collaboration may have only been three films in the space of 2 or 3 years but their work on; "Sixteen Candles" (1984), "The Breakfast Club" (1985) and "Weird Science" (1985) has left a significant impact on teen audiences of the decade. As with most John Hughes films "Weird Science" comes complete with a nice blend of 80s pop and rock tunes, most notably, the catchy title track by new wave rock band Oingo Boingo that will have you humming along to the beat after the credits roll.

With "Weird Science" John Hughes introduced a dash of fantasy into his teen film series. The result is a fun, tongue-in-cheek; leave your brain at home joyride into the lives of male teens and their quest for the perfect woman.

Gary and Wyatt (Anthony Michael Hall, Ilan Mitchell-Smith) are two geeky teenagers who are having difficulty fitting in at school. One night while watching an old Frankenstein movie on TV they are inspired to use their home computer to create a dream girl who they hope will help them overcome their insecurities and boost their popularity with the opposite sex. After feeding in various bits of information, predominately, images, measurements and tons of 80s pop culture references, they also tap into a government mainframe before a freak electrical storm strikes and pushes everything into overdrive. The end result is a house that looks like it has just come out of a war-zone but the icing on the cake is the arrival of the seductively stunning Lisa, played by the beautiful Kelly LeBrock, fresh from her success in "The Woman in Red" (1984). With Lisa part of their daily lives, Gary and Wyatt are soon thrown into a lifestyle that is faster and flashier than they could ever have imagined.

To add to the fun, Bill Paxton, complete with crew-cut hairstyle, is brought in as Wyatt's domineering older brother Chet. He plays a cigar chomping, singlet-clad, sergeant-major type-character. His over-the-top comedic-performance gives him some of the film's funniest and most outrageous lines. Who can forget, "That's not a joke, that's a severe behavioral disorder" and his suspicious reply to his brother after he is served breakfast, "Did you spit in this?". Also, look out for Robert Downey Jr (Tuff Turf) and Robert Rusler (Thrashin') in supporting roles as the school bullies. They humiliate Gary and Wyatt by pulling down their shorts in gym class and later attack them in a shopping mall by pouring a slurpee on their heads. Comedic situations and confrontations may be a key to the film's success but what gives the film its heart is the interesting twist to it all. The so-called woman of Gary and Wyatt's dreams may look like the sex object of their desires but rather turns out to be a guiding fairy godmother figure that helps them through their coming of age saga. With Lisa's help, Wyatt and Gary move from the awkwardness of nerd-hood to finding their feet and becoming confident young men.

"Weird Science" may have been extremely popular with teens that grew up in the 1980's but who would have guessed that the 1990's would see an overflow effect of the film. Almost 10 years after the success of the feature film, a spin-off TV series debuted in 1994 and ran for 88 episodes before coming to an end in 1997. The series was simliar in plot and starred Michael Manasseri as Wyatt, John Mallory Asher as Gary, Lee Tergesen as Chet and

English model turned actress Vanessa Angel as Lisa. A new generation of teens could now experience the same fantasy. The success of "Weird Science" is unquestionable; its special effects and hilarious situations continue to thrill teens and now a further 10 years after the popular TV series debuted, there is talk of the complete TV series getting a DVD release. Even John Hughes could not have imagined this when he first sat down to pen the story.

My Science Project **

US Release Date: 9th August 1985
Running Time: 94 min
US Classification: PG
Director: Jonathan R. Betuel
Starring: John Stockwell, Danielle von Zerneck, Fisher Stevens, Raphael Sbarge, Richard Masur, Barry Corbin, Ann Wedgeworth, Dennis Hopper, Candace Silvers, Beau Dremann, Pat Simmons, John Vidor, Vincent Barbour, Jaime Alba

Taglines:

* We must not destroy the world.
* The funniest sci-fi movie of the summer
* They discovered the most powerful time weapon known to man
* Eighteen-year-old Michael Harlan has to save the world - and finish high school.

Film Review:

"My Science Project" is a bizarre teen sci-fi flick and although plodding at times, it still manages to keep you watching until the very end. The funny thing is, the more you watch of it, the less sense it makes but maybe that's the intention of the film, very little explanation and a lot of cheesy B-grade special effects. The film stars John Stockwell, a young actor who chalked up a number of film credits during the 80s, most notably, "Losin' It (1983), "Eddie And The Cruisers" (1983), "Christine" (1983) and "Top Gun" (1986). In the new millennium Stockwell has become a teen movie director in his own right, with films such as "Crazy/Beautiful" (2001), "Blue Crush" (2002),

"Into The Blue" (2005) and the thriller "Turistas" (2006). For Stockwell, "My Science Project" could have been his breakthrough film, but unfortunately it didn't reach the heights of other 80s teen fantasy flicks such as "The Last Starfighter" (1984), "Back To The Future" (1985) or "Weird Science" (1985) for that matter.

In "My Science Project", Stockwell plays Michael Harlan a high school student and car nut on the verge of failure if he doesn't hand in a high quality science project. His hippie teacher Bob Roberts, played over-the-top by Dennis Hopper, threatens to flunk him if the project doesn't make the grade. Desperate to succeed Stockwell and his girlfriend Ellie Sawyer (Danielle Von Zerneck) go scavenging for something "scientific" in a nearby air-force military base. What they find in the military junkyard is much more than they can handle; an alien artifact that opens a doorway into a Time-space continuum that allows objects, people and animals from the past to interact with the present. As a result the teens have to confront Viet-cong soldiers, an ape-man, a roman gladiator and even a T-Rex dinosaur before saving their high school and their hometown from destruction.

To give the production some scope the film begins in the 1950s and then quickly time shifts to the 1980s a few minutes later. Unfortunately, it still takes another 40 minutes before the film really kicks into gear, the suspense of it all was killing me and then when something eventually did happen it was a bit of a letdown. Ultimately, the film becomes an excuse for a series of campy sound-stage special effects sequences as the teens take the audience from one set piece to the next like a back-lot tour in a theme park. To make things worse the entire final act is filmed at night with dull lighting. This may have looked okay on the big cinema screen when first released but sadly all the effort and the effects are diminished even further when viewed on a small TV screen. And if that's not enough the film even has its own cornball title song performed by The Tubes, but for some reason or other the song is not played on the opening credits, instead we hear it on the closing credits, why I am not sure, maybe the song was an afterthought when principal editing was finished, whatever the case maybe, the song wasn't a contender come Oscar time. Nevertheless "My Science Project" can boast a title song, many films can't. Also, the film's end credits are in fact quite interesting as they come with a stills montage and off-cuts featuring the film's comedy relief Vince Latello played by Fisher Stevens of "Short Circuit" fame. Stevens is given some of the film's best one-liners with the most memorable one delivered when he is arrested by a female cop who says to him, "Hey kid, why do you wear sunglasses at night?" Stevens replies," Because when you're cool, the sun shines on you 24 hours a day".

Yes, the film does have its funny moments between all the time warps, scientific havoc and mumbo jumbo.

When "My Science Project" hit cinemas it was sandwiched between "Weird Science" and "Real Genius" with both competitors doing better at the box office. Also, "Back To The Future" was still going strong in cinemas so it faced stiff competition left right and center. Nevertheless, made on a small budget the film still managed to bring in a neat $4 million at the US box office. Although, it was caught in the cinema shuffle on release, the video boom of the mid-80s was kind to it. As expected "My Science Project" is predictable teen entertainment. Everything works out just fine in the end. Mike Harlan saves his girl, his teacher, his town and of course he gets an A for his science project. More importantly, "My Science Project" delivers the right message to teen viewers; don't mess with scientific gizmos that you find in military junkyards, enough said.

Real Genius ***

US Release Date: 9th August 1985
Running Time: 108 min
US Classification: PG
Director: Martha Coolidge
Starring: Val Kilmer, Gabriel Jarret, Michelle Meyrink, William Atherton, Ed Lauter, Jon Gries, Patti D'Arbanville

Taglines:

* When he gets mad, he doesn't get even... he gets creative.
* Meet Chris Knight, the Einstein of the 80's. He can turn the simple into the simply amazing, and now he turns revenge into high comedy.
* It's yet another in a long series of diversions in an attempt to avoid responsibility.
* You need brains to act this crazy!
* Meet Chris Knight, the Einstein of the 80's. He can turn lasers into light shows, armchairs into aircraft, and high tech into high jinks. But when his professor steals his prize invention he turns revenge into high comedy.

Film Review:

"Real Genius" is a unique if not goofy teen comedy about two teenage Einstein's partnered in a bizarre plot to develop a high-powered laser weapon capable of vaporizing a target from outer space. Their professor misleads them into believing that the laser is for a class project but in reality he intends to sell the laser to the government for use as a weapon. The narration in the film's trailer says it all…."When the military runs short on brains, they go hunting at Pacific Tech, an exclusive institution for outstanding intellects. Where the superstar of smarts is Chris Knight. His hobbies violate the laws of gravity. His homework could win a noble prize. He is one of the ten finest minds in the country. His IQ is higher than most people can count. But when Chris makes the scientific discovery of the century, his classmates want the credit, his professor wants the publicity and the military wants to use his discovery as the ultimate weapon. So Chris is about to turn getting even into a science and show them they should never try to outsmart a real genius". Is the film a true reflection of the trailer, you bet and more! It is also an unexpected gag-fest, plus Val Kilmer makes a great Chris Knight.

If seeing a young Val Kilmer with a blonde Elvis-hairdo, wearing bunny slippers and an "I Love Toxic Waste" t-shirt tickles your fancy…then "Real Genius" is just the ticket for you, that's right, a trip back to 80s lunacy at its wackiest. Fresh from his stint in the Zucker Bros comedy "Top Secret", Kilmer yet again shows a flair for comedy with this indifferent teen fantasy about teenage Einstein's. "Real Genius" can be challenging at times, some may find the jokes hit and miss, as they aren't always obvious and are mostly of the verbal variety. You will have to listen carefully and not get distracted in order to absorb the essence of the film's banter. Smart-alec humour and wise cracks are a plenty. When Professor Hathaway tells Kilmer he needs to be "seeing more of him at the lab," Kilmer replies, "Fine. I'll gain weight." If this style of humour tickles your funny bone then Real Genius is an absolute howl. For some viewers, whether or not they get something out of this unusual film may also be a little dependent on how much they can take of watching Kilmer acting the goat for 100 minutes or so. Whether you enjoy it or not, becomes a matter of taste, just like the party scene with the aerated slippery slide into a swimming pool, you never know what's going to "pop up" next in this irreverent 80s lab experiment.

The Los Angeles Times describes "Real Genius" as "A brisk, smart, satirical comedy from the writers of Police Academy and the Director of Valley Girl". Whatever the case, "Real Genius" is a teen movie like no other, you will never see another one quite like it and for this reason alone it has developed a strong cult following over the years with many fans considering it Kilmer's best work. The performances are great all round with Kilmer's co-star Gabriel Jarret proving to be a standout by winning the "Best Actor" award at the Paris Film Festival. Director, Martha Coolidge also picked up the "Grand Prix" award for the film. "Real Genius" didn't only score points with the critics but clocked up a neat $13 million at the US box office, not bad considering the stiff competition at the time from "Back To The Future", "Weird Science" and "Teen Wolf". The bottom line is "Real Genius" is a wacky, way-out, one of a kind fantasy that comes with a real popcorn finale…. literally! And the pop ballad "Everybody Wants To Rule The World" by Tears For Fears is a fitting cap as the end credits roll.

Teen Wolf ***

US Release Date: 23rd August 1985
Running Time: 91 min
US Classification: PG
Director: Rod Daniel
Starring: Michael J. Fox, James Hampton, Susan Ursitti, Jerry Levine, Matt Adler, Lorie Griffin, Jim McKrell, Mark Arnold, Jay Tarses, Mark Holton, Scott Paulin, Elizabeth Gorcey, Melanie Manos, Doug Savant, Charles Zucker.

Tagline:

He always wanted to be special… but he never expected this!

Film Review:

If you grew up in the 1980's chances are pretty high that you got to see the werewolf comedy "Teen Wolf" on the big screen. Although made before "Back To The Future", this campy low budget teen film starring Michael J. Fox of "Family Ties" fame was held back and given a major release in August 1985, just after the massive box office success of "Back To The Future". While "Back To The Future" was packing houses and becoming the number 1 film across America, "Teen Wolf" opened and capitalized on its success and everybody's enthusiasm for Fox. With "Back To The Future" at number 1 & "Teen Wolf" at number 2, a new teen star had been born. "Teen Wolf" is a campy tale of a teenage basketball player who discovers that he is a descendent of a family of werewolves. This premise was originally used in the 1957 Michael Landon classic "I Was A Teenage Werewolf", but this time round it is given a 1980's spin with more emphasis on comedy and romance rather than horror.

While everything in the film is totally implausible the presence of Fox is the glue that holds this fantasy tale together. The film has enough situations to keep audiences watching, some of the more memorable ones include, the dog whistle in the hardware store that sends Fox nuts, Fox tearing his girlfriend's shirt with his claws when the two are locked in a closet, the basketball match when Fox first turns into the wolf, Fox's Dad revealing that he is also a werewolf and who can forget the moment when Fox sinks his teeth into the beer can at the bowling alley. "Teen Wolf" is literally littered with standout scenes and like some special films this one also comes with a signature scene. In this case, it is the scene where Fox van surfs on the roof of his best friend's wolf-mobile to the sound of The Beach Boys classic Surfin' USA and if that isn't enough to keep your attention there's the school dance finale with Fox wearing the "Saturday Night Fever" inspired suit strutting it out to the beat of "Big Bad Wolf" by Bunny and the Wolf Sisters. "Teen Wolf" also comes with a number of classic one-liners, the most memorable being the line Fox delivers to the liquor storeowner, "Give me, a keg, of beer" he says with his glowing red eyes that are enough to scare the most fearless of humans. Yes, "Teen Wolf" has everything that 80s teen movie fans are looking for.

On its cinema release "Teen Wolf" was extremely popular with audiences everywhere, grossing over $33 million at the US box office and ranking 26th in its year. When it was later released on videocassette it became one of those films that teens wanted to re-watch over and over again. With the big-time success of "Teen Wolf" it was inevitable that a sequel would follow. Two years later "Teen Wolf Too" was released in theatres with a new werewolf in the role. Jason Bateman the popular star of the TV series "Valerie's Family" and later the spin-off series "The Hogan Family", replaced Michael J. Fox in this sequel. Bateman plays the cousin of the Michael J. Fox character of the original film. "Teen Wolf Too", although not as good as the original, was nevertheless a success. The sequel sadly lacks the presence of Michael J. Fox, who at the time of its release was starring in the much bigger box office smash "The Secret Of My Success". Both "Teen Wolf" & "Teen Wolf Too" are essential viewing for 1980's fans. If you are looking for campy light-hearted entertainment on a Saturday night then they don't come much better than this double-bill. "Teen Wolf" is and always will be howling good fun.

Better Off Dead *** ½

US Release Date: 11ᵗʰ October 1985
Running Time: 97 min
US Classification: PG
Director: Savage Steve Holland
Starring: John Cusack, Kim Darby, Diane Franklin, Curtis Armstrong, Amanda Wyss, Chuck Mitchell, David Ogden Stiers, Scooter Stevens, Aaron Dozier, Yuji Okumoto

Taglines:

* Teenage life has never been darker...or funnier...
* You've blown up your neighbour's mom. Your seven-year-old brother has better luck with women than you do. Your girlfriend has a new boyfriend. Relax, you're never... Better Off Dead.
* Insanity doesn't run in the family, it gallops.

Film Review:

"Better Off Dead" is a quirky teen comedy that you could either love or hate, for many there is not much room for middle-ground. According to a comment on the DVD case cover, "writer / director Savage Steve Holland say's Better Off Dead is semi-autobiographical". "After his high school love ditched him, he picked up an 8-millimeter camera and made some depressing movies that had the exact opposite effect on his friends - they laughed". One thing is for sure, when Holland put pen to paper for this screenplay, his creative juices must have been in overdrive. Seldom does a Director's film debut turn out to be this wacky and outrageously unique.

High school student Lane Meyer (John Cusack) is broken-hearted when his sweetheart Beth Truss (Amanda Wyss) leaves him for popular jock Roy Stalin (Aaron Dozier) who just happens to be the top dog of the ski slopes. Lane's obsession with his girlfriend (his bedroom is plastered wall to wall with her pictures) leads him to contemplate suicide, hence the title of the film "Better Off Dead". However, someone always interrupts Lane's lackluster attempts at ending his life, usually in an unexpected comedic way.

When Lane is trying to hang himself behind a door, his mother opens the door when she is vacuuming; this causes him to fall with the noose around his neck, almost choking to death he is forced to save himself. In another incident he is about to jump off an overpass but falls victim to a pat on the back by his best-friend Charles De Mar (Curtis Armstrong or Booger from "Revenge Of The Nerds") who just happens to pass by. Charles is obviously not much help; he wears a top hat, sniffs jelly, sniffs snow or sniffs anything he can get his hands on for that matter. In this instance, the pat on the back causes Lane to fall, but instead of falling to his death he lands in the back of a garbage truck and lives to see another day. The crazy situations continue when Lane attempts to set himself alight but instead accidentally blows up a family dinner guest after she mistakenly drinks his lighter fluid and strikes a cigarette. You just get the feeling that if left to his own-devices Lane would never be successful in killing himself. Maybe that's because, in his sub-conscious, he knows that this is not the right thing to do.

To add insult to injury, after the break-up every song that pops up on Lane's car stereo is a depressing break-up ballad from "Breaking Up Is Hard To Do" to "50 Ways To Leave Your Lover" the songs just keep on coming. This causes Lane to remove the stereo and throw it out of the window. If this isn't enough, every-time Lane gets behind the wheel he comes across some Japanese car nuts keen to drag race. They taunt him via a giant mega-phone on the roof of their vehicle and sound like leftovers from a poorly dubbed Godzilla movie. Also, in two instances, Lane is the victim of road rage by none other than Chuck Mitchell of "Porky's" fame. Chuck plays Rocko, owner of Pig Burgers, a hamburger restaurant that Lane later gets a job at. When Lane asks Rocko can he wash his hands before he begins making the burgers Rocko's reply is something to the effect of, "No, you can do that in your own time, now get back to work". Hygiene is obviously not a priority at Pig Burgers. At various points of the film Lane's imagination runs wild, his sketches come to life and talk to him at the school cafeteria, while at the hamburger joint the burgers and fries get their own song and dance routine through the use of clay-animation. By the time Lane snaps out of his dream world the burgers are burnt and Rocko fires him. Later, Lane challenges Roy, the school bully, to a ski-competition in a bid to win back his girlfriend but in the meantime begins to fall for a French Exchange student, Monique Junot (Diane Franklin from "The Last American Virgin"), who is staying with his nerdy be-spectacled neighbour Ricky Smith (Dan Schneider).

Oddball characters are certainly the norm in this one and Lane's family members are no exception, they may even be the worst offenders. Lane's father battles it out with the local paperboy who smashes his garage windows and persistently demands, "I want my 2 dollars". Lane's mother would have to be the worst cook in the world. She boils bacon and serves mystery food (resembling jelly) that simply moves off the plate and if that's not enough, the giant moving tentacles hanging out of her saucepan are enough to make anyone squirm and head for the nearest takeaway outlet. Also, to the annoyance of the entire family, Lane's mother cuts holes in the boxes of breakfast cereals to remove the coupons; hence more cereal hits the floor than hits the bowl. Lane's parents even try to help him out by arranging a date for him. The hilarious consequences are brief but carefully calculated. You will have to view the scene to appreciate why. Lane's even has an 8-Year old little brother. He is a wannabe-inventor, who builds and shoots laser guns (Lane is almost vaporized in one sequence), reads books on how to pick up trashy women and by the film's closing credits has unleashed his space shuttle that flies up; crashing through the roof of the house and into space. That's right, the film is over-the-top from start to finish, even the film's final screen credit is an attempt at humour with its statement, "The film's over….you can go now".

"Better Off Dead" is unique, maybe even a bit strange but certainly one of the most original teen movies of the decade. Writer / director Savage Steve Holland has gone to the nth degree to make every scene funny. When you try to inject that much comedy into every frame it is not easy to make every scene work, it is inevitable that the comedy will be hit and miss. Every character is a caricature, from the leads to the supports and the absurdity of it all may be loved or hated, dependent on the mood or tastes of the audience. One thing is for sure; I don't think you'll ever see another teen movie like it. The Los Angeles Times describes it as "An inventive, oddball gem..." that "lovingly recreates all the worst traumas of teenage life." John Cusack is known for choosing quirky roles, but this one would have to take the cake. "Better Off Dead" is a Cusack classic with originality plus.

Chapter 7:

TEEN MOVIES OF 1986

Iron Eagle **

US Release Date: 17th January 1986
Running Time: 117 min
US Classification: PG-13
Director: Sidney J. Furie
Starring: Louis Gossett Jr., Jason Gedrick, Tim Thomerson, Larry B. Scott, Jerry Levine, Michael Bowen, Melora Hardin

Taglines:

* Break the sound barrier. Break the speed barrier.
* Heroes with attitude. Adventure with altitude.
* Doug is 18. Raised on an air base and born to fly. His father has been shot down 6000 miles away, and has been sentenced to death... for the crime of being an American. Everyone's telling Doug to sit tight and wait. Everyone but Retired Air Force Colonel Chappy Sinclair. They know what they have to do. And they've "borrowed" a pair of F-16s to do it. For them, waiting time is over.

Film Review:

Before "Top Gun", there was "Iron Eagle", the story of a teenage fighter-pilot who takes to the skies to rescue his father who is being held captive in a middle-eastern country after his plane was brought down when it ventured into foreign air space. The plot's an excuse for some spectacular aerial acrobatics, stunts, explosions, teenage heroics and aviator sunglasses. Director Sidney J. Furie was no newcomer to teen movies when he signed up to do this one, having already made two popular teen musicals in the 1960s, "The Young Ones" (1961) and "Wonderful Life" (1964) with British pop star

Cliff Richard. This time round the teens are still there but Furie has to forgo song and dance for action and adventure; he even gets his name down in the writing credits for the film.

Jason Gedrick from "The Heavenly Kid" plays Doug Masters the teen air force cadet who sets out on the rescue mission. Academy Award winner Louis Gosset Jr ("An Officer And A Gentleman") plays a retired Air Force Colonel who decides to assist Gedrick in his quest to rescue his father (Tim Thomerson). Other familiar teen movie faces pop up as Gedrick's school friends including Larry B. Scott ("Revenge Of The Nerds"), Jerry Levine ("Teen Wolf"), Michael Bowen ("Valley Girl") and Melora Hardin ("Soul Man").

"Iron Eagle" ranked in the top 50 US Box Office earners of 1986. The film came in at 41st and grossed $24,159,872 not bad for a film that is often described as "Top Gun for teens". It is interesting to note that "Top Gun" was released a couple of months later and became the year's top money-spinner bringing in $176,786,701 at the US box office. Strangely, there were no sequels to "Top Gun" but the success of "Iron Eagle" at the box office ensured that the saga continued into the next decade with 3 sequels, "Iron Eagle II" (1988), "Aces: Iron Eagle III" (1992) and "Iron Eagle IV" (1995). All the sequels starred Louis Gossett Jr. with the most notable change being different teenagers playing the young pilot, Doug Masters.

"Iron Eagle" maybe a bit far-fetched for mature audiences, but its mindless fun has generated a fan base over the years, and why not, what teenage boy wouldn't want to take to the skies like Doug Masters? He looks cool in aviator sunglasses, knows how to fly an F-16 fighter plane and with his finger on the trigger, he's a crack shot at taking down the enemy. Now, if that's not enough, he takes his walkman with him into battle claiming that the music helps him with his aim.... silly we know, but remember, this is the "totally awesome" 80s.

Pretty In Pink ****

US Release Date: 28th February 1986
Running Time: 96 min
US Classification: PG-13
Director: Howard Deutch
Starring: Molly Ringwald, Andrew McCarthy, Jon Cryer, James Spader

Taglines:

* Blane's a pretty cool guy. Andie's pretty in pink. And Ducky's pretty crazy.

* He's crazy about her. She's crazy about him. He's just crazy.
* He's good. She's good. He's just Duckie.
* The laughter. The lovers. The friends. The fights. The talk. The hurt. The jealousy. The passion. The pressure. The Real World.

Film Review:

"Pretty In Pink" is considered by many to be one of the best teen films of the 1980's, thanks to an excellent script by John Hughes, first-rate direction by Howard Deutch and solid performances by the cast. Molly Ringwald shines in her role as Andie and Jon Cryer is brilliant as Duckie, her best friend. The film looks at the relationships and emotions between several characters and the social barriers they must confront. Andie lives with her unemployed father Jack (Harry Dean Stanton) in a poor neighborhood. Life has been difficult since Andie's mother left them. Andie's best friend, Duckie is secretly in love with her and the plot intensifies when Andie meets and falls in love with rich kid, Blaine

(Andrew McCarthy). Lurking in the background is Steff (James Spader), Blane's creepy best friend who also has a thing for Andie. Who will Andie end up with at the film's end? That is the question, in this charming, character study of first love among high school students.

"Pretty In Pink" is one of those emotional romance dramas that captures your attention right from the word go and keeps you interested all the way to the end. It has all the elements of a quality teen film, love triangles, proms, secrets, broken promises, class differences, trendy clothes, great music and of course an outstanding performance from its star…. Molly Ringwald. The film's soundtrack features a good blend of hip 80s pop and rock tunes. From the title track by The Psychedelic Furs, to mood setters like "Wouldn't It Be Good" by Nik Kershaw and "Round Round" by Belouise Some, to the film's passionate love theme "If You Leave" by OMD (Orchestral Manoeuvres in the Dark). It's no surprise that fans loved the LP just as much as the movie. The drama in the film is complemented not only by the music but also by many comedic moments. One of the film's standout sequences is Jon Cryer lip-synching in the record store to Otis Redding's "Try A Little Tenderness". From the moment he slides across the floor in those Duckman shoes, you know that you are in for a treat. It's almost too much for Molly Ringwald and her best friend Iona (Annie Potts) to take in. In fact, Jon Cryer almost steals the show with some the film's best one-liners, including "Drinking and driving don't mix. That's why I ride a bike" (after he downs a juice box) and "I'm off like a dirty shirt" (after he has a one on one conversation with Molly's father). Also, look out for comedian Andrew "Dice" Clay in a small role as a bouncer at CATS nightclub. How he handles a cigarette is an eyebrow raiser and it leaves one to ponder how he would handle a drunken guest…but I guess in a small role like this there is simply no time to take his character further.

When I sat down to review this film, my first thoughts were, how can you put pen to paper and review a film that you love and adore so much? What's its appeal? Why has it stood the test of time? Here is a short list of "10 Things I Like About Pretty In Pink"! Here goes…One; the John Hughes script is brilliant, Two; the love triangle is totally captivating, Three; Molly Ringwald meets the expectations of the title and is at her very best, Four; Jon Cryer's performance is an absolute knockout, Five; Andrew McCarthy is at his sweetest, Six; James Spader is at his creepiest, Seven; the film's color and fashion are impressive, Eight; the soundtrack captures the mood of the film beautifully, Nine; the movie poster is a dead-set classic, Ten; the film has an ending that has been debated ever since it hit the screens. "Pretty In Pink" has now reached cult status and there are fans of this movie all around the world. If you haven't seen it, don't wait any longer, get the DVD and see this classic movie today. "Pretty In Pink" is one of those special films that can give you goose bumps just thinking about it!

Lucas *** ½

US Release Date: 28th March 1986
Running Time: 100 min
US Classification: PG-13
Director: David Seltzer
Starring: Corey Haim, Kerri Green, Charlie Sheen, Courtney Thorne-Smith, Winona Ryder, Tom Hodges, Ciro Poppiti, Guy Boyd, Jeremy Piven, Kevin Wixted, Emily Seltzer, Erika Leigh, Anne Ryan, Jason Alderman, Tom Mackie.

Taglines:

* There's nothing wrong with being different.
* It's about falling in love...for the first time.
* A boy that just won't be beaten.

Film Review:

"Lucas" was a late inclusion into this book. We knew of the films existence but for some reason or another we never seemed to find an opportunity to watch it. We missed it on its initial release at the cinemas, we never had the desire to pick it up off the video rental shelves and we can't ever recall seeing it advertised on normal free to air TV. Eventually we caught up with the film in February 2003 when it began doing the rounds on cable TV. Even then it was only by chance, as we had to forfeit an invitation to see the new "Star Trek" movie in order to finally view this 17 year old gem of a film. The wait was worth it. We were both pleasantly surprised to discover the quality of the film and also to see young stars such as Corey Haim, Kerri Green, Charlie Sheen and Winona Ryder in their early beginnings. After watching the film we both decided that "Lucas" was a well worth inclusion in the "80 from the 80s".

After small appearances during the mid-80's in films such as "Secret Admirer" (1985) and "Murphy's Romance" (1985), 15 year-old Corey Haim was given the opportunity to star in "Lucas" as the film's sympathetic 14 year-old title character. "Lucas" is a heart-warming high school drama, with dashes of comedy and romance thrown into the mix. Bullied youngster Lucas knows what it's like to be on the outside, but when he befriends an older new girl in town (2 years his senior) his life seems to take a turn for the better until she falls in love with the school football star. Lucas' rejection hits him hard and the lovelorn little fellow must now pick up the pieces and regain his self-worth.

As the credits begin to roll Lucas' character is set up immediately. He is a bespectacled youngster, an "accelerated" loner, who would prefer to spend his time searching for and catching insects, especially locusts, rather than mixing with the in-crowd of jocks and cheerleaders. As Lucas wonders around with a backpack full of junk and an insect catcher in his hand, his lonely existence changes focus when he stumbles on to a tennis court and spots a beautiful redhead (Maggie played by Kerri Green) practicing her tennis swing. Lucas is immediately smitten by her beauty and simply can't take his eyes off her. When a tennis ball rolls in Lucas' direction, their eyes meet and the two youngsters spark up a conversation. It is not long before a friendship develops and Maggie offers Lucas a ride home. Lucas tells her that he lives in a nearby mansion and that his parents are workaholics (we later find out that Lucas lives in a trailer park with his alcoholic father, who we never see in the film). It is summer vacation and Maggie is the new girl in town with time to spare. She is soon swept into Lucas's world of bugs, opera and his "superficial" attitude towards football heroes, cheerleaders and parties. As the two sit back to back in an underground sewer listening to classical music that resonates from an outdoor concert above them, Lucas mutters the phrase, "I just wish that school would never start". In the next scene the school bell rings and his summer of bliss is over.

For Lucas, going back to school is one humiliation after the next. It is only day one and the bullying begins. At the school assembly a blond-haired jock bails him out of the crowd, puts him over his shoulder and dumps him on to the stage to a huge roar from his fellow students. Lucas' true genius comes through however as he makes the most of a bad situation with his impromptu attention seeking hand gestures at the expense of the school football coach (Guy Boyd). To his credit Lucas succeeds in getting the crowd to laugh with him rather than at him, not an easy task when the entire school population is mocking you. Despite his peculiar personality and indifferent behaviour Lucas does have a secret admirer. Shy girl Rina (played by Winona Ryder in her debut role), secretly loves Lucas from afar.

For poor old Lucas the bullying never ends. Even outside the schoolyard the torment continues. At the local cinema Lucas is taunted and picked on at the candy bar, by a bunch of dumb jocks. Luckily for Lucas every oddball has to have a protector and in this film he comes in the form of Cappie (Charlie Sheen) the school football captain. As the film develops, sadly for Lucas, the inevitable happens. Maggie becomes a cheerleader and falls in love with Cappie. Lucas is heartbroken and desperately tries to win her back by leaving the school band and joining the competitive school football team. Unfortunately, Lucas just doesn't fit in, his intellect and diminutive stature are his handicap and now even the football locker-room becomes an avenue for the jocks to make Lucas the brunt of all their practical jokes. As the film moves into the final quarter and a big football game showdown, one may begin to think that the film is heading into predictability, but "Lucas" is much more than that. The film's finale is touching to say the least, emotions run hot, both on and off the screen and the experience is ultimately uplifting.

"Lucas" is a sensitive teen drama, full of likeable characters and obviously a labour of love for writer/director David Seltzer, who with this film made his directorial debut. If you didn't know Seltzer was responsible for this delightful character driven film, one could be excused for believing it might have come from the John Hughes stable of 80's teen flicks. The key to the film's success is in its writing, all the characters are multi-dimensional, but for a script to work you need outstanding performances. The film's talented cast achieves this in spades; they are successful in making each character their own. For Corey Haim, "Lucas" may even be his finest hour. His performance as the skinny, downtrodden, "accelerated" youngster is nothing short of superb. Remember, this is Corey Haim long before he became one-half of the infamous "Corey double-team" of Haim and Feldman. The two Corey's reigned as a team in the late 80's with films such as "License To Drive" (1988) and "Dream A Little Dream" (1989) but by the mid-90's the team had run its course. Red-haired sweetheart Kerri Green, fresh from "The Goonies", gives a convincing and very natural performance as the girl caught between the affections of the two boys. Charlie Sheen, who would later that year go on to star in Oliver Stone's Oscar wining Vietnam masterpiece "Platoon" (1986), is believable in the difficult role of the football star who falls in love with Lucas' girl while trying to maintain his friendship with Lucas by continuing to protect and care for him. "Lucas" may not have brought in big bucks at the US box office ($8.2 million) but the critics loved it. At the "Young Artist Awards", Corey Haim, Kerri Green and the film itself were all nominated for awards. "Lucas" is not your stereotypical teen film, nor is it an exploitation film; it shies away from using bad language, nudity, violence and sex to tell its story, for that the film is a breath of fresh air, it exudes a unique quality and charm of its own, that should be applauded.

Ferris Bueller's Day Off ****

US Release Date: 11th June 1986
Running Time: 102 min
US Classification: PG-13
Director: John Hughes
Starring: Matthew Broderick, Alan Ruck, Mia Sara, Jennifer Grey, Jeffrey Jones, Charlie Sheen, Cindy Pickett, Lyman Ward, Ben Stein

Taglines:

* One Man's Struggle To Take It Easy
* Leisure Rules

Film Review:

Everybody at some stage in their lives has cut classes in school to do extra-curricular activities? Well, "Ferris Bueller's Day Off" uses that theme to great effect. Many teen movies were released during 1986 but Ferris was definitely a standout from the pack. A film that is still favourably watched today, it has become a classic film of youth. For some, Mathew Broderick's character has emerged as a likeable hero. At the 1987 Golden Globe Awards Broderick was nominated for "Best Actor in a Comedy or Musical". Yes, Broderick's performance in the film is exceptional and the nomination was well deserved. For Writer / Director John Hughes this was his fourth and final teen movie in the director's chair. He has once again crafted a highly entertaining film about the rebelliousness of youth that connects well with its target audience.

The story is simple, but effective. 17-year-old Ferris Bueller (Matthew Broderick) pretends to be ill in order to get a day off school. His parents decide to let him stay home provided he remains in bed, but Ferris has other ideas. He sums up his philosophy on life when he says, "Life goes by pretty fast. If you don't stop and look around once in a while, you could miss it." He talks his best friend Cameron Frye (Alan Ruck) into taking his father's Red Ferrari for a spin around town and he also uses foul means to successfully pull his girlfriend Sloane Peterson (Mia Sara) out of school. The three of them spend their "day off" running wild through the streets of Chicago. The film's cinematographers take full advantage of capturing all the sights and sounds of Chicago's eye-catching landmarks. Hot on Ferris' trail is the high school Principal Ed Rooney (played hilariously over- the-top by Jeffrey Jones) who is not about to let Ferris get away with his truancy. Look out for Charlie Sheen ("Lucas") in a cameo as the druggie in the police station and Jennifer Grey ("Dirty Dancing") makes brief appearances as Ferris' sister Jeanie. Also, Ben Stein is memorable as the Economics teacher with the distinct monotone voice. His role-call sequence when he calls out...

"Bueller?... Bueller?... Bueller?" is now firmly established in the book of classic film quotes.

"Ferris Bueller's Day Off" keeps the audience engaged from the first to the last frame because Director John Hughes manages to keep the film fast-paced and full of laughs. The film features many memorable moments, Ferris's monologues to the audience are grabbing and Ed Rooney's misadventures in his hunt for Ferris are stupefying. The teens' dining experience in a ritzy restaurant is a hoot while the valet's that take the Ferrari for a joyride are hilarious. However, one of the best sequences would have to be when Ferris, standing on top of a float in a passing street parade, delivers a fun version of "The Beatles" classic "Twist & Shout". Ferris' lip-synching of Wayne Newton's "Danke Schoen" isn't too bad either. There are just so many standout moments in this movie that the list could go on and on and on. No wonder, in 2005 an Empire Magazine article named it "The Number One Teen Film Of All-Time".

"Ferris Bueller's Day Off" enjoyed enormous success at the box office grossing over $70 million in the US alone. Not bad for a teen movie with a $6 million budget. In 1990 a short-lived situation comedy titled "Ferris Bueller" hit the small screen. Enjoying only a lukewarm reception, it lasted only one season and starred Charlie Schlatter as Ferris Bueller, Jennifer Aniston as Jeanie Bueller, Ami Dolenz as Sloan Peterson and Brandon Douglas as Cameron Frye. For fans however, the big screen version of "Ferris Bueller's Day Off" is the ultimate 1980's teen classic, a fun film that can be enjoyed time and time again because of its innocent charm, likeable characters and hilarious situations. Finally, if you haven't already seen it, make sure you stay to the very end of the film's credits to see Ferris return briefly and tell viewers to "go home the film has finished".

Never Too Young To Die ** ½

US Release Date: 13th June 1986
Running Time: 92 min
US Classification: R
Director: Gil Bettman
Starring: John Stamos, Vanity, Gene Simmons, George Lazenby, Robert Englund, Peter Kwong, Ed Brock, John Anderson, Tara Buckman, Curtis Taylor, Jon Greene, Tim Colceri, John Miranda Patrick M. Wright, Art Payton.

Taglines:

* He Inherited All His Father's Enemies And Only One Of His Friends.
* Stargrove: the new American hero.
* Vanity: The New Breed Of Temptress!
* Stamos: The New Breed Of Hero!
* Action: Bond Style
* Beauty: Vanity Style
* Hero: American Style
* At the age of 18, every government agency wanted him... dead or alive.

Film Review:

"Never Too Young To Die" is a real curiosity piece if ever there was one. One part Bond, one part Stamos, one part Vanity, one part Gene Simmons and a whole lot of camp make this film a unique entry into the 1980s teen movie genre. For teen heartthrob John Stamos, "Never Too Young To Die" was his first starring role and what better way to make his film debut than to play the son of former James Bond star, George Lazenby ("On Her Majesty's Secret Service"), in this action-packed Bond-style teen thriller. Australian born Lazenby plays secret agent Drew Stargrove and when he is brutally murdered by the ruthless Van Ragnar (Gene Simmons from the rock band Kiss), his teenage son, high school gymnast Lance Stargrove (John Stamos) is thrust into the dangerous and intriguing world of secret agents and espionage. Villainous Simmons and his cronies who look like leftovers from a second-rate "Mad Max" movie are out to poison the cities water supply and will stop at nothing to get the job done. Stamos' mission is to stop Simmons and at the same time avenge his father's death. To add to the fun, real-life Motown pop-star Vanity, fresh from her success in "The Last Dragon" (1985), co-stars as Stamos' sidekick & love interest. The two leads look good together and share a great on-screen chemistry while Simmons hams it up to the nth degree as the maniacal hermaphrodite hell bent on global domination.

"Never Too Young To Die" is a matinee-style popcorn film and even features its own cheesy theme song titled "Stargrove" with music and lyrics by Chip Taylor, Ralph Lane, Michael Kingsley, and Iren Koster. That's right, it took 4 people to write this 80s secret agent track. The campy song is played over the opening gymnastic credit sequence with Stamos (complete with mullet) bouncing on the school trampoline while other real gymnasts demonstrate their skills on various pieces of equipment. Now if you want a taste of what the song is like, the chorus goes something like this:

Stargrove! Flying like you've never flown

Stargrove! Runnin' through a danger zone

Stargrove! Are you gonna stand alone?

Stargrove! Stargrove!

That's certainly 80s song-writing at its cheesiest and yes, you guessed it, "Stargrove" did not get a nomination for "Best Song" at the 1986 Academy Awards but it did set up the tone of the film very nicely. Before "Never Too Young To Die" John Stamos was a regular on TV appearing in shows such as "General Hospital", "Dreams" and "You Again?". "Never Too Young To Die" was supposed to kick off his movie career but somehow it just didn't happen. Instead Stamos wound up back on the small screen, this time playing second fiddle to "The Olsen Twins" in the hugely successful TV series "Full House" (1987 – 1995).

As far as teen Bond spoofs go "Never Too Young To Die" stands tall, as it was the first of its kind and although there were no sequels it nevertheless left its mark and paved the way for others to follow. The concept of a teen secret agent saving the world has popped up a number of times since in films such as "If Looks Could Kill" (1991) and "Stormbreaker" (2006) and like its predecessor these films also enjoyed only mediocre success. "Never Too Young To Die" may not have won any critical accolades or made much money at the box office but if you don't take the film too seriously you might just enjoy it for what it is and find this low-budget piece of escapism quite entertaining. Maybe all it lacked was a bigger budget and a better script as it certainly had a colourful cast and an interesting concept. A unique quality of "Never Too Young To Die" is that it shares its appeal with 5 different fan bases, the secret agent fans, the John Stamos fans, the Vanity fans, the Gene Simmons fans and of course the teen movie fans. In fact, "Never Too Young To Die" has something to offer for most people, it is fast-paced, action-filled entertainment, with lots of explosions, battles, chases, stunts and a dash of romance. Stamos makes an appealing teenage James Bond and the film is a fun alternative to the conventional Bond flick or teen flick for that matter.

Thrashin' ** ½

US Release Date: 29th August 1986
Running Time: 92 min
US Classification: PG-13
Director: David Winters
Starring: Josh Brolin, Robert Rusler, Pamela Gidley, Josh Rickman, Brett Marx, Sherilyn Fenn

Taglines:

* Hot. Reckless. Totally Insane.
* It's not a kid's game anymore.
* He's in for the ride of his life.

Film Review:

Thrashin' is the ultimate skateboarding extravaganza. What Breakin' did for breakdancing and what "Rad" did for bike riding, Thrashin' did for skateboarding. The film may feature minimal plot and mediocre performances but the highly charged skateboarding sequences are nothing short of electrifying. The skateboarding craze was all the rage during the 1980s and skateboards were showcased in a number of high profile teen movies of the decade. Scott Baio was a skateboard kid in "Foxes", Matthew Broderick had one in "WarGames", Fred Savage had one in "The Wizard" and of course who can forget Michael J. Fox and his skateboard in "Back To The Future". Thrashin' marked the first major motion picture to center totally around the sport of skateboarding, the second film being "Gleaming The Cube" (1989) with Christian Slater. While "Gleaming The Cube" tried to feature an engaging murder mystery plotline, Thrashin' is 110% die-hard skateboarding from start to finish, nothing more, nothing less. Nearly everyone in Thrashin' has a skateboard and barely a frame of film goes by without one in view. If the boys aren't riding them, they carry them everywhere they go, you name it, into cafes and even dance venues. It's like the cowboy with his gun and holster or a nerd with his calculator and pocket pen or a surfer with his board and wax. For the teens in Thrashin' the skateboard is their weapon of choice.

Now, maybe the term Thrashin' is self-explanatory for some, but if you are wondering what it means there is a brief reference to the term in the movie describing it as "an aggressive form of skateboarding". The film's throwaway plotline sees two rival skateboarding gangs, The Ramp Locals and The Daggers, pitted against one another for supremacy. Josh Brolin fresh from his success in "The Goonies" headlines this skateboard-fest as Corey Webster, the good guy skateboarder from the valley who falls in love with Chrissy (Pamela Gidley) the sister of bad boy skateboarder, Tommy Hook (Robert Rusler). For Pamela Gidley, Thrashin' marked her feature film debut but for Robert Rusler, Thrashin' was just another teen movie supporting role. Rusler, had already appeared in films such as "Weird Science" (1985), "A Nightmare On Elm Street 2" (1985) and "Dangerously Close" (1986) before freestyling his way through this one. Aside from these three young actors, Thrashin' features small appearances by a number of stars of the skateboarding world including Tony Hawk, Tony Alva, Chris Cook, Lance Mountain and Alan Losi with some of these skaters performing as stunt doubles for Josh Brolin.

What Thrashin' lacks in plot and acting performances it makes up for with kinetic skateboarding sequences and excellent use of California locations such as Malibu, Venice Beach and Hollywood Boulevard. The skateboarding sequence along the Hollywood Walk of Fame is a hoot and certainly one of the film's highlights. Thrashin' never gets caught up with lengthy dialogue sequences, it's like these teens don't talk to their parents, they don't attend school and all their time is spent on the streets with their boards. Skateboarding is their life. The pacing and momentum of the film is maintained throughout with frequent highflying skateboarding montages, slowing down only on odd occasions for brief dialogue exchanges and in one instance a brief love scene. After any brief lull, the film quickly kicks up a gear with more skateboarding antics and stunts. The cinematographers have gone all out to capture the feel of the ride with multiple angle photography that will keep viewers on the edge of their boards. If the downhill skateboarding finale doesn't grab you, then maybe the film's rock music soundtrack will, featuring songs from Meatloaf, Devo, The Bangles and The Fine Young Cannibals. Also included is an energetic on-stage appearance by the Red Hot Chili Peppers. Film critic Leonard Maltin describes Thrashin' as "West Side Story on wheels". No small co-incidence as Thrashin' Director David Winters actually appeared in "West Side Story" in 1961. The film may not have won any Academy Awards like "West Side Story" and it may not have done very well at the box office but it has certainly developed a cult following among skateboarding enthusiasts around the world. Known as "Skate Gang" in France, Trashin' in West Germany and Thrashin' almost everywhere else in the world, this hip film achieves exactly what it sets out to do and that is entertain and thrill the skateboard crowd.

Chapter 8:

TEEN MOVIES OF 1987

Hotshot ** ½

US Release Date: 23rd January 1987
Running Time: 94 min
US Classification: PG
Director: Rick King
Starring: Pelé, Jim Youngs, Penelope Ann Miller, Mario Van Peebles, Billy Warlock

Taglines:

* They've got nothing in common but the determination to be the best.
* It takes more than talent to become a winner.

Film Review:

Soccer may be considered "The World Game" but movies about the sport are few and far between. When "Hotshot" was released in 1987 the only film of substance about the sport that came before it was the WWII drama "Victory" (1981) starring Sylvester Stallone, Michael Caine, Max Von Sydow and of course Pele, arguably the greatest soccer player of all-time. Unlike "Victory", "Hotshot" was aimed totally at the teen market and in particular young soccer players. The film may not have had the star-power of "Victory" but it still had legendary soccer superstar Pele. "Hotshot" is "The Karate Kid" of soccer films. In "The Karate Kid" we had Pat Morita play the master or wise one. In "Hotshot", Pele plays the mentor who guides a young wannabe soccer star and teaches him not only how to play better soccer but also how to conduct himself in life. Although the storyline is cliqued and the performances routine, the soccer sequences are well done and as far as soccer films go they don't get much better than this one.

Jim Youngs ("Footloose", "The Wanderers") stars as hot headed Jimmy Kristidis, a young American with a passion for soccer. When Jimmy's tryout with the New York Rockers fails he travels to Brazil to seek out his idol, the legendary Santos (Pele). Santos, once the world's greatest soccer player, now lives the life of a recluse in the hills of Rio de Janeiro. In the company of Santos, Jimmy learns new skills both on and off the field, including the famed bicycle kick. It is interesting to note that Pele's character name "Santos" is, in reality, the name of the Brazilian Soccer club that Pele played for during his long career in professional football. Jim Youngs was an excellent choice for the lead role, his acting is adequate but more importantly he possesses the necessary soccer skills that are required to make his character believable. Look out for Mario Van Peebles ("Heartbreak Ridge", "Posse") in dreadlocks and Billy Warlock ("Baywatch") both as Jimmy's teammates.

"Hot Shot" is about one man's determination to be the best at what he enjoys most and that is, playing soccer. Writer / Director Rick King has successfully moulded a story full of emotion and excitement that looks closely at the themes of heroism, friendship and loyalty while Pele's presence is the key ingredient that adds authenticity to the project. Despite its low-budget and predicable plot, the film is still an excellent blend of sporting action and drama, featuring a nail-biting soccer finale that will have you on the edge of your seat, right through to the referee's final whistle. "Hotshot" is a film everybody can enjoy, but for young soccer players and soccer fans this film is an absolute treat.

Some Kind Of Wonderful *** ½

US Release Date: 27th February 1987
Running Time: 95 min
US Classification: PG-13
Director: Howard Deutch
Starring: Eric Stoltz, Mary Stuart Masterson, Lea Thompson, Craig Sheffer, John Ashton, Elias Koteas, Molly Hagan, Maddie Corman, Jane Elliot, Candace Cameron, Chynna Phillips, Scott Coffey, Carmine Caridi, Lee Garlington, Laura Leigh Hughes.

Tagline:

Before they could stand together, They had to stand alone.

Film Review:

Director Howard Deutch and writer John Hughes follow up their "Pretty In Pink" success with another teen movie gem. "Some Kind Of Wonderful" takes the plot of "Pretty In Pink" and switches the sexes. Eric Stoltz replaces Molly Ringwald and Mary Stuart Masterson replaces Jon Cryer. This involving teen melodrama features winning performances by the entire cast, with Mary Stuart Masterson being nothing short of exceptional in her sensitive portrayal of the drum playing tomboy who is madly in love with her best friend, Stoltz. Unfortunately Stoltz pays little attention to Masterson, as he is infatuated with the most popular girl in school, played by "Back To The Future's" Lea Thompson (who won Best Actress at the "Young Artist Awards" for her portrayal). When Thompson has an argument with her rich hotshot boyfriend (Craig Sheffer from "Fire With Fire"), Stoltz manages to score a date with her on the rebound. Emotions run hot and jealousies come to the fore when Masterson offers to act as chauffeur for Stoltz's date with Thompson. Also, tensions heighten further when bully Sheffer plans to get back at Stoltz by inviting him to his party with the intention of bashing him up. The stage is set for an emotionally charged finale but when the dust settles will true romance prevail?

"Some Kind of Wonderful" has a fine supporting cast including, John Ashton of "Beverly Hills Cop" fame as Stoltz's demanding, yet understanding father, Elias Koteas ("Teenage Mutant Ninja Turtles") is menacing as the tough but likeable school delinquent and look out for Candice Cameron (From TV's "Full House") in a few comedic moments as Stoltz's little sister. It is interesting to note that Molly Ringwald was offered the Lea Thompson role but refused it and thus marked the end of her involvement with John Hughes movies. Also of interest is the fact that Lea Thompson would go on to marry Director, Howard Deutch and the two would work together again on the hospital drama "Article 99" (1992). "Some Kind Of Wonderful" features an easy-listening soundtrack that complements the mood and tone of the films romanticism. The March Violets' version of the Rolling Stones' song "Miss Amanda Jones" adds flavour to Thompson's characterisation and the film's concluding soundtrack is an interesting gravel-voiced version of the famous Elvis Presley hit "Can't Help Falling In Love". The Elvis song is performed by 80's band "Lick The Tins" and adds a nice cap to the film's touching finale.

"Some Kind of Wonderful" is easily one of the most outstanding teen films of the 1980's. Masterson is an absolute standout and steals the film with a captivating performance. It is her beautiful portrayal of the love-struck teen that resonates on audiences long after the film is over. Apart from the compelling performances, the key ingredient to the film's success is that writer John Hughes has given all the characters enough depth for teen audiences to easily identify with them. All the emotions are on show, ranging from, love, hate, jealously, insecurity, rejection, peer pressure and self-discovery. "Some Kind Of Wonderful" is one of those special films that ooze charm, sensitivity and a unique quality that leaves both the audience and the film's characters understanding themselves a little better.

Adventures In Babysitting *** ½

US Release Date: 3rd July 1987
Running Time: 102 min
US Classification: PG-13
Director: Chris Columbus
Starring: Elisabeth Shue, Maia Brewton, Keith Coogan, Anthony Rapp, Calvin Levels, Vincent D'Onofrio, Penelope Ann Miller, George Newbern, John Ford Noonan, Bradley Whitford, Ron Canada, John Davis Chandler, Dan Ziskie, Lolita Davidovich, Allan Aarons.

Tagline:

She thought babysitting was easy money -until she started hanging out with the Andersons.

Film Review:

After making an impression as Ralph Macchio's love interest in "The Karate Kid" (1984), Elisabeth Shue was given her first opportunity to headline a film; the result was Chris Columbus' directorial debut "Adventures In Babysitting" (aka "A Night On The Town" in Australia and UK). Elisabeth Shue plays Chris, a babysitter who takes her two charges and their friend to downtown Chicago to help out her girlfriend Brenda (Penelope Ann Miller) who has run away from home and is now stranded at a bus station, with an assortment of seedy characters and without any money. After their car breaks down the fun begins and never lets up for a minute as Shue and the kids go from one madcap disaster to another. They encounter; jealous husbands, thieves, gangs, hoods and a giant garage attendant that resembles "The Mighty Thor", all before returning home safe and sound.

Shue is perfectly cast as the teenage babysitter who after being stood up by her slime-ball boyfriend Mike (who tells all his dates "Girls like you come along once in a lifetime"), reluctantly accepts the job of looking after the two Anderson kids (pre-teen Sara and young-teen Brad) while the parents go to a work party. Sara (Maia Brewton) is a big fan of comic-book superhero Thor and in most of the film she is seen wearing a silver Thor helmet. Older brother Brad (Keith Coogan) munches away at his chocolate bars while desperately trying to conceal his zits because he is madly in love with babysitter, Shue. To add to the mix Brad's smart-aleck friend Daryl (Anthony Rapp) turns up and weasels his way into joining them by blackmailing Shue with threats of telling Mr. and Mrs. Anderson about their planned night tour of Chicago.

The style and comedic situations of "Adventures in Babysitting" are reminiscent of John Hughes' "Ferris Bueller's Day Off" (1986) and Chris Columbus' later film "Home Alone" (1990). Anything and everything imaginable goes wrong, from the moment the crew hit the expressway in their station wagon. After their car has a tire blowout, Shue discovers that she has left her purse and money back at the house. They reluctantly accept a lift from a crazy tow-truck driver (John Ford Noonan) who turns out to have a hook-hand and a gun hidden in his glove box. It is not long before the trucker gets a message on his two-way that his wife is cheating on him, so he grabs his gun and heads straight for home. When they arrive at the house bullets start flying and the youngsters narrowly escape into a nearby vehicle, only to discover that there is a car thief at the wheel (Calvin Levels, who strangely enough looks and sounds like a male version of Whoopi Goldberg). Things go from bad to worse when they are taken to a nearby warehouse where a mafia crime ring is running a car theft operation. "Take the Brady Bunch upstairs", snarls the mafia boss, but before too long the kids find an escape route, along a tightrope walk on the rafters of the warehouse. With the villains in hot pursuit the youngsters stumble through the backdoor of a Blues nightclub and onto the stage just before the bandleader makes the film's most memorable quote "Nobody leaves this place without singing the blues". What follows is easily one of the film's standout scenes as we see the foursome reluctantly talk and sing their way through an impromptu performance of the memorable "Babysitting Blues". Another standout musical moment is the film's opening credit sequence in which the attractive Elisabeth Shue energetically dances and mimes to the tune of "Then He Kissed Me" by The Crystals.

"Adventures in Babysitting" scores high marks for its pacing. Just when you think everything is about to slow down something else happens. Before the end of the film the kids get caught up in a scuffle between two-rival gangs on a train carriage (in which Keith ends up in hospital with a stab wound), Maia ends up dangling on the window of a skyscraper at her parents work party and Shue somehow, still manages to find time to sought out her love life, by putting her old boyfriend (Bradley Whitford) in his place (when she discovers him two-timing her in a restaurant) and finding a new boyfriend (George Newbern) when she and the kids stumble into a rowdy frat party.

"Adventures In Babysitting" is definitely one of the more enjoyable teen comedies to come out of the 1980's and many of the film's stars went on to bigger and better things. The film proved to be the perfect vehicle to kick-start Elisabeth Shue's rising career. Shue would later go on to star opposite Tom Cruise in "Cocktail" (1988), with Michael J. Fox in the "Back To The Future" sequels (1989 & 1990) and by the mid-90's, Shue received an Oscar nomination for her performance as a prostitute, opposite Nicolas Cage in the critically acclaimed drama "Leaving Las Vegas" (1995). After "Babysitting", Keith Coogan's career continued with appearances in teen movies such as "Hiding Out" (1987), "Book Of Love" (1990), "Toy Soldiers" (1991), "Don't Tell Mom The Babysitter's Dead" (1991) and the Disney family/adventure "Cheetah" (1989).

Penelope Ann Miller, who spends most of the film stranded at the bus station, may have only been given a handful of comedic scenes but some of them are real standouts. Her scenes are interspersed throughout the story and used very effectively for pacing. The best of these scenes include, the telephone booth scene (the old man tells Penelope to "Get out of my house"), the sewer rat scene (after losing her glasses Penelope mistakes a sewer-rat for a kitten) and of course the very funny hot dog scene (Penelope's attempt to buy a hot dog with a used cheque). Although her role was only small, the film did prove to be a steppingstone for Penelope. She would later go on to star opposite some of Hollywood's A-list leading men such as, Arnold Schwarzenegger in "Kindergarten Cop" (1990), Danny DeVito in "Other People's Money" (1991) and Al Pacino in "Carlito's Way" (1993).

"Adventures In Babysitting" was released by Disney's "Touchstone" label and went on to gross over $34 million at the US box office. The film also received some critical acclaim with Elisabeth Shue winning the award for "Best Actress" at the "Paris Film Festival". At the "Young Artist Awards", Maia Brewton won the award for "Best Young Actress In A Comedy" while co-star Keith Coogan and the film itself both received nominations for "Best Young Actor" and "Best Family Comedy" respectively. "Adventures In Babysitting" is a fun film that doesn't try to take itself too seriously; it makes good use of Blues music, it takes advantage of Chicago's great locations, it extracts winning performances from its likeable young stars and the film's all-round light-hearted approach makes it appealing not only to teenagers but also to adults.

The Lost Boys ***

US Release Date: 31ˢᵗ July 1987
Running Time: 97 min
US Classification: R
Director: Joel Schumacher
Starring: Jason Patric, Corey Haim, Dianne Wiest, Barnard Hughes, Edward Herrmann, Kiefer Sutherland, Jami Gertz, Corey Feldman, Jamison Newlander, Brooke McCarter, Billy Wirth, Alex Winter, Chance Michael Corbitt, Alexander Bacon Chapman, Nori Morgan

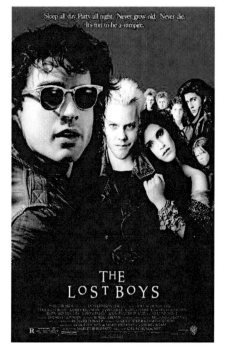

Taglines:

* Sleep all day. Party all night. Never grow old. Never die. It's fun to be a vampire.
* Being wild is in their Blood.

Film Review:

While "The Goonies" was a perfect fit for young teens and family audiences, "The Lost Boys" offered something different, a much wilder, scarier ride that was suitable only for older teens. Traditionally, vampire films are aimed at mature adult audiences who enjoy the horror genre but "The Lost Boys" broke the mould and became the first vampire film that was clearly marketed at a teenage audience. It was cooler, hipper and slicker than any vampire film that came before it. "Goonies" Director, Richard Donnor was originally slated for the project but dropped out to work on "Lethal Weapon" and handed over directing duties to Joel Schumacher who had previously directed The Brat Pack in "St. Elmo's Fire". According to the commentary on "The Lost Boys" 2004 Special Edition DVD release, the boys in the film were originally meant to be similar in age to those in "The Goonies", however, considering the horror concept Schumacher thought it would work much better if the young teens were older teens, this would allow more scope with boy girl relationships and would also give the film a much sexier look and feel overall. With a hot young cast and an atmospheric rock soundtrack, "The Lost Boys" became a teen movie soufflé, blending horror, comedy, romance, adventure and suspense all with the style of cutting edge MTV music videos.

Jason Patric and Corey Haim star as Michael and Sam Emmerson, two brothers who move to Santa Carla, California with their divorcee mother, Lucy (Diane Wiest), to live with their eccentric old grandfather (Barnard Hughes). When older brother Michael visits the local fairground, he meets an attractive but mysterious girl called Star (Jami Gertz). He begins to fall in love with her only to discover that she has a dangerously psychotic boyfriend called David, played with un-denying creepiness by Kiefer Sutherland. David is the leader of a biker gang who tear up streets in and around the fairground at night. It tuns out that David and his crew have something dark and sinister lurking beneath their punk attitude and leather-clad veneer. Meanwhile younger brother Sam befriends the "Frog Brothers", Edgar and Alan Frog (Corey Feldman and Jamison Newlander), two boys who run the local comic-book store and claim to be vampire hunters. Feldman's spoof-like portrayal of Edgar Frog is more than a nod & a wink to Stallone's "Rambo" or even Chuck Norris's "Missing In Action". To add to the intrigue Mrs Emmerson starts dating Max (Edward Herrman) whom the boys suspect may be a vampire. As the drama unfolds, Michael's newfound thirst jeopardises his life and the lives of those around him. In a gut-wrenching, thrill-packed finale, the teenage vampires converge onto the grandfather's house for one final act of bloodletting that will have viewers on the edge-of-their-seats.

"The Lost Boys" marked the first pairing of Corey Haim and Corey Feldman who after this film were dubbed, "The Two Coreys". Before the 1980s were over, Haim and Feldman would go on to star in another two films together, "License To Drive" (1988) and "Dream A Little Dream" (1989). Throughout the 90s "The Two Coreys" continued their collaboration with countless direct-to-video projects but for many "The Lost Boys" is considered their best work as a duo. There are enough situations and script elements in "The Lost Boys" for "The Two Coreys" to shine as the dramatics and danger of Patric's initiation into Sutherland's vampire-biker gang unfolds. With a well-equipped and talented cast, that includes Oscar winner Diane Wiest ("Hannah And Her Sisters") it is, however, Barnard Hughes as the grandfather who brings some light-hearted fun to the proceedings, with some of the film's best lines. He doesn't own a TV and explains to the boys, "If you read the T.V. Guide, you don't need a T.V.". He also has a few strict house rules "Second shelf is mine. That's where I keep my root beers and my double-thick Oreo cookies. Nobody touches the second shelf but me". When the body count is over and the film draws to a close, the grandfather pops up for one last time and almost steals the show with the film's most memorable line, "One thing about living in Santa Carla, I never could stomach, all the damn vampires". At this point the audience believe that he has been oblivious to the existence of vampires but with this quip it seems the old Grandfather knew a lot more about what was going on than he made out to.

In general critics were fairly kind to the "The Lost Boys" and the film featured strongly at some of the awards shows. At the "Academy Of Science Fiction Horror and Fantasy Films", it was nominated for 5 Awards, "Best Horror Film", "Best Costumes", "Best Make-Up", "Best Performance by a Younger Actor – Corey Haim and "Best Supporting Actor – Barnard Hughes", with the film winning the award for "Best Horror Film". At the "Young Artist Awards", the film won for "Favourite Teenage Horror/Drama" while the two Corey's were both nominated in the acting categories with Corey Feldman winning the award for "Best Young Actor in a Horror Motion Picture". It was no surprise "The Lost Boys" proved a hit for Warners Bros. grossing over $32 million at the US box office. Strong video rentals followed, cable TV has been kind to it and fans also welcomed the 2004 Special Edition DVD release. In the years since there have often been talks of a sequel with titles such as "The Lost Boys 2" and even the "The Lost Girls" thrown-around as possibilities. At the time of writing a direct to DVD sequel called "The Lost Boys 2: Tribes" was in the works, whether or not the project with come to fruition or whether or not any of the original cast will return is yet to be known. Whatever the case, "The Lost Boys" broadened the Vampire concept and presented it to a wider audience. If you are after a bit of horror, teen style, then "The Lost Boys" will more than fill your craving. With its 97-minute concoction of terror, laughs and bites it will give even the most anaemic viewers something to chew on. Today, "The Lost Boys" still remains the definitive teen vampire tale.

Footnote: By the time of publication two official direct-to-DVD sequels were released, "The Lost Boys 2: Tribes" (2008) and "The Lost Boys 3: The Thirst" (2010). Corey Feldman reprised his role as Edgar Frog in both sequels while Corey Haim appeared only briefly on the end credits of "The Lost Boys 2: Tribes". Haim's untimely death in March 2010 means he will be sadly missed if there are any further instalments of the popular film series.

Back To The Beach *** ½

US Release Date: 7th August 1987
Running Time: 92 min
US Classification: PG
Director: Lyndall Hobbs
Starring: Frankie Avalon, Annette Funicello, Lori Loughlin, Tommy Hinkley, Demian Slade, Connie Stevens, Joe Holland, John Calvin, David Bowe, Laura Urstein, Linda Carol, Marjorie Gross, Hartley Silver, Alan Barry, Thomas David Parker.

Taglines:

* Fasten your seatbelts and get ready for a totally NEW WAVE motion picture experience.
* Frankie and Annette. All the wave you can crave & all the sand you can stand!

Film Review:

"Back To The Beach" is a teen movie that successfully bridges the generation gap, that's right; it brought the teenagers of the 1960s and the teenagers of the 1980s into the cinemas at the same time. In 1963 a phenomenon called the "Beach Party" film began. Singer Frankie Avalon and Mouseketeer Annette Funicello were teamed up for the first instalment of a long running film series that would entertain and amuse audiences for most of the decade. Amazingly, more than 20 years later the idea still had some kick left in it, so Frankie and Annette were reunited for one last beach bash, this time round 80s teenagers could take their mums and dads to watch a teen movie that they could all enjoy together. As it turned out this 80s update is even better than any of the 60s "Beach Party" films that came before it. What made it work was that Frankie and Annette were able to spoof their former personas and bring new life into their old characters.

In this sand and surf update, Frankie and Annette are happily married with two kids, Bobby (Demian Slade) and Sandi (Lori Loughlin). Frankie, still sporting his famous hair-helmet is now working as a car salesman, while Annette is a spic-an-span stress-free housewife who is convinced that

Skippy Peanut butter is the answer to healthy living. Their son Bobby is a wannabe punk rocker, complete with leather jacket, sunglasses, earrings, spiked hair and flick knife, while their teenage daughter Sandi lives in an LA beach house with her surfer boyfriend Michael (Tommy Hinkley). The plot thickens when Frankie and Annette head "Back To The Beach" to visit their daughter who has kept her boyfriend a secret. To add to the fun, enter Connie (Connie Stevens), one of Frankie's ex-girlfriend's who runs the local beach shack/nightclub that heavily remembers the good old surf days of the 60s when Frankie earned his reputation as The Big Kahuna. Jealousies run hot and sparks fly when Connie flirts with Frankie and Annette feels the pinch. Will Frankie and Annette be able to stick together through this whirlwind summer at the beach or is there relationship doomed? "Back To The Beach" has all the answers and more.

For Australian Director Lyndall Hobbs, "Back To The Beach" was her first and last feature film and it's a mystery as to why she didn't do anything else because she handles the material in this teen sand and surf adventure with the finesse of a veteran filmmaker. She obviously had enthusiasm for the project and must have done her homework thoroughly to create this brilliant satire of the Frankie and Annette "Beach Party" films of the 1960's. Audiences enjoyed Frankie and Annette's comeback and "Back To The Beach" clocked up over $13 million at the US box office. The film was popular enough to warrant a sequel and was talked about but never eventuated because Annette became ill shortly after its release. Sadly, Annette was diagnosed with multiple sclerosis and was unable to be involved in further films. Nevertheless, "Back To The Beach" remains a lively, colourful and harmless film, full of laughs and great songs (California Sun, Jamaica Ska and Surfer Bird). It also makes good use of Californian beach locations in Malibu and Santa Cruz.

"Back To The Beach" sees Frankie and Annette in top form for one last time, poking fun at their old personas and hamming it up with a fantastic supporting cast of who's who from the fabulous 60s that includes, Don Adams (Get Smart), Bob Denver (Gilligan's Island), Alan Hale Jr (Gilligan's Land) and Edd Byrnes (77 Sunset Strip). Thrown into the mix is wacky 80s comedian Pee-Wee Herman (Pee-Wee's Big Adventure) whose rendition of Surfin' Bird adds a little extra fun to this sand and surf cocktail. Also, look out for the stars of "Leave It To Beaver", Jerry Mathers and Tony Dow as judges while Barbara Billingsley (Beaver's mum) appears as an announcer in the exciting, action-packed, surf finale. In true tongue-in-cheek style the finale sees Frankie slip into his Bermuda shorts, dust off his giant surfboard and hit the waves for one last ride. Why? To win back Annette of course, plus he must reclaim his title as "The Big Kahuna" and teach the new beach punks a lesson or two. Frankie proves once and for all, that not only does his character have what it takes but he does as well. This film was the perfect vehicle for Frankie and Annette's return to the surf and a fitting finale that allows them to hang up their surfboards in style. "Back To The Beach" is a great piece of nostalgia that complements the 1960's films and proves that the old "Beach Party" formula can still cut it with the best of them.

Can't Buy Me Love ****

US Release Date: 14th August 1987
Running Time: 94 min
US Classification: PG-13
Director: Steve Rash
Starring: Patrick Dempsey, Amanda Peterson, Courtney Gains, Tina Caspary, Seth Green, Sharon Farrell, Darcy DeMoss, Dennis Dugan, Ami Dolenz

Taglines:

* Ronald is making an investment in his senior year. He's hiring the prettiest cheerleader in school to be his girlfriend.
* Money can buy popularity but it can't buy me love.

Film Review:

It was 1988 when I (Tony) first sat down to watch director Steve Rash's romantic teen comedy "Can't Buy Me Love". It had just been released on home video. I had missed it the previous year in the cinema but I knew of the films existence. I had seen the movie posters and the TV marketing campaign that included TV spots, trailers, a film review by a local TV critic and of course that infamous Beatles song. From the moment I set eyes on the TV promos I was hooked, I am not sure exactly why. Maybe it was that catchy Beatles song used in the TV marketing blurbs or maybe it was because I was fairly young at the time? I still don't know, but one thing is for sure I wanted to see the film at all costs so when it came out on video there was no holding me back. To this day I still fondly remember the first time I saw the movie, it was at my uncles, with a couple of giggling young girls that were about my age. I have watched it many times since and I enjoy it every time. Fine characterisations and winning performances from the entire cast make it work. It was the first time I had seen Patrick Dempsey in a film and he left an immediate impression. I knew then that this actor was a major talent. From "Can't Buy Me Love" onwards I have made an effort to watch all his films. With this film Patrick Dempsey proved he was a charming actor with a fine flair for comedy. Some Audiences are only just discovering Dempsey's talent now, in the new millennium, due his role as Dr. McDreamy in the highly popular TV series "Grey's Anatomy".

In "Can't Buy Me Love" Patrick Dempsey plays lovable geek Ronald Miller, the unpopular guy in school who would like to fit in with the so-called in-crowd of popular jocks and cheerleaders. Dempsey could only dream of one day maybe dating the most popular girl in school, Cindy Mancini (played by then-newcomer Amanda Peterson). Dempsey already mows her family's lawn but has not yet made an impression on her. Cindy and her friends virtually don't even know of his existence but their ignorance of him is about to change. One night at a party Cindy is wearing her mother's suede outfit without permission. The unthinkable happens to Cindy, a popular jock-friend accidentally spills red wine on her clothes. She now has the dilemma of trying to replace the outfit for her mother, without her mother knowing, but a new outfit is priced at an extravagant $1,000 dollars, a price that a young high school girl can simply not afford. Cindy even offers to work for the shopkeeper after school every-day until she can afford to pay for a new outfit but he tells her this is not possible. Nearby in the shopping centre Dempsey notices what's going on whilst shopping for a scientific telescope. He decides to part with his hard earned lawn mowing money to pay for Cindy's outfit. The deal however, is for her to spend the next month going out with him at school and thus Mrs. Popularity will turn geek Ronald Miller into Mr. Popularity. She agrees and there we have it, the premise for a delightfully enjoyable teen comedy.

"Can't Buy Me Love", also known as "Boy Rents Girl", works well on a number of levels. Like many of the John Hughes films that came before it, this one has a similar quality about it. The plot is simple but effective. The acting, the direction and the script are all above average for a teen film. "Can't Buy Me Love" deals with many issues; fitting in with the popular crowd, first-time love, discrimination, friendship, loyalty, honesty, acceptance and of course the central theme which suggests that in life it is best for one to be yourself and not try to act like someone you're not. "Can't Buy Me Love" is charming, fast-paced and features an excellent supporting cast. Dennis Dugan, star of the Walt Disney classic "The Unidentified Flying Oddball" (aka "The Spaceman & King Arthur" 1979) plays Dempsey's father. In recent years Dugan has become a director in his own right and has made the Adam Sandler comedies "Happy Gilmore" and "Big Daddy", along with Jason Biggs' "Saving Silverman" (aka "Evil Woman"). Seth Green plays Dempsey's younger troublemaking brother to great comedic effect. I don't know exactly why, but one quote I have always remembered from this film is when Seth looks at the TV in amazement and says "Now That Ain't Dick Clark". I don't know what effect the line has on others but it has me in stitches every time I see it, I even find myself repeating it at the strangest times, I can't explain it but maybe it's just me. Those of you that have seen the "Austin Powers" films will remember Seth playing Dr Evil's son Scott Evil. Also, another plus for 80's teen fans is the brief appearance of Ami Dolenz, the "She's Out of Control" star and daughter of Monkee's drummer Mickey Dolenz. Ami appears throughout the movie in a few brief scenes, most notably the one where Cindy's outfit gets ruined.

There are many highlights in "Can't Buy Me Love" but one that stands out is the "African Ant Eater Ritual" performed by Dempsey at the school dance. If you don't know what that is you will have to see the film to find out. No matter how many times I see it, that sequence always brings a smile to my face. "Can't Buy Me Love" also features a great soundtrack. From the vibrant Beatles title song, to the Johnny Rivers novelty track "Secret Agent Man" to Billy Idol's "Dancin' With Myself" to the classic Beach Boys hit Surfin' Safari, we have a soundtrack that adds tremendously to the atmosphere and pacing of the film, while blending in well with the storyline.

From touching moments at the aeroplane graveyard to the rise and demise of a wannabe "Mr. Popularity", "Can't Buy Me Love" has every ingredient a good teen comedy needs. No wonder the film went on to gross over $31 million at the U.S. Box office making it one of the big hits of the year. This affectionately remembered gem of a film is a real charmer and is the one that made a teen movie star of Patrick Dempsey. It was no surprise to discover that he went on to win "Best Young Actor" at the Young Artist Awards for his performance in this film. Dempsey's talent has always been there but some audiences are just discovering it now on the TV show "Grey's Anatomy". As for Dempsey's co-star Amanda Peterson, she may not be a name that pops up very much today but her work in this film stands tall, so much so, that Amanda would have to be the perfect candidate for an episode of "Where Are They Now?." All in all, "Can't Buy Me Love" is a bright, yet emotionally charged teen film that has rightfully earned a place as a 1980's teen comedy classic.

North Shore ** ½

US Release Date: 14th August 1987
Running Time: 96 min
US Classification: PG
Director: William Phelps
Starring: Matt Adler, Gregory Harrison, Nia Peeples, John Philbin, Gerry Lopez, Laird Hamilton, Robbie Page, Mark Occhilupo, John Paragon, Rocky Kauanoe, Lokelani Lau, Cristina Raines, Tiffany Pestana, Corky Carroll.

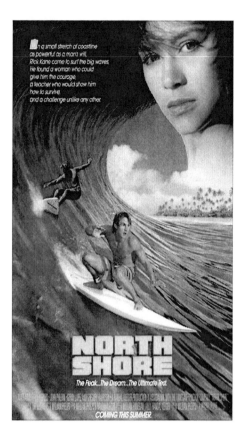

Taglines:

* On a small stretch of coastline as powerful as a man's will, Rick Kane came to surf the big waves. He found a woman who would show him how to survive, and a challenge unlike any other.
* The Peak... The Dream... The Ultimate Test.

Film Review:

"North Shore" is a coming of age surf drama set to the backdrop of Hawaii's surfing sub-culture. What sets it aside from other Hollywood-style sand and surf flicks is the authenticity of the surf action and the stunning Hawaiian locations. The best previous representations of this film-type were 1960s "Ride The Wild Surf" (Starring Fabian and Barbara Eden), which was shot in the wild waters of Hawaii's Waimea Bay and of course the big daddy of surf flicks, the 1970s classic "Big Wednesday" (Starring Jan-Michael Vincent and Gary Busey) filmed on the sunny Californian coastline. "North Shore" is straightforward storytelling with some great waves and rides thrown in for pacing. Rick Kane (Matt Adler) is a teenage surfer from Arizona who wins the local wave pool surf championship. He decides to use his prize winnings on a trip to Hawaii to surf the real waves off Oahu's North Shore. After a few misadventures with some tough waves and some tough locals, Rick earns a side-job creating a surfboard logo for Chandler (Gregory Harrison), a surf guru who designs and sells surfboards. As Chandler takes young Rick under his wing, a friendship soon develops and Chandler becomes somewhat of a mentor to Rick. Whilst on the island Rick still finds time to attract the affections of a beautiful Hawaiian girl Kiani (Nia Peepples) much to the displeasure of her family that includes a protective cousin (Gerry Lopez) and three brothers.

For any Hollywood surf movie, getting the right balance between actor and surfer is always a challenge for casting agents but with "North Shore" the filmmakers were spot on. Both male leads, Gregory Harrison and Matt Adler where cast not just because of their acting ability but also for their surfing skills and passion for the sport. For Matt Adler, "North Shore" was a dream-come true. After a few TV appearances and a supporting role as Michael J. Fox's friend in "Teen Wolf", Adler scored big when he was given the two thumbs up to jump on his surfboard and star in this teen surf fantasy. Like Adler, Gregory Harrison had always been a keen surfer so taking on the role of Chandler was a once in a lifetime opportunity. In fact, on the DVD release Gregory Harrison makes a point of saying that out of all the characters he has portrayed on film, Chandler is his most favourite and that playing Chandler was like playing himself. Another good casting choice was that of Nia Peeples as Adler's love interest. It is interesting to note that about three quarters of the film was shot with a different actress in the lead role. Peeples was a last minute inclusion and all her scenes had to be re-shot and slotted in to the final cut. Sadly, the end result of this is that the romance element isn't given enough time to develop and does feel like a tack-in and secondary to the surfing plotline. Nevertheless, Peeples was definitely the right choice for the role. She possesses a sensual innocence and the alluring charm of a native princess. Her natural beauty more than matches any surfer boy's fantasy of the ideal Hawaiian dream-girl. The DVD release features an alternate ending with the original "unknown" actress in the role. To round out the cast and add even more authenticity to the project real-life surfing greats such as Laird Hamilton, Gerry Lopez, Mark Occhilupo, Shaun Tomson and Derek Ho were thrown into the surf with the actors.

For Writer/Director William Phelps, "North Shore" marked his feature film debut. Phelps captures the laid-back atmosphere of Hawaii well with exotic locations, superb photography, traditional hula dancing, local cuisine, a Halloween beach bash and of course the obligatory surf comp which caps the film's finale. Also, if you can maintain concentration throughout you will be treated to an amazing but brief novelty moment of pushbike surfing, a real eye-opener if ever there was one. "North Shore" was not a box office bonanza, grossing just over $3.8 million in US cinemas; nevertheless it has become a cult classic due to VHS and DVD releases. Surf crowds love it and why not; the film has all the elements that make the surfing culture likeable and accessible to a movie-going audience. As far as Hollywood surf movies go, "North Shore" succeeds where it counts, the acting may be just adequate but more importantly the locales are breathtaking and the surfing footage is an absolute blast.

Dirty Dancing ****

US Release Date: 21st August 1987
Running Time: 100 min
US Classification: PG-13
Director: Emile Ardolino
Starring: Patrick Swayze, Jennifer Grey, Cynthia Rhodes, Jerry Orbach, Jack Weston, Kelly Bishop, Jane Brucker

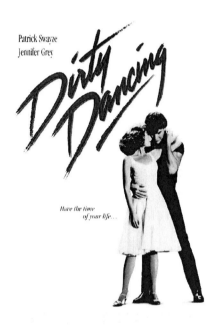

Taglines:

* Have The Time Of Your Life
* First dance. First love. The time of your life.
* Dancing to the beat of their hearts.

Film Review:

"Dirty Dancing" is an appealing dance musical with a strong love story and a toe-tapping soundtrack. It is this perfect blend of dance; romance and music that has elevated the films appeal to female audiences the world over. The story takes place in a resort hotel in the early 1960's. Jennifer Grey plays Baby Houseman, the innocent teenage daughter of a wealthy doctor, Jake Houseman (Jerry Orbach). Patrick Swayze stars as the dynamic Johnny Castle, the working-class hotel dance instructor who she falls madly in love with. It's the steps the film takes in getting these two characters together that make it so interesting. At the evening dance Baby sees Johnny perform a Latin dance routine with Penny (Cynthia Rhodes) and is instantly smitten. Later, Baby carries a watermelon to gain entry into the darkened staff quarters where "Dirty Dancing" is the popular pass-time. Here, her first dance with Johnny takes place and by now she is madly in love. Next, we find out that Johnny's dance partner Penny is pregnant and cannot perform in a dance exhibition at a nearby hotel. Baby agrees to help out by taking her place. At first Johnny is skeptical but eventually agrees. Johnny begins to train Baby and the romance blossoms.

Tensions mount when Baby's, Dr. father, has to save Penny's life after a botched up abortion. Baby's father believes that Johnny is responsible for the pregnancy and tries to stop Baby from seeing Johnny. All of these things culminate in a captivating finale, involving the two lovers performing in the resort's end of season show.

"Dirty Dancing" features some raw, energetic dance sequences and has a spectacular soundtrack as a backdrop. From new songs such as "I've Had The Time Of My Life" by Jennifer Warnes and Bill Medley to "Hungry Eyes" by Eric Carmen to "She's Like The Wind" by Patrick Swayze and a collection of old 60s favorites such as "Hey Baby" by Bruce Channel, "Big Girls Don't Cry" by Frankie Valli, "Do You Love Me" by The Contours and "Wipe Out" by the Surfaris. When it comes to great music, "Dirty Dancing" has it all and it is no surprise that record sales went through the roof. Patrick Swayze is a dancer in real-life and this film gave him the opportunity to put those hot dance moves to good use. This was his star-making performance and for many years after he was a household name. Jennifer Grey's innocence and girl-next-door quality was what female audiences connected with and her work on this film has become her signature role. Dancer turned actress Cynthia Rhodes (Staying Alive, Flashdance) is also very good in her small role, especially in the opening mambo dance sequence with heartthrob Swayze. They are electrifying together and it's a shame the film's storyline kept them apart most of the time. The film's climactic dance sequence featuring Swayze and Grey is nothing short of spectacular. This show-stopping finale makes you want to jump out of your seat and start dancing yourself or simply sit there with a big goofy smile on your face wishing that you could dance like that. It has that feel-good quality that makes you want to watch it again and again.

Made on a shoestring budget of $5 million, "Dirty Dancing" was the surprise box office smash of 1987 grossing over $300 million worldwide. The film's theme song, "I've Had The Time Of My Life" added to its success and deservedly won the Academy Award for "Best Song In A Motion Picture". The film was so popular around the world that there was a demand for more. Fans just couldn't get enough of "Dirty Dancing" so in Los Angeles some of the film's musicians and dancers went on tour for what was to become, "Dirty Dancing – The Live Concert" (1987). Fans loved it, but this still wasn't enough, they wanted a big screen sequel with Swayze and Grey but unfortunately they didn't get one. Instead the result was a short-lived 1988 TV series starring an entirely different cast, with Patrick Cassidy and Melora Hardin playing Johnny and Baby this time round. In 2004 a sequel of sorts was released to moderate success. It was titled "Dirty Dancing: Havana Nights" with Swayze making a brief guest appearance as a dance class instructor. In 2004-2005 an international "Dirty Dancing" stage-show hit the scene with shows in the UK, Australia, New Zealand and Germany. In 2006 the search for a new "Baby" began when "Dirty Dancing" became part of the reality TV fad. Jennifer Lopez's ex-husband Cris Judd hosted this dance series that lasted one season. In 2007, Dirty Dancing celebrated its 20th Anniversary with a new DVD launch, a brief US cinemas re-release and "Dirty Dancing – The Classic Story On Stage" went to Canada. "Dirty Dancing" remains a favourite film for many people and is the ultimate crowd-pleaser. It is the perfect example of what a teen dance musical should be.

Three O'Clock High ** ½

US Release Date: 9th October 1987
Running Time: 90 min
US Classification: PG-13
Director: Phil Joanou
Starring: Casey Siemaszko, Anne Ryan, Richard Tyson, Stacey Glick, Jonathan Wise, Jeffrey Tambor, Philip Baker Hall

Taglines:

* Jerry Mitchell just bumped into Buddy Revell. Now Jerry isn't thinking about Math or English. Because at three o'clock, he's history.
* When school's over, it's all over.

Film Review:

"Three O'Clock High" is one of those forgotten teen movies that you don't often hear very much about. The film did not feature a well-known cast, nor was it a big box office earner (US $3.6 million) in its day, but the film certainly has uniqueness about it, when compared with other teen movies. "Three O'Clock High" is "High Noon" in a high school and plays out like an old-fashioned-Hollywood western. In fact there are a number of references throughout the film to westerns, "Gunsmoke" is one that comes to mind and in one scene the lead's predicament is compared to that of a gunfighter preparing for a shootout. A clock is even shown throughout the film at various intervals to show the passing of time right through to the 3pm showdown. "Three O'Clock High's" entire story (apart from the opening credits at the house) is set in and around the high school campus. The film's stylised cinematography highlights the suspense and tension that mounts as the clock ticks away in this teen potboiler where romance and raunchiness take a back seat to "survival" in the blackboard jungle of the schoolyard.

Like "The Breakfast Club" (1985) and "Ferris Bueller's Day Off" (1986) before it, "Three O'Clock High" takes place in just one single school day. Casey Siemaszko plays Jerry Mitchell, the unlikely hero of the piece, a conservative, strictly-by-the-book-type-of-kid who helps out in the school store and writes for the school newspaper, he also has a neat-hairstyle to boot. When the film kicks off, Jerry is having a very bad day but it soon gets worse. After arriving at school late, due to a flat tyre, Jerry is asked to interview the new kid at school, Buddy Revell (Richard Tyson), a leather-clad, long-haired, muscle-bound heavy, with the scariest reputation on campus. Jerry isn't one to go looking for trouble but somehow on this dog of a day trouble was about to find him. During Jerry's impromptu attempt to interview Buddy in the boy's toilets, he accidentally puts his hand on Buddy's shoulder. This sparks off a reaction of gigantic proportions when Buddy challenges Jerry to a fight at the close of the school day, 3pm. Buddy doesn't say very much but the message he delivers to Jerry hits home loud and clear, "You and me, we're gonna have a fight. Today. After school. Three o'clock. In the parking lot. You try and run, I'm gonna track you down. You go to a teacher, it's only gonna get worse. You sneak home, I'm gonna be under your bed".

Every attempt by Jerry to pacify Buddy and end this David and Goliath battle before it begins is unsuccessful. In a last ditch effort to save himself from destruction, Jerry, even steals money from the school store cash register to hire a behemoth jock to confront Buddy before the 3pm deadline. To Jerry's shock and disbelief, Buddy smashes the jock in the face with a sledgehammer punch, causing a domino effect that brings down all the bookshelves in the school library. The jock gets a bloodied nose for his trouble and now Jerry is more terrified than ever. Now, even the school authorities are on Jerry's trail as they search for the culprit who stole the money from the store. All the action in the film is great, visually, but unfortunately the bully's character is very one-dimensional throughout. He's just like a wrecking machine. You never really get to find out what makes him tick, you just see the end result of his actions, having said that, the problem is with the inadequacy of the script and not with Richard Tyson's steely performance as Buddy. Strangely, one of Buddy's infamous lines is "I don't like people knowing about me", and that includes the audience. Funnily enough, Buddy's look at times reminds you of Heath

Ledger in "10 Things I Hate About You" (1999), but that's where the character resemblance stops.

The set-up and premise of "Three O'Clock High" is an interesting one, however, the big misstep is with its conclusion. In the film's showdown, the entire school turns up to witness the battle. The bully punches a teacher, smashes a video camera, punches a security guard and even tosses a girl that tries to stand in his way. The pay-off is typical-Hollywood-stuff; Jerry fights the bully and beats him, but only after resorting to the use of brass knuckles for the victory. What could have lifted the film above the norm is if the scriptwriters devised a way in which the hero defeated the villain using his intelligence and wit rather than resorting to physicality and foul means for the win. A clever, brains against brawn victory would have been a much better way to go. Instead, the film comes to a cliched ending, where all reputations are reversed, Jerry is now the alpha-male, the tough-guy, the top-gun, or the fastest-draw in the west, so-to-speak, everyone wants to know him and the girls want to date him. Let's just hope that Jerry doesn't let everything go to his head! Casey Siemaszko's performance as Jerry is good but maybe a higher profile actor could have lifted the film somewhat. Whilst watching the film I couldn't help but think that the lead-role seemed tailor-made for someone like Michael J. Fox who would have fitted the bill perfectly. Despite some of its shortcomings "Three O' Clock High" is nevertheless a fairly enjoyable film, a missed opportunity of sorts, that certainly doesn't deserve to be completely forgotten. One thing is for sure the film achieves its objective of presenting an-age-old western theme in a modern-day teen movie setting.

Chapter 9:

TEEN MOVIES OF 1988

*For Keeps? ** ½*

US Release Date: January 15th 1988
Running Time: 98 min
US Classification: PG-13
Director: John G. Avildsen
Starring: Molly Ringwald, Randall Batinkoff, Kenneth Mars, Miriam Flynn, Conchata Ferrell, Sharon Brown, John Zarchen, Pauly Shore, Michelle Downey, Patricia Barry, Janet MacLachlan

Taglines:

* From Backpacks to Strollers
* They have their plans. They have each other. And a little something they weren't expecting
* It's about sticking around, no matter what.

Film Review:

It was inevitable that the teen queen of the 1980s, Molly Ringwald, would be required to take romance one step further so by 1988 teen audiences were ready to see Molly move on into parenthood. "For Keeps" is a sweet-natured, teen romance film that should hold a special appeal with teenage girls. Unfortunately, for director, John G. Avildsen ("Rocky" and "The Karate Kid"), "For Keeps" was definitely a step down. The film's storyline is straightforward and everything that happens is fairly predictable. They fall in love, Molly unexpectedly gets pregnant, they get married without their parents' permission, have the child, attempt to juggle their studies while caring for the baby, have a few disagreements and fights along the way and eventually make-up and live happily ever after. In real-life, when teenagers are faced with adult responsibilities, the loose ends don't always tie up this neatly. The plot is so routine and contrived that the film's watch-ability factor relies totally on the presence of Molly Ringwald. She has blossomed in her appearance and has somewhat matured since her earlier teen movies of the 80s. In this one Molly looks better than ever and as always puts in a well-rounded performance. In fact, Molly won a "Best Actress Award" for her work in this film. She came in equal first alongside fellow teen star Elisabeth Shue ("Adventures In Babysitting") at the "Paris Film Festival" in 1988.

"For Keeps" features a few standout moments, in particular, the scene at the dinner table when Molly is pressured into revealing that she is pregnant. Everyone is present, her mother, her boyfriend's parents and of course the younger siblings who spark Molly into revealing the news sooner than she wanted to. Everyone is shocked to say the least and absolute mayhem breaks out. Ringwald's love-interest, pretty boy, Randall Batinkoff, overacts at times but his overall performance is adequate. The film also features brief appearances by Renee Estevez (Emilio's younger sister) and Pauly Shore (Encino Man) in a blink and you'll miss him role as a character called Retro. "For Keeps" did not enjoy the box office success of some of Molly's earlier teen films such as "The Breakfast Club" or "Pretty In Pink" but it still brought in a tidy $17,514,553 at the US Box Office and ranked 60th in its year. "For Keeps" may lack realism at times. It may even be a little sappy and plodding but it's nevertheless an engaging little teen film that should keep young teenagers on their toes.

The Night Before ** ½

US Release Date: 15th April 1988
Running Time: 85 min
US Classification: PG-13
Director: Thom Eberhardt
Starring: Keanu Reeves, Lori Loughlin, Theresa Saldana, Trinidad Silva, Michael Greene, Suzanne Snyder, Morgan Lofting

Taglines:

* You lost your father's car. Sold your prom date. And a guy named 'Tito' wants you dead. So what did happen 'The Night Before?'
* A Guy can get into serious trouble after dark

Film Review:

Before "Bill & Ted's Excellent Adventure" Keanu Reeves starred as Winston Connelly in "The Night Before", a teen adventure romance that is an unusual blend of mystery and suspense with comedy and slapstick thrown in for good measure. "The Night Before" could also be described as a teen version of Martin Scorsese's "After Hours", as the lead character spends the entire film, wandering at night, in a dangerous part of town, in a state of constant distress, due to nightmarish situations and events that he is confronted with. "The Night Before" moves from one misadventure to another brimming with crazy characters in outrageous situations. From the moment Winston picks up his prom date Tara (Lori Loughlin) everything starts to go wrong, her father (Michael Greene) is a gun-happy policeman ready to shoot first and ask questions later, the couple take a wrong turn and end up in the barrio, an underprivileged, seedy Latin/Hispanic neighbourhood riddled with crime, drugs, prostitution, hoods and pimps. To add to their predicament the couple wind up in a creepy bar where Winston is drugged and accidentally sells his prom date to a notorious pimp named Tito (Trinidad Silva). Tara is quickly dumped into the trunk of car, taken to a nearby brothel, stripped to her lingerie and handcuffed to a bed. For Winston this means a race against time to rescue his prom date before Tito sells her to a chain-smoking, slave trader named Fat Jack. As the clock ticks away, the crazy scenarios all come to a head in a car chase finale and showdown with Tito and his cronies.

"The Night Before" does not follow a traditional linear format, the story starts in the middle and quickly jumps to the beginning and then both parts play out simultaneously, cutting from one to the other until they eventually come together about three quarters of the way into the film. "The Night Before" may suffer from too much style over substance and for some viewers its flashback structure may be annoying. The disjointed flow of the material that chops and changes from the present to earlier in the night may be a little bit put offish but if you give it some time and allow the two strands to come together in the film's last 25 minutes or so the finale becomes quite entertaining and proves to be the film's most engaging section. The film also features a couple famous faces in small roles during the bar sequence, singer George Clinton appears as the on-stage entertainment and former WWF Wrestler Zeus (aka Tommy 'Tiny' Lister) is seen as a bartender. "The Night Before" may not have reached its full potential but it nevertheless intrigues us with what it could have been. The film is certainly an ambitious piece of filmmaking, complete with absurd humour, bizarre situations and a cavalcade of weird and wonderful characters. One thing is for sure, if the notion of seeing a young Keanu Reeves trudging around a battered neighbourhood wearing a beat-up tuxedo and battling society's most unsavoury characters in a desperate attempt to save his prom date from slave traders is your idea of a fun night's entertainment, then "The Night Before" will more than satisfy your craving.

License To Drive *** ½

US Release Date: 8th July 1988
Running Time: 88 min
US Classification: PG-13
Director: Greg Beeman
Starring: Corey Haim, Corey Feldman, Carol Kane, Richard Masur, Heather Graham, Michael Manasseri, Harvey Miller, Michael A. Nickles, Nina Siemaszko, Grant Goodeve, James Avery, Grant Heslov, Michael Ensign, Helen Hanft, Christopher Burton.

Tagline:

Some guys get all the brakes!

Film Review:

The first time "License To Drive" captured our attention was not at the cinema, but at the local drive-in, on a double-bill with the Tom Hanks comedy "Big". In those days the main feature was always shown first as many people would either fall asleep or go home early during the second feature. After sitting through "Big" and Hanks' Oscar nominated performance, which was the main reason why we went, we were treated to "License To Drive", a teen comedy film starring Corey Haim and Corey Feldman, two young actors that were relatively unknown at the time. "License To Drive" turned out to be equally as entertaining as "Big" and although we knew very little about the two new stars we were nevertheless impressed by their enthusiastic performances. As it turned out "License To Drive" became the springboard that would establish the two-Corey's, as a formidable comedic duo for younger audiences.

"License To Drive" looks at the trials and tribulations of a teenager trying to get his hands on the one thing he believes he needs the most, a driver's license. The look and sound of the opening credit sequence; complete with road sign graphics and upbeat soundtrack, sets up the tone and carefree nature of the film that is to follow. As the names of the two stars slide across the screen to the sound of roaring engines, screeching brakes and "The Beatles" song, "Drive My Car" performed by "The Breakfast Club", you know you're in for a wild ride. "License To Drive" is reminiscent of films such as "Ferris Bueller's Day Off" (1986) and "Adventures In Babysitting" (1987). All three films feature similar plotlines, comedic situations and hi-jinks. The teens go out on the town without parents knowing. They need to get back home before parents find out and of course in all three films the car gets trashed. Also, dating rituals, car chases, stunts and slapstick style-humour are in abundance.

"License To Drive" begins with a mysterious dream sequence in which Haim and other students are shackled together on a school bus with a maniacal driver. Haim escapes by breaking his chains and crashing through the back window of the bus, what ensues is a James Bond-style chase sequence, in which a beautiful blonde in a red corvette rescues Haim. As they drive-off, with the bus in hot-pursuit, Haim throws a match out of the car into a petrol spillage that sees the bus explode into a ball of flames. When Haim awakes he is at a driving class with his head on the desk.

Corey Haim stars as Les Anderson, a school student who becomes preoccupied with the notion that getting his license will be the solution to all of his problems, his main concern being winning a date with his dream girl, Mercedes (Heather Graham). His need to get a license is reinforced on a number of occasions by comedic sidekick Dean (Corey Feldman). When the two boys see Mercedes with her boyfriend, Dean says to Les, "Anderson, the only difference between you and that grease-ball is that he has a license and you don't". Later on in a comedic inspirational speech, Dean explains to Les what a license means to him, "A license to live, a license to be free, a license to go wherever, whenever and with whoever you choose".

At a birthday party Les spots his dream-girl Mercedes who is having an argument with her boyfriend. In retaliation to his complaints she points to the nearest guy possible, in this case Les and states that she has a date with him on Saturday night. Les can't believe his luck but realizes now, more than ever, that he must pass his driver's test. In one of the film's funnier moments, when Les gets picked up from school, he convinces his father (Richard Masur) into letting him drive so he can give Mercedes a ride home. His father reluctantly steps out of the car, groceries and all, expecting the trip to be only short. As it turns out Mercedes is not going home but to a friend's house that is a considerable distance away. The father is left stranded and has to make his way home on foot. The look on his face and his reaction to Les when he returns home is priceless. Richard Masur is excellent as the understanding father who is pushed to the limit not only by his son's crazy misadventures but also by his wife's pregnancy. Also, Carol Kane is amusing as Les' loopy mother who believes mashed potato and ketchup is the ideal food for a successful pregnancy.

Les' twin-sister Natalie (Nina Siemaszko) breezes through the computer knowledge part of the driving test while Les struggles, with the simplest of multiple-choice questions. After finding out he has failed the exam, Les belts the computer, all the test screens cut out, thus rendering his test score irretrievable. Luckily Natalie aced the test so the examiner decides to base Les' test score on hers and awards him a pass. "License To Drive" features not just one, but a number of support characters that are so funny that they almost steal the show from the leads. The testing officer, the driving instructor, the tow truck driver, the old drunk and even the grandfather are all-played over the top to hysterical effect. Of all the support characters, the most memorable would have to be the driving instructor (James Avery) with his "don't spill a drop coffee routine". He determines pass or fail on the basis of his coffee cup that sits prominently on the dashboard during the driving test. His motto is, "You burn me, you fail, you don't, you pass, it's as simple as that". After muddling through the road test and passing by the skin of his teeth (coffee cup tips up but luckily it was empty), Les' bliss is short-lived when the examiner (Helen Hanft) retrieves the lost test results and deems him a failure.

Les lies to his parents and friends about his license and when Mercedes calls him on the phone, he decides to take his grandfather's prized Cadillac, for a night on the town, without permission. In the film's most memorable quote Les turns to the camera and utters the words "An innocent girl, a harmless drive. What could possibly go wrong?" Well anything and everything goes wrong, his car gets towed away, it costs him $80 to get it back, his tape gets chewed up in the cassette player, Mercedes gets drunk, she dances on the car and scratches the hood, she passes out, they get caught up in a protest march, get pulled over by cops and finally their car gets stolen by an old drunk who vomits in it and trashes it. Just went you think the crazy antics are over, in the film's nail-biting finale, Les has to drive his pregnant mother to the hospital in reverse!

Not all great teen films have a message or serious overtone. "License To Drive" is one such film. It delivers what it sets out to achieve and that is light-hearted, carefree entertainment. With an excellent movie poster and two hot young stars how could the film go wrong? Also, an 80's pop soundtrack with a few oldies thrown in for good measure compliments "License To Drive". Who can forget Heather Graham and Corey Haim dancing on the hood of the car to the sound of Frank Sinatra singing "Strangers In The Night" or the film's appropriate conclusion to Billy Ocean's "Get outta my dreams, get into my car". At the US box office "License To Drive" grossed $22.4 million and later proved to be a popular rental on the video circuit. This enjoyable romp was even a critical success for it young stars. Both Corey Haim and Corey Feldman won the "Young Artist Award" for "Best Young Actor in a Motion Picture Comedy" (in a rare tie). Also, Heather Graham was nominated for "Best Young Actress".

For Haim and Feldman "License To Drive" is still considered by many to be their best work as a team. In fact, Haim's dream was to a do a follow-up film titled "License To Fly". This idea had the potential and promise of being something special but sadly it just didn't materialise. Their catalogue of work together began in the 1980's with the big studio productions, "The Lost Boys" (1987), "License To Drive" (1988) and "Dream A Little Dream" (1989). During the 1990's the two Corey's were re-united on at least four occasions in low-budget productions that included; "Blown Away" (1992), "National Lampoon's Last Resort" (1994), "Dream A Little Dream 2" (1994) & "Busted" (1996) in which Feldman also wrote and directed. For the best of Haim and Feldman see "License To Drive", a teen comedy than can be summed up in two very simple words, "Good Fun".

Young Guns ***

US Release Date: 12th August 1988
Running Time: 102 min
US Classification: R
Director: Christopher Cain
Starring: Emilio Estevez, Kiefer Sutherland, Lou Diamond Phillips, Charlie Sheen, Dermot Mulroney, Casey Siemaszko, Terence Stamp, Jack Palance, Patrick Wayne, Brian Keith

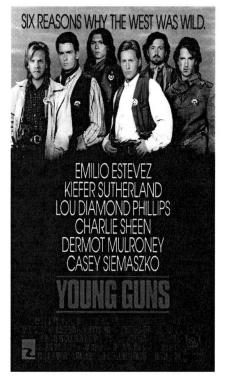

Taglines:

* Six reasons why the west was wild.
* Don't count the odds, count the bodies.
* The odds were a hundred to one.

Film Review:

"Young Guns" or "The Brat Pack Goes West", as some may think of it as, is an action-packed western tailored especially for the 1980s youth crowd. With some of the most popular young actors of the decade assembled together in the one film, the filmmakers were guaranteed of a box office bonanza. Grossing over $45 million at the US Box office and ranking 22nd in its year, "Young Guns" proved that the western was back in style with a new marketability factor. Emilio Estevez and his brother Charlie Sheen headlined a cast of who's who from the pages of teen magazines of the day. The other hot young stars included in the gang were Lou Diamond Phillips ("La Bamba"), Kiefer Sutherland ("The Lost Boys") and Casey Siemaszko ("Three O'Clock High") and given their worldwide popularity at the time, the film was assured of success not only in the US but also around the globe. To round off the cast and add quality to the production producers saddled up some veteran actors in supporting roles including Terence Stamp, Jack Palance, Brian Keith and Patrick Wayne, son of famous American icon John Wayne plays lawman Pat Garrett. With a blockbuster cast like this and a story about America's most famous outlaw how could the filmmakers go wrong? Well they didn't go wrong on an entertainment basis. On the other hand, if you are looking for historical accuracy grab a history book, you'll be much better off but if history isn't an issue then this blazing western will do the trick.

"Young Guns" tells the story of a bunch of young homeless cowboys who are taken in by a British gentleman, John Tunstall (Terence Stamp). He tries to educate them, teaching them to read, write and to treat each other with respect. In return the young men are to guard him and his ranch from local outlaws. When their master, Tunstall, is murdered by the ruthless Lawrence Murphy (Jack Palance) and his thugs, the boys are left to fend for themselves under the influence of William Bonney (Emilio Estevez) who later becomes known as, Billy The Kid. At first, all they want is to avenge the death of their master, but in doing so they end up taking the law into their own hands and become notorious outlaws. As the rampage continues and the body count piles up, the boys are relentlessly pursued until they wind up taking refuge in an old barn house where they make their final stand in the film's explosive finale.

"Young Guns" was not the first time the screen was ablaze by the gunfire of Billy The Kid but it was the first time that the character was marketed for a teen audience. Previously this "real" American legend had been depicted on the silver screen numerous times popping up again and again for each new generation of filmgoers. The most notable films featuring Billy The Kid include, "Billy The Kid" (1930) with Johnny Mack Brown, "Billy The Kid" (1941) with Robert Taylor, "The Outlaw" (1943) with Jack Buetel, "The Kid From Texas" (1950) with Audie Murphy, "The Left-Handed Gun" (1958) with Paul Newman, Sam Peckinpah's "Pat Garrett And Billy The Kid" (1973) with Kris Kristofferson and "Gore Vidal's Billy The Kid" (1989) with Val Kilmer. Now, if you think that's a lot of Billy The Kids, we haven't even scratched the surface without mentioning beefcake Buster Crabbe's (Flash Gordon & Buck Rogers) contribution to the Billy The Kid legend. Buster starred as the infamous outlaw in over a dozen Billy films throughout the 1940s kicking his film series off with "Billy The Kid Wanted" (1941).

"Young Guns" marks the 1980's film version of the Billy The Kid tale. With its over-the-top characterizations, brutal confrontations and sadistic humor it possibly stands out as the most violent depiction of them all. It was inevitable that the films popularity and recipe for success would spawn a sequel, "Young Guns II" (1990). The only stars that didn't return for the sequel were the ones that were killed off in the first film. Emilio of course reprised his role with Christian Slater and Balthazar Getty joining the regulators for the next rampage. Like the original, "Young Guns II" was a hit at the box office, this time round the film's popularity was helped along by its Oscar nominated rock inspired soundtrack "Blaze Of Glory" by Jon Bon Jovi. The Billy The Kid story in "Young Guns" may not be told exactly by the book but it is nevertheless a thrilling, shoot-em-up piece of western entertainment, 80s teen style.

Chapter 10:

TEEN MOVIES OF 1989

*Gleaming The Cube ** ½*

US Release Date: 13ᵗʰ January 1989
Running Time: 100 min
US Classification: PG-13
Director: Graeme Clifford
Starring: Christian Slater, Steven Bauer, Richard Herd, Le Tuan, Ed Lauter, Art Chudabala, Tony Hawk, Tommy Guerrero.

Taglines:

* When getting even means risking it all
*All he cared about was Gleaming the Cube...until the night they killed his brother.

Film Review:

Filmed on location in California with Australian director Graeme Clifford at the helm, "Gleaming The Cube" is a teen action thriller featuring some of the most spectacular skateboarding sequences ever put on the screen. Christian Slater heads out the cast in his first major starring role as the rebellious skater punk who takes matters into his own hands when arms dealers kill his adopted Vietnamese brother. Slater puts in a fine performance but it's the skateboarding sequences that emerge as the true stars of the film. Elaborate skateboarding moments take place at every turn, at an airstrip, inside an empty swimming pool, at a skate ramp, in a street chase involving bikies and of course a number of exciting freestyle sequences are featured. To maintain authenticity and a high standard of skateboarding, professional skaters Rodney Mullen and Mike McGill were called in to stunt double for Slater, while champion skateboarders Tony Hawk and Tommy Guerrero were added to the cast in small roles. Also, to add fine-tuning to the skateboarding sequences legendary skateboarder Stacy Peralta was hired to serve as technical advisor and second unit director. On another note, "Pizza Hut" must have cut a good product-placement deal with this film, as the fast food chain's logo features prominently throughout, most notably in the finale when the skateboarders all pile into a "Pizza Hut" vehicle that is headed for a showdown.

The title "Gleaming The Cube" is a term that has generated discussion since the film's release. Some say it's a piece of skating jargon that means doing the impossible or achieving the ultimate. Others say that it's not skating jargon but a term that was developed especially for the film. Whichever way you look at it, the title gives the film that something extra. For a skater "Gleaming The Cube" could be going to that special place of peace within yourself that gives you that feeling of calm and freedom that is only achieved whilst pushing yourself and the board to the nth degree. For Christian Slater's character "Gleaming The Cube" meant he had to achieve the impossible. He was told that his brother had committed suicide, something he refused to believe. Now he had no alternative but to think out of the box and push himself beyond the boundaries of reason so that he could solve his brother's murder. "Gleaming The Cube" is a full-on teen detective story with Christian Slater as a so-called "Skateboard Cop". The film may not have set the box office on fire when first released but it did do well as a video rental. Over the years it has developed a strong cult following and holds a special place in the hearts of skateboarders worldwide. Like any good action film, the hero overcomes every hurdle, rises to the occasion and in this case, "Gleams The Cube". It is certainly a fun, teen action film that's great entertainment for everyone but perfect entertainment for the skateboarding crowd.

Bill & Ted's Excellent Adventure ***

US Release Date: 17th February 1989
Running Time: 90 min
US Classification: PG
Director: Stephen Herek
Starring: Keanu Reeves, Alex Winter, George Carlin, Bernie Casey, Terry Camilleri, Dan Shor, Tony Steedman, Al Leong, Jane Wiedlin, Clifford David

Taglines:

* The funniest comedy in the history of history.
* Time flies when you're having fun.
* Party on, dudes!
* History is about to be rewritten by two guys who can't spell...

Film Review:

When "Bill And Ted's Excellent Adventure" hit cinemas in 1989 it turned the teen movie genre on its head with the introduction of two unique characters that would re-define the meaning of the word dudes. To the uninitiated, how could one best sum up a film like "Bill And Ted's Excellent Adventure"? Well here goes, take Wayne and Garth from "Wayne's World", throw in Jesse and Chester from "Dude, Where's My Car", add one part Spicoli from "Fast Times At Ridgemont High" and throw in a dash of "Napoleon Dynamite" for good measure, stir gently for 5 minutes and what do you get, Bill & Ted from "Bill And Ted's Excellent Adventure", arguably the most wacko teen movie fantasy of the 80s. It's surprise success at the US box office ($40 million plus) could be attributed to a number of things; the time travel element, the cheesy special effects, the general crazy-ness of the storyline but most importantly the whacked-out banter between the two leads that is surprisingly infectious.

Alex Winter and Keanu Reeves play teenagers Bill and Ted, two wannabe rock musicians who are not the sharpest tools in the shed. They produce a "noise" on their guitars that is pounding to the ears and are struggling in their studies at San Demis High School. When their History teacher Mr. Ryan (Bernie Casey) threatens to flunk them unless they turn in a first rate report, the two boys go to extreme measures to learn their history, pass their assignment and of course have some fun along the way. To add to their desperation, Ted's Dad threatens to send him away to Military school if he doesn't pass history. The boys know that failure would mean the end of their partnership and their band the Wyld Stallyns. With a stroke of luck, Rufus (George Carlin), a time traveller from the future comes to their aid by giving them access to a phone booth that will transport them through time. The boys use their newfound toy to round up some of history's most famous and influential figures including, Napoleon Bonaparte, Socrates, Billy The Kid, Sigmund Freud, Genghis Kahn, Joan Of Arc and Abraham Lincoln just to name a few. The film may be unbelievable and overflowing with silliness but what is does offer amongst all its craziness is a history lesson that is sure to make some teens inquisitive about the historical characters that it presents. The film's finale involves Bill and Ted's history presentation, live on stage with all of history's famous faces present in the flesh. Will Bill & Ted's time travelling escapades earn them a passing grade? Finding out is all the fun.

The success of "Bill and Ted's Excellent Adventure" led to a sequel, "Bill And Ted's Bogus Journey" two years later, which also proved to be a hit at the US box office. A third film was talked about but never eventuated.

For Keanu Reeves, Bill and Ted was a catalyst to bigger and better things such as "Speed" and "The Matrix" film series. For Alex Winter, "Bill and Ted" has become his signature film, as his acting career seems to have stagnated somewhat since. Like all good films "Bill And Ted's Excellent Adventure" leaves its audience with a catchphrase to take with them, "Be excellent to each other and party on dudes". Just like the famous people in Bill and Ted's story who have left their mark in world history, so to, Bill and Ted have left their mark in film history with their memorable one-liner. An important historical footnote if ever there was one.

Dream A Little Dream **

US Release Date: 3rd March 1989
Running Time: 114 min
US Classification: PG-13
Director: Marc Rocco
Starring: Corey Haim, Corey Feldman, Jason Robards, Piper Laurie, Harry Dean Stanton, Meredith Salenger, William McNamara, Ria Pavia, Lala Sloatman, Laura Lee Norton, John Ward, Matt Adler, Josh Evans, Jody Smith, Kent Faulcon.

Tagline:

With dreams like these who needs reality?

Film Review:

"Dream A Little Dream" is another entry in the 1980's body swap genre but sadly it just doesn't measure up to any of the others that came before it, such as, "Freaky Friday" with Jodie Foster, "Vice Versa" with Judge Reinhold, "Big" with Tom Hanks, "Like Father, Like Son" with Dudley Moore and "18 Again" with George Burns. Even those that came after it are better such as "Freaky Friday" with Lindsay Lohan and "The Hot Chick" with Rob Schneider. "Dream A Little Dream" tries hard but unfortunately it is a disjointed, disorganised, jumbled jigsaw of scenes that lack a sense of fun. The film is too caught up in its own dream world to become really engaging. In "Dream A Little Dream" the stars of "License To Drive", Corey Haim and Corey Feldman are back together again for another wild adventure. In "License To Drive" Haim was the star and Feldman was the support but this time round Feldman steps up to the mark to take centre-stage but audiences looking for the free-wheeling fun, romance and comedy of their previous film will be disappointed as this film is just too bizarre for its own good. Also, along for the ride are Meredith Salenger ("The Journey of Natty Gann"), Matt Adler ("North Shore") and Victoria Jackson ("Casual Sex?"), together with screen veterans Jason Robards (Once Upon A Time In The West), Piper Laurie ("The Hustler") and Harry Dean Stanton ("Pretty In Pink").

Feldman plays teenager, Bobby Keller, who seems to have everything a young guy could possibly want, a good buddy (Corey Haim), a hot girlfriend and loving parents but somehow he just isn't happy. He's having problems at school and has a crush on Lainie Diamond (Meredith Salenger), a girl who already has a boyfriend. When an older couple, Gena and Coleman Ettinger (Laurie & Robards) who live down the road from Bobby dabble in an experiment aimed to extend their lives, something goes dramatically wrong. Coleman is a philosophical old man searching for the fountain of youth. He sums up the film's confusing premise when he says to his neighbour, Ike Baker (Dean Stanton), "I'm conducting a scientific experiment, nobody knows what dreams really are, now if I can find the point where they intersect with reality and enter one's consciousness, if I can really enter the dream-state, who knows, maybe I can live forever". One night while Coleman and his wife are meditating in their front yard, Bobby and his dream girl Lainie come through the yard and collide with them in a freak bike accident. As a result Coleman's personality becomes trapped in Bobby's body while Lainie is partially trapped in Gena's body.

This film is the body swap scenario but with a difference, because it is not a two-way swap. Only one side of the swap is focused upon. In this case the old man's personality is in the teenager's body but we don't see the reverse. The old man is never shown acting like a teenager, so it's only a one-way swap. When the old man is shown it is like he is in a state of imprisonment trying to breakout or wake up from a dream but he can't until he solves the teenager's personal problems that include helping him win the love of his dream girl. The body swappers enter into periodic discussions about their progress. These scenes are dream-like and are shown in a different colour tone to the rest of the film. It becomes evident that the teenager doesn't want out until the old man can rectify all his problems. Feldman tries hard playing the mixed up teenager with the old man's personality but some -how the idea just doesn't work. Maybe, it's the script or Feldman's performance, but whatever the case, some viewers may be blown away by it originality and uniqueness while others may be bamboozled by its weirdness and general craziness.

When "Dream A Little Dream" kicks off it gives fans what they want, but with something a little different thrown in. The hip introduction involves exchanges of cool dialogue between the two Corey's, alternating between title credits. The sequence culminates with an on-stage musical performance of the film's title song by Robards. The film soon cuts to a musical montage set to the beat of "The Future's So Bright I Gotta Wear Shades" involving the two Corey's getting dressed for school in their punk outfits, complete with ripped jeans, trendy jackets, earrings, gloves, headbands, sunglasses and of course lots of hair mousse. Unfortunately, the film's style soon becomes indifferent and the general fun doesn't last. In no time at all the films nonsensical plotline comes to the fore and takes over what could have been a much more entertaining film.

"Dream A Little Dream" does however feature a solid soundtrack that includes artists such as Van Morrison, R.E.M., Mickey Thomas, Otis Redding and the hit track "Rock On" by Michael Damian. Despite the abundance of music and the use of musical montages for pacing the film still drags and is heavy going for most of the near 2 hour running time. Even Feldman's Michael Jackson routine in the school's basketball stadium and Robards and Feldman's title song duet on the end credits can't save the film from mediocrity. Also, Haim is wasted in support, he is given very little to do and spends most of the film hobbling around aimlessly with a walking cane, dressed in a military-style jacket, wearing an earring and sporting a frizzed red hair-do. Nevertheless, this teen fantasy grossed just over $5.5 million at the US box office and generated enough interest to warrant a direct-to-video sequel in 1995 pairing the two Corey's once again. The low-budget sequel is more nonsense with a lesser supporting cast and a plot revolving around a pair of magical sunglasses. For fans of the two Corey's "Dream a Little Dream" provides the goods some of the time but unfortunately is disappointing a lot of time. In the end it is somewhat of a missed opportunity for something that could of been better. "Dream A Little Dream" remains Haim and Feldman's last big-screen collaboration and marked the end of an era for this 1980s teen duo.

Say Anything... ****

US Release Date: 14th April 1989
Running Time: 100 min
US Classification: PG-13
Director: Cameron Crowe

Starring: John Cusack, Ione Skye, John Mahoney, Lili Taylor, Amy Brooks, Pamela Segall, Jason Gould, Loren Dean.

Tagline:

* To know Lloyd Dobler is to love him. Diane Court is about to know Lloyd Dobler.
* She's got everything going for her. He's going for her with everything he's got.
* A Lloyd meets girl story

Film Review:

Teen romance films don't come much better than this. "Say Anything" is a thoughtful, witty, love story with real heart. The film predominately focuses on three central characters and their interaction with each other, two young lovers and a father that will do anything to protect and provide for his daughter, even if it means going above the law. John Cusack plays Lloyd Dobler, a slightly hyperactive but optimistic High school graduate who believes that "kickboxing is the sport of the future" and is always "looking for a dare to be great situation". Lloyd falls for attractive Diane Court (Ione Skye), an intelligent honours student who has just won a scholarship to study in England. Diane lives with her divorced father, James Court (John Mahoney), who runs a nursing home for the elderly. Lloyd knows that Diane is way out of his league, his friends tell him "Diane Court doesn't go out with guys like you. She's a brain", but nevertheless Lloyd decides to take a chance and make a play for her affections. When he finally works up enough courage to ring Diane at home, she is not there. Her father answers the phone instead. As Lloyd speaks to him, he paces up-and-down. He is so wound up and fast-talking that he is almost incomprehensible. It is a wonder that the father passes the message on to his daughter. Diane later returns Lloyd's call and this sets the ball rolling.

On their first date they attend an end of school party but it is not until they leave the party that their personalities begin to connect. They realize that their attraction is not just physical; it is also mental, they actually enjoy each other's company. When a friend asks Diane, why she agreed to go out with Lloyd, her response is simple, "he made me laugh". When her disapproving father asks why she likes Lloyd, she explains how he protected her from some broken glass on the street. Lloyd's caring nature and true love for Diane is unquestionable but there are obstacles he will have to overcome in his quest to win her, the biggest one being Diane's father. When Diane's father convinces her to break up with Lloyd he tells her to give him a pen as a parting gift. Diane reluctantly does exactly as her father requests. Lloyd is heartbroken and later tells his sister (Joan Cusack also his real-life sister), "I gave her my heart and she gave me a pen". Lloyd tries to win her back by standing outside her bedroom window, holding a boom-box over his head, playing the Peter Gabriel song "In Your Eyes". In this signature scene Lloyd's true love for Diane is deeply felt by the audience and is the essence of the film's quality. Also, the pen scenario is well book-ended when Diane later hands her father a pen, just before she leaves for England with Lloyd.

The star of "Say Anything" is the characterization of Lloyd and the presentation of all his idiosyncrasies. The film features a number of standout dialogue moments all executed with precision by Cusack. The discussion on the phone as Lloyd tries to snag a date with Diane is a gem; Lloyd's persistence pays off even after he is told that she is too busy to go out with him. Lloyd's first meeting with Diane's father is a hoot, he arrives wearing a long overcoat reminiscent of a character from an Italian spaghetti western and nervously explains, via rapid-fire dialogue, that his daughter will be "safe with him for the next 7 or 8 hours" because of his kickboxing skills. Later, when Lloyd is invited to dinner with Diane's family he is asked, "What are your plans for the future?" Lloyd's reply to this clichéd question is one of the most inventive responses ever put on the screen "I don't want to sell anything, buy anything, or process anything as a career. I don't want to sell anything bought or processed, or buy anything sold or processed, or process anything sold, bought, or processed, or repair anything sold, bought, or processed. You know, as a career, I don't want to do that". When "Say Anything" finally comes to a conclusion and Diane's father makes one last ditch effort to separate the two lovers by stating, "You're not a permanent part of her life, you're a distraction", Llyod's reply is a beautifully crafted piece of dialogue, "I'm the distraction that's going with her to England, sir", a fitting end note to his relationship with Diane's father.

"Say Anything" is an emotionally charged romance drama with sensitivity and charm to burn. Carefully written and directed by Cameron Crowe ("Almost Famous") this script driven teen film packs a punch with engaging performances from the entire cast, particularly its two young stars, Cusack and Skye. Other actors that were considered but missed out on the Lloyd role were Kirk Cameron, Christian Slater and Robert Downey Jr. Also, in contention for the Diane role was actress Jennifer Connelly. Cusack and

Skye are such a winning combination that it is hard to imagine anyone else projecting that great chemistry. Finally, the film's appeal comes down to a simple notion; the likeability factor of Lloyd, both Diane and the audience can't help but fall in love with him. As for the significance of the title, Diane's father has always taught her that she can "say anything" to him, but unfortunately he is not prepared to "say anything" to her. However, Lloyd is prepared to "say anything" to anyone and everyone and more importantly he is sincere in what he says. Ultimately this is how Lloyd wins.

She's Out Of Control ***

US Release Date: 14th April 1989
Running Time: 90 min
US Classification: PG
Director: Stan Dragoti
Starring: Tony Danza, Ami Dolenz, Catherine Hicks, Wallace Shawn, Dick O'Neill, Matthew Perry, Laura Mooney, Derek McGrath, Dana Ashbrook, Marcie Barkin.

Taglines:

* How can you protect your daughter when boys think about sex 652 times a day!
* Girls go wild, boys go crazy, and dads go nuts!
* She was Daddy's little girl. Now she's at that age, when girls go wild, guys go crazy & Dads go nuts.

Film Review:

"She's Out Of Control" is a charming, feel-good, teen movie, starring TV favourite Tony Danza ("Who's The Boss", "Taxi") in a rare big screen outing. Danza plays Doug Simpson an overprotective father whose life is thrown into a whirlwind when his 15-year old daughter Katie, played by Ami Dolenz (daughter of famous Monkee's rocker Mickey Dolenz) gets a complete makeover while he is away on business. It is Danza's girlfriend Janet Pearson (Catherine Hicks), who encourages Katie to do something about her appearance. In a musical montage Katie quickly replaces her glasses with contact lenses, has her braces removed, gets a new hairstyle and to top it off a new wardrobe of clothes. When Danza arrives home from his business trip he is shocked to see his daughter's transformation. In no time at all the phone runs hot and boys start lining up at the front door to take her out. The young suitors come in all shapes and sizes, from creepy to weird, from geeky to sleazy, from mullets to Mohawks, they're all here, even a set of twins come to the door, but most of them are just plain bizarre.

Situations get out of control and so does his daughter as her dates clock up and Danza's blood pressure reaches boiling point. Danza is so affected that he seeks advice from his local psychiatrist, Doctor Fishbinder (Wallace Shawn) whose unorthodox methods seem to aggravate his problem rather than solve it. With almost every boy in town vying for her affections Katie eventually settles on one to take her to the school prom. Her prom date comes in the form of Timothy, a sly playboy-type, played by a-young Matthew Perry in a pre-"Friends" role. As prom night approaches, Doctor Fishbinder informs Danza that a high percentage of girls lose their virginity on that night. This pushes Danza's frenzy into hyper-drive and prepares the audience for a "saving one's virtue" finale.

"She's Out Of Control" came at the end of the 80's teen movie craze and became an under-appreciated teen flick that deserved more recognition than it received on its initial release. Grossing just over $12 million at the US box office it wasn't enough to turn sitcom star Tony Danza into a big screen movie star. Nevertheless, the comedic performances are spot on, Danza is in top form, Dolenz makes an attractive teenage lead and Wallace Shawn as Danza's psychiatrist puts in yet another wacky performance. The film's pacing is complemented by a neat soundtrack that comes complete with a few oldies thrown in to add atmosphere to the proceedings, such as, "Venus" by Frankie Avalon, "Secret Agent Man" by Johnny Rivers and "You Really Got Me" by The Kinks. Ultimately, "She's Out Control" is a light-hearted re-telling of the age-old ugly duckling story. The father-daughter scenarios are pushed to the limit with the comedy revolving totally on Danza's obsessive hysteria about his daughter's coming of age. Not an easy role to pull off for any actor especially in a teen comedy framework such as this. It works in this case, due to the buoyancy of Danza's personality. Maybe "She's Out Of Control" could have been called "Dad's Out Of Control", whatever the case, it is one of those films that teenage daughters can watch with their dad's and have a real laugh together, all at Tony Danza's expense. If you missed this one at the cinemas in 1989, don't let it slip away, catch up with it on DVD; it is certainly well worth a look at.

Loverboy ***

US Release Date: 28th April 1989
Running Time: 98 min
US Classification: PG-13
Director: Joan Micklin Silver
Starring: Patrick Dempsey, Kate Jackson, Robert Ginty, Nancy Valen, Dylan Walsh, Barbara Carrera, Kirstie Alley, Carrie Fisher, Bernie Coulson, Ray Girardin, Rob Camilletti, Vic Tayback, Kim Miyori, Robert Picardo

Taglines:

* When Randy delivers pizza to the uppercrust of Beverly Hills... Watch out for the extras!!

* He Delivers

* There are a lot of hungry housewives in Beverly Hills. Some of them even like pizza.

Film Review:

"Loverboy" is a light-hearted teen farce with plenty of madcap gags and an outrageous plotline to boot. It features Patrick Dempsey ("Grey's Anatomy") in possibly his best-remembered film after "Can't Buy Me Love" (1987). In this one, Dempsey plays Randy Bodek, a college student who returns home for the summer and lands a job at the local pizza joint. His boss insists that he must wear his stick on moustache at all times and make his deliveries in a sombrero-shaped truck. After a few plot twists and turns the pizza delivery store becomes a front for a male gigolo service. Female customers requiring some intimate affection on the side simply order a pizza with extra anchovies. In no time at all, Dempsey becomes the most popular delivery guy in town and a sure-fire hit with the Beverly Hills lady customers that include, Barbara Carrera, Kirstie Alley and Carrie Fisher in great supporting roles. The film's female characters are complemented by the jealous antics of their oddball husbands who go all out to hunt down Dempsey in spectacular style. Carrie Fisher's gym junkie husband, Peter Koch is like a pumped-up-clone of actor Patrick Swayze, he bears such as striking resemblance that he could easily pass as his brother. Thrown into the mix for fun is Dempsey's pizza shop buddy Tony, the Italian Romeo (played by Sylvester Stallone look-alike Rob Camilletti) who has an eye for Dempsey's mom, Kate Jackson of "Charlie's Angels" fame in a rare big screen outing. After a series of bumbling escapades and misunderstandings everything and everyone culminates in a rollicking restaurant finale that will leave you breathless.

"Loverboy" and its lunacy may not have set the box office alight but it certainly delivers all the right ingredients for its target audience. "Loverboy" plays out like Richard Gere's "American Gigolo" but in true teen-movie-style. Instead of "Gigolo's" high drama, murder and suspense, "Loverboy" presents lots of laughs, romance and a good ole helping of slapstick humour, with Dempsey clearly performing all his own stunts. Watching Dempsey juggle his activities and trying to maintain his responsibilities while hiding his reputation, as the "love doctor of Beverly Hills" from both his parents and his girlfriend is an absolute hoot. The film is well directed and thanks to Dempsey's charm and on-screen naivety it manages to achieve all the fun without becoming a crude and rude bedroom farce. The bottom line is "Loverboy" is genuinely funny and without-all-the smut one might expect from a plotline such as this. This feel-good entertainment even features a few nice dance moments involving Dempsey and Alley, not to mention at least three tunes on the soundtrack provided by Beach Boy, Brian Wilson. If you are a Patrick Demspey fan from way back or have only just discovered him on TV's "Grey's Anatomy" or you simply missed this comic romp at the cinemas back in 1989, the good news is you can now catch up with "Loverboy" on DVD but before you watch it, order a pizza and if you are a female fan, don't forget to ask for extra anchovies.

Teen Witch *

US Release Date: 28th April 1989
Running Time: 90 min
US Classification: PG-13
Director: Dorian Walker
Starring: Robyn Lively, Dan Gauthier, Joshua John Miller, Caren Kaye, Dick Sargent, Tina Caspary, Zelda Rubinstein, Noah Blake

Taglines:

* Fall under her spell.
* To her, trouble comes super-naturally.
* When You're Young, Boys Are A Mystery. And Love Is Pure Magic
* Winning is a magical feeling (Trailer)

Film Review:

Seven years before "Sabrina The Teenage Witch" hit the small screen in 1996, there was "Teen Witch" a film that breezed in and out of cinemas in 1989 so fast that when the film hit the video rental stands in 1990, audiences didn't even know of the film's existence. Bringing in almost nothing at the US box office ($27,843), the film quickly won over a new audience thanks to the video boom. "Teen Witch" is a juvenile teen fantasy that tries hard to please but more often than not it simply misses the mark. Its plotline is flimsy, the characters are cardboard and the script is sadly unengaging. On the plus side it features, some vibrant song and dance numbers, colourful 80s fashions and redhead Robin Lively as the "Teen Witch" of the title.

Lively looks great, she's suited for the role and her performance earned her a nomination for "Best Young Actress" at the Young Artist Awards but even this wasn't enough to save the film from relative obscurity.

Predictability sums up the storyline in this one. Louise Miller (Robin Lively) is not the most popular girl at her school but she does have a crush on the most popular boy at her school, Brad Powell (Dan Gauthier). I am sure a lot of young girls can identify with a problem like this. Louise even goes on to describe her own life of misery when she says "My life is a walking, talking tragedy", while her little brother Richie (Joshua John Miller) takes it one step further when he tells her "No one wants to date you because you're a dog". One day by chance, Louise meets Madame Serena (Zelda Rubinstein), a fortune teller who claims that she "knows all, sees all and tells all", what a pity she couldn't give the filmmakers a few pointers. After talking to Serena, Louise discovers that, like Serena, she herself is in fact a descendent from a tribe of witches and will inherit their powers when she turns 16 years of age. It takes about 30 minutes before her powers kick in and when they do they suffer the same fate as the crummy plotline. When Louise's brother calls her a dog, she in return uses her powers to turn him into one. In another scene, Louise undresses her teacher with the aid of a voodoo doll. Her teacher makes an absolute fool of himself shedding his clothes in the classroom, he later falls down some stairs and finally to top it off walks through a car wash. These are just some of the cheesy special effects moments in the film. Louise even zaps away her geeky-blind-date by making him disappear when he comes on to her too strongly, but the question remains, should Louise use her newfound powers to win the affections of the most popular boy in school or not? That is the premise of this pointless, low-budget teenybopper piece of fluff.

The supporting cast don't exactly help the film stay afloat either. Lively's parents are played by Dick Sergent ("Bewitched") and Caren Kaye ("My Tudor"). For one, they are not a great matrimonial match but worse still, both actors give possibly the most uninspired performances of teenage parents that came out of the decade, either that, or the script they had to work with was almost non-existent. "Teen Witch" also comes with the obligatory sex education teacher, featured in arguably the silliest sex-ed class scene in cinema history. The actress playing the teacher should have demanded a script re-write and her student's descriptors for the male appendage would have to be some of most ridiculous words spoken in a classroom scene. You have to see it to believe. Yes, it really is that awful and for that reason it may even have you doubling over in howls of laughter due to the stupidity of it all. As for Lively's younger brother he gives one of the most over-the-top, crazy performances that you will see from a youngster in any teen movie. His scene with the gigantic pizza and the disgusting mess he makes in the kitchen takes absurdity to a new level. He also has some of the film's corniest one-liners, "I'm rubber your glue whatever you call me sticks back on you", some of the most sarcastic, "Nobody's comin' to your sweet sixteen party Louise", not to mention some of the most idiotic, "I took the liberty of ironing your homework". Also of interest is the appearance of Valentine Leone, niece of famous Italian director Sergio Leone. Valentine plays Shana the lead singer in a band sequence and like her role in the film she is a musician in real-life.

"Teen Witch" may be tacky from start to finish and not very involving for mature audiences but it does hold special appeal with teenage girls. 1980s aficionados will also get a lot from this film, the look, the sound, the feel and all the cheese is totally 80s. Boys and girls sporting the big hair-dos of the day, the Madonna-inspired outfits, not to mention the campy song and dance routines, involving the girls singing "I like boys" in the change rooms while the boys sing the "high school blues" in the corridors and of course, the white boys trying to rap, only to be hilariously upstaged by a girl. Only in a film like this will you see scenes like these, bursting with that real 80s flavour. For the boys there was "Teen Wolf" and for the girls there is "Teen Witch". This lightweight teen fantasy may lack depth and the performances may be clumsy but the film's sheer simplicity is what gives it a sense of fun.

CONCLUSION

80 from the 80s - In a Nutshell

Foxes (1980)
"A gritty, realistic time capsule of teenage girls growing up tuff in L.A.'s fast lane"

<u>Above:</u> Lobby Card for the Jodie Foster flick "Foxes" (1980)

Little Darlings (1980)
"An engaging summer camp movie featuring a superb screenplay with thought-provoking teen issues"

Fame (1980)
"Landmark dance flick with raw energy & a timeless title track"

The Blue Lagoon (1980)
"Pretty-as-a-picture, exploitation flick with an innocent charm that continues to resonate"

My Bodyguard (1980)
"A bully film with heart that will make you want to stand-up & cheer"

The Idolmaker (1980)
"The 60s period flavor with an 80s groove will have you tapping to the beat"

Endless Love (1981)

"An emotional rollercoaster with heartbreak and tragedy at every turn"

Private Lessons (1981)

"A controversial sleeper hit that sparked the teen sex-comedy craze of the 80s"

Taps (1981)

"A compelling human drama highlighting the consequences of military discipline & ideals"

Porky's (1982)

"A yard-stick by which all other teen sex comedies are measured"

Above: Lobby Card featuring the rowdy young boys from "Porky's" (1982)

Paradise (1982)

"A teen version of Tarzan & Jane substituting school, students & teachers, with exotic locations & adventure"

Zapped (1982)

"Cheezy special-effects with a telekinetic wackiness that will have teenage boys hooked"

Tex (1982)

"A compelling, coming-of-age tale with characters so real that you can't help but feel for them"

The Last American Virgin (1982)

"A teen sex comedy that becomes an emotional drama with an unforgettable suprise ending"

Fast Times At Ridgemont (1982)

"Fast, funny but also serious, an honest attempt to tell it how it was, or maybe how it is"

Above: The girls from "Fast Times At Ridgemont High" (1982)

Class of 1984 (1982)

"Over-the-top with excessive violence & mayhem, it's Death Wish in a high school"

Liar's Moon (1982)

"A teen melodrama with an underbelly of lies & deceit spanning a couple of decades"

My Tutor (1983)

"Raunchy, teacher-student fling with all the usual trappings & teenybopper fluff"

The Outsiders (1983)

"S.E. Hinton's most famous novel introduces a dynamic cast & becomes a J.D. film of raw power"

Spring Break (1983)

"A return to the Beach Party formula but now the innocence has gone & the raunchiness has begun"

Share the suds, a familiar SPRING BREAK pastime. Perry Lang, Paul Land, David Knell and Steve Bassett play four wily, willing, wide eyed, would be womenizers in this raucous, raunchy comedy. A Columbia Pictures release, produced and directed by Sean S. Cunningham from an original screenplay by David Smilow. SPRING BREAK also stars Jayne Modean and Corinne Alphen. Executive producers were Mitch Leigh and Milton Henson in association with Fogbound, Inc.

Copyright © 1983 Columbia Pictures Industries, Inc. All rights Reserved.   #4

Above: Fun in the sun with the boys from "Spring Break" (1983)

Bad Boys (1983)

"This brutal portrayal of teens in prison is tough hard-hitting entertainment"

Losin' It (1983)

"South-of-the-border, teen sex comedy with hair-raising road trip antics & a pre-stardom Tom Cruise"

Valley Girl (1983)

"Definitive 80s love story pushed into hyper-drive by Cage's wacky portrayal of a way-out teen"

WarGames (1983)

"Ferris Bueller saves the world in this first-rate teen computer thriller that will have you glued to your seat"

Class (1983)

"A Graduate-lite romance drama with snappy performances from a likeable cast"

Private School (1983)

"A teen-male fantasy piece that fleshes out its competitors with non-stop dormitory hi-jinks"

Risky Business (1983)

"A stylish study of american youth with unbridled ambition that is both outrageous & thought-provoking"

Above: Rebecca DeMornay & Tom Cruise heat up the screen in "Risky Business" (1983)

All The Right Moves (1983)

"Strictly-by-the-numbers high school football drama that is nothing more, nothing less"

Reckless (1984)

"A raw, rebellious love story that is a throwback to the J.D. films of the 1950s & 60s"

Footloose (1984)

"Lithgow roars & Bacon's cool-factor soars while the soundtrack & theatrics are a match made in heaven"

Where The Boys Are '84 (1984)

"Light & breezy, air-headed entertainment that proves some originals are better left untouched"

Breakin' (1984)

"Fresh, fab & kinetic, a youthful combo of new faces & spectacular dance numbers"

Making The Grade (1984)

"Trading Places goes college & the hi-jinks earn a passing grade for the target audience"

Above: Judd Nelson & Jonna Lee hit the highway in "Making The Grade" (1984)

Sixteen Candles (1984)

"Characters with sensitivity, charm & a beating heart, Molly & friends shine in this Hughes original"

The Karate Kid (1984)

"Martial arts philosophies & heartwarming storytelling combine to produce a crowd-pleasing classic"

The Last Starfighter (1984)

"Sci-fi fun for arcade freaks featuring a powerhouse music score as big as the film itself"

Revenge Of The Nerds (1984)

"Mad-cap hysterics in this raunchy geek-fest of laughs, tears & fraternity woes"

No Small Affair (1984)

"A cute, romantic comedy about age-difference that echoes Moore's real-life"

Above: Jon Cryer & Demi Moore light up San Francisco in "No Small Affair" (1984)

Tuff Turf (1985)

"A gritty, teen gang-drama with a dash of music, romance & an abundance of angry youths"

Mischief (1985)

"A 1950s time capsule, think TVs Happy Days meets 1980s raunch"

Above: Doug McKeon & Kelly Preston having a little car trouble in "Mischief" (1985)

The Breakfast Club (1985)

"An insightful peak into the teenage psyche that continues to intrigue audiences"

The Sure Thing (1985)

"A coming-of-age story on a road trip where the feelings & emotions of the characters ring true"

Girls Just Want To Have Fun (1985)

"Laughs, love & footwork combine in this zippy dance flick that with have you rollicking from start to finish"

Just One Of The Guys (1985)

"Tootsie is reversed for the teen crowd in this laugh-out loud romantic gender-bender"

Private Resort (1985)

"Low-budget teen sexploitation flick that is easy on the eyes & melodic to the ears"

The Goonies (1985)

"Old-fashioned, matinee-style adventure flick that can be enjoyed by people of all ages"

Secret Admirer (1985)

"Teens will love it because it makes their parents look like bigger idiots than them"

Back To The Future (1985)

"An intelligent teen fantasy that will have you believing that time travel is possible"

The Heavenly Kid (1985)

"A cool, inventive, feel-good film with a father & son dynamic that you will want to revist"

Better Off Dead (1985)

"Qwirky teen comedy with additives that you will either love or hate"

CAFETERIA CONFRONTATION — AARON DOZIER (l. center) is told off by JOHN CUSACK (r. center) with AMANDA WYSS at the center of the controversy while front (l. to r.) DANIEL SCHNEIDER and DIANE FRANKLIN look on in 'Better Off Dead' the new comedy from Warner Bros.

BK 5

Above: John Cusack in a cafeteria confrontation in "Better Off Dead" (1985)

Weird Science (1985)

"A tongue-in-cheek, leave your brain at home joyride into the teen male psyche"

My Science Project (1985)

"Scientific gizmos, time warps & mumbo-jumbo unite in this bizarre teen sci-fi flick"

Real Genius (1985)

"Goofball Kilmer excels in this wacky, way-out, fantasy that explodes with a real popcorn finale"

Teen Wolf (19805)

"Fox in make-up leads to howling good fun in this campy slam-dunk creature feature"

Iron Eagle (1986)

"Armed for combat, high-flying fighter pilot fun with its finger on the trigger"

Lucas (1986)

"A breath of fresh air, it exudes a unique quality & charm that should be applauded"

Above: Kerri Green, Corey Haim & Charlie Sheen in "Lucas" (1986)

Pretty In Pink (1986)

"A special teen romance that can give you goosebumps just thinking about it"

Ferris Bueller's Day Off (1986)

"Definately a stand-out from the pack. You will want to take this day off, over & over again"

Never Too Young To Die (1986)

"One-part-Stamos, one-part Vanity, two-parts-Bond & an avalanche of secret agent cheese"

Thrashin' (1986)

"Skaters unite for the ultimate 110% die-hard skateboarding extravagazna"

Hotshot (1987)

"A bicycle kick of a flick, this Karate Kid of Soccer, scores a full-time winner"

Some Kind Of Wonderful (1987)

"Charming, sensitive & unique, takes the plot of Pretty In Pink & switches the sexes"

Adventures In Babysitting (1987)

"Fun in the big-city kids-style, with a dash of danger, excitement & whole lot of laughs"

Above: Elisabeth Shue takes charge in "Adventures In Babysitting" (1987)

The Lost Boys (1987)

"Teen vampires leave an intoxicating trail of bloodlust, romance & laughs"

Back To The Beach (1987)

"Retro-freaks eat-your-heart out, Frankie & Annette bring a nostalgic charm to an 80s wave"

Can't Buy Me Love (1987)

"Charming, fast-paced, teen romance with big laughs & even bigger-heart"

North Shore (1987)

"Surfing & scenery are an absolute blast in this coming-of-age surf drama"

Dirty Dancing (1987)

"A perfect blend, of dance, romance & music makes this the ultimate crowd-pleaser"

Above: Jennifer Grey & Patrick Swayze lock lips in "Dirty Dancing" (1987)

Three O'Clock High (1987)

"High Noon in a high school, a funny, suspenseful story about teen-angst & survival"

For Keeps (1988)

"A teen Pregnancy yarn that presents the questions but doesn't have all the answers"

The Night Before (1988)

"A teen adventure romance with an unusual blend of mystery, suspense & slapstick"

License To Drive (1988)

"The 2-Coreys are at their peak & can be summed up in 2 simple words....Good Fun"

Young Guns (1988)

"The Brat-Pack goes west in this thrilling, cowboys with attitude shoot-em-up"

Gleaming The Cube (1989)

"Slater plays Skateboard cop in this exciting, stunt-filled teen detective yarn"

Bill & Ted's Excellent Adventure (1989)

"A teen sci-fi spectacular headlined by air-heads with a trippy vernacular"

Dream A Little Dream (1989)

"The two-Coreys ham-it-up in this nonsensical body-swap dramedy"

Say Anything... (1989)

"An emotionally charged teen romance drama with sensitivity & charm to burn"

Above: Ione Skye & John Cusack in "Say Anything..." (1989)

She's Out Of Control (1989)

"Dad's out of control in this fast-paced dating comedy that is every parents' worst nightmare"

SHE'S OUT OF CONTROL

AMI DOLENZ (Katie Simpson) suddenly comes of age and realizes she is no longer an awkward teenager in 'She's Out Of Control'

Above: Ami Dolenz shines in "She's Out Of Control" (1989)

Loverboy (1989)

"Outrageous, mad-cap gags a-plenty in this light-hearted teen farce with extra anchovies"

Teen Witch (1989)

"Bewitched for the teen set, the look, the sound, the feel is totally 1980s cheese"

TEEN STARS OF THE 80s

A Cross-Reference of Actors & Movies

Aames, Willie – Born 15th July 1960
* Paradise (1982)
* Zapped (1982)

Adler, Matt – Born 8th December 1966
* Teen Wolf (1985)
* North Shore (1987)
* Dream A Little Dream (1989)

Armstrong, Curtis – Born 27th November 1953
* Risky Business (1983)
* Revenge Of The Nerds (1984)
* Better Off Dead (1985)

Astin, Sean – Born 25th February 1971
The Goonies (1985)

Atkins, Christopher – Born 21st February 1961
* The Blue Lagoon (1980)

Bacon, Kevin – Born 8th July 1958
* Footloose (1984)

Baio, Scott – Born 22nd September 1961
* Foxes (1980)
* Zapped! (1982)

Baldwin, Adam – Born 27th February 1962
* My Bodyguard (1980)
* Reckless (1984)

Bowen, Michael – Born 21st June 1953
* Valley Girl (1983)
* Private Resort (1985)
* Iron Eagle (1986)

Broderick, Matthew - Born 21st March 1962
* WarGames (1983)
* Ferris Bueller's Day Off (1986)

Brolin Josh – Born 12th February 1968
* The Goonies (1985)
* Thrashin' (1986)

Cage, Nicolas – Born 7th January 1964
* Fast Times At Ridgemont High (1982)
* Valley Girl (1983)

Above: Deborah Foreman & Nicolas Cage in "Valley Girl" (1983)

Cates, Phoebe – Born 16th July 1963
* Paradise (1982)
* Fast Times At Ridgemont High (1982)
* Private School (1983)

Clay, Andrew "Dice" – Born 29th September 1957
* Making The Grade (1984)
* Private Resort (1985)
* Pretty In Pink (1986)

Cruise, Tom – Born 3rd July 1962
* Endless Love (1981)
* Taps (1981)

* The Outsiders (1983)
* Losin' It (1983)
* Risky Business (1983)
* All The Right Moves (1983)

Cryer, Jon – Born 16th April 1965
* No Small Affair (1984)
* Pretty In Pink (1986)

Cusack, Joan – Born 11th October 1962
* My Bodyguard (1980)
* Class (1983)
* Sixteen Candles (1984)
* Say Anything (1989)

Cusack, John – Born 28th June 1966
* Class (1983)
* Sixteen Candles (1984)
* The Sure Thing (1985)
* Better Off Dead (1985)
* Say Anything (1989)

Dempsey, Patrick – Born 13th January 1966
* Can't Buy Me Love (1987)
* Loverboy (1989)

Depp, Johnny – Born 9th June 1963
* Private Resort (1985)

Dickey, Lucinda – Born 14th August 1960
* Breakin' (1984)

Dillon, Matt – Born 18th February 1964
* Little Darlings (1980)
* My Bodyguard (1980
* Tex (1982)
* Liar's Moon (1982)
* The Outsiders (1983)

Dolenz, Ami – Born 8th January 1969
* Can't Buy Me Love (1987)
* She's Out Of Control (1989)

Downey Jr, Robert – Born 4th April 1965
* Tuff Turf (1985)
* Weird Science (1985)

Edwards, Anthony – Born 19th July 1962
* Fast Times At Ridgemont High (1982)
* Revenge Of The Nerds (1984)
* The Sure Thing (1985)

Estevez, Emilio – Born 12th May 1962
* Tex (1982)
* The Outsiders (1983)
* The Breakfast Club (1985)
* Young Guns (1988)

Feldman, Corey – Born 16th July 1971
* The Goonies (1985)
* The Lost Boys (1987)
* License To Drive (1988)
* Dream A Little Dream (1989)

Above: Corey Haim, Heather Graham & Corey Feldman in "License To Drive" (1988)

Fenn, Sherilyn – Born 1st February 1965
* Just One Of The Guys (1985)
* Thrashin' (1986)

Foreman, Deborah – Born 12 October 1962
* Valley Girl (1983)

Foster, Jodie - Born 19th November 1962
* Foxes (1980)

Fox, Michael J. – Born 9th June 1961
* Class Of 1984 (1982)
* Back To The Future (1985)
* Teen Wolf (1985)

Franklin, Diane – Born 11th February 1963
* The Last American Virgin (1982)
* Better Off Dead (1985)
* Bill & Ted's Excellent Adventure (1989)

Gedrick, Jason – Born 7th February 1965
* The Heavenly Kid (1985)
* Iron Eagle (1986)

Gertz, Jami – Born 28th October 1965
* Endless Love (1981)
* Sixteen Candles (1984)
* Mischief (1985)
* The Lost Boys (1987)

Glover, Crispin – Born 20th April 1964
* My Tutor (1983)
* Back To The Future (1985)

Green, Kerri - Born 14th January 1967
* The Goonies (1985)
* Lucas (1986

Grey, Jennifer – Born 26th March 1960
* Reckless (1984)
* Ferris Bueller's Day Off (1986)

* Dirty Dancing (1987)

Guest, Lance – Born 21st July 1960
* The Last Starfighter (1984)

Haim, Corey – Born 23rd December 1971 / Died 10th March 2010
* Secret Admirer (1985)
* Lucas (1986)
* The Lost Boys (1987)
* License To Drive (1988)
* Dream A Little Dream (1989)

Hall, Anthony Michael – Born 14th April 1968
* Sixteen Candles (1984)
* The Breakfast Club (1985)
* Weird Science (1985)

Hannah, Daryl – Born 3rd December 1960
* Reckless (1984)

Hewitt, Martin – Born 19th February 1958
* Endless Love (1981)

Above: Martin Hewitt & Brooke Shields in "Endless Love" (1981)

Howell, C. Thomas – Born 7th December 1966
* The Outsiders (1983)
* Secret Admirer (1985)

Hunt, Helen – Born 15th June 1963
* Girls Just Want To Have Fun (1985)

Hutton, Timothy – Born 16th August 1960
* Taps (1981)

Kilmer, Val – Born 31st December 1959
* Real Genius (1985)

Land, Paul – 31st January 1956
* The Idolmaker (1980)
* Spring Break (1983)

Lane, Diane - 22nd January 1965
* The Outsiders (1983)

Lattanzi, Matt – 1st February 1959
* My Tutor (1983)

Leigh, Jennifer Jason – Born 5th February 1962
* Fast Times At Ridgemont High (1982)

Loughlin, Lori – Born 28th July 1964
* Secret Admirer (1985)
* Back To The Beach (1987)
* The Night Before (1988)

Lowe, Rob – Born 17th March 1964
* The Outsiders (1983)
* Class (1983)

Macchio, Ralph - Born 4th November 1961
* The Outsiders (1983)
* The Karate Kid (1984)

Masterson, Mary Stuart - Born 28th June 1966
* Some Kind Of Wonderful (1987)

McCarthy, Andrew – Born 29th November 1962
* Class (1983)
* Pretty In Pink (1986)

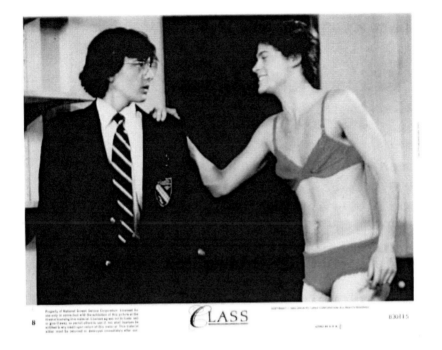

Above: Andrew McCarthy & Rob Lowe (in drag) ham it up in "Class" (1983)

McNichol, Kristy – Born 11th September 1962
* Little Darlings (1980)

Modine, Matthew – Born 22nd March 1959
* Private School (1983)

Montgomery , Lee – Born 3rd November 1961
* Girls Just Want To Have Fun (1985)

Moore, Demi – Born 11th November 1962
* No Small Affair (1984)

Nelson, Judd – Born 28th November 1959
* Making The Grade (1984)
* The Breakfast Club (1985)

O'Neal, Tatum - Born 5th November 1963
* Little Darlings (1980)

Parker, Sarah Jessica – Born 25th March 1965
* Footloose (1984)
* Girls Just Want To Have Fun (1985)

Patric, Jason – Born 17th June 1966
* The Lost Boys (1987)

Penn, Chris – Born 10th October 1965 / Died 24 January 2006
* All The Right Moves (1983)
* Footloose (1984)

Penn, Sean – Born 17th August 1960
* Taps (1981)
* Fast Times At Ridgemont High (1982)
* Bad Boys (1983)

Preston, Kelly – Born 13th October 1962
* Mischief (1985)
* Secret Admirer (1985)

Quinn, Aidan – Born 8th March 1959
* Reckless (1984)

Reeves, Keanu – Born 2nd September 1964
* The Night Before (1988)
* Bill & Ted's Excellent Adventure (1988)

Reinhold, Judge – 21st May 1957
* Fast Times At Ridgemont High (1982)

Ringwald, Molly – Born 18th February 1968
* Sixteen Candles (1984)
* The Breakfast Club (1985)
* Pretty In Pink (1986)
* For Keeps? (1988)

Romanus, Robert – Born 17th July 1956
* Foxes (1980)
* Fast Times At Ridgemont High (1982)

Ruck, Alan – Born 1ˢᵗ July 1956

* Bad Boys (1983)
* Class (1983)
* Ferris Bueller's Day Off (1986)

Sheedy, Ally - Born 13th June 1962

* Bad Boys (1983)
* WarGames (1983)
* The Breakfast Club (1985)

Sheen, Charlie – Born 3rd September 1965

* Lucas (1986)
* Ferris Bueller's Day Off (1986)
* Young Guns (1988)

Sheffer, Craig – Born 23rd April 1960

* Some Kind Of Wonderful (1987)

Shields, Brooke – Born 31st May 1965

* The Blue Lagoon (1980)
* Endless Love (1981)

Shue, Elisabeth - Born 6th October 1963

* The Karate Kid (1984)
* Adventures In Babysitting (1987)

Above: Elisabeth Shue & Ralph Macchio in "The Karate Kid" (1984)

Siemaszko, Casey – Born 17th March 1961
* Class (1983)
* Secret Admirer (1985)
* Back To The Future (1985)
* Three O'Clock High (1987)
* Young Guns (1988)

Singer, Lori - Born 6th November 1957
* Footloose (1984)

Slater, Christian - Born 18th August 1969
* Gleaming The Cube (1989)

Spader, James – Born 7th February 1960
* Endless Love (1981)
* Tuff Turf (1985)
* Pretty In Pink (1986)

Stewart, Catherine Mary - Born 22th April 1959
* The Last Starfighter (1984)
* Mischief (1985)

Stockwell, John – Born 25th March 1961
* Losin' It (1983)
* My Science Project (1985)

Stoltz, Eric – Born 30th September 1961
* Fast Times At Ridgemont High (1982)
* Some Kind Of Wonderful (1987)
* Say Anything (1989)

Sutherland, Keifer – Born 21st December 1966
* The Lost Boys (1987)
* Young Guns (1988)

Swayze, Patrick - Born 18th August 1952 / Died 14th September 2009
* The Outsiders (1983
* Dirty Dancing (1987)

Thompson, Lea – Born 31st May 1961

* All The Right Moves (1983)
* Back To The Future (1985)
* Some Kind Of Wonderful (1987)

Youngs, Jim – Born 16th October 1956

* Footloose (1984)
* Hotshot (1987)

Zabka, William - Born 20th October 1965

* The Karate Kid (1984)
* Just One Of The Guys (1985)

Above & Below: William Zabka with Macchio & Shue in "The Karate Kid" (1984)

Zuniga, Daphne – Born 28th October 1962

* The Sure Thing (1985)

HOLLYWOOD TEEN MOVIES 80 FROM THE 80s

U.S. Box Office Ranking

Rank / Film Title	YEAR	GROSS
1. Back To The Future	1985	$210,609,762
2. Porky's	1982	$105,492,483
3. The Karate Kid	1984	$90,815,558
4. Footloose	1984	$80,035,402
5. War Games	1983	$79,567,667
6. Ferris Bueller's Day Off	1986	$70,136,369
7. Risky Business	1983	$63,541,777
8. Dirty Dancing	1987	$63,446,382
9. The Goonies	1985	$61,389,680
10. The Blue Lagoon	1980	$58,853,106
11. The Breakfast Club	1985	$45,875,171
12. Young Guns	1988	$45,661,556
13. Revenge Of The Nerds	1984	$40,874,452
14. Bill & Ted's Excellent Adventure	1989	$40,485,039
15. Pretty In Pink	1986	$40,471,663
16. Breakin'	1984	$38,682,707
17. Taps	1981	$35,856,053
18. Adventures In Babysitting	1987	$34,368,475
19. Little Darlings	1980	$34,326,249
20. Teen Wolf	1985	$33,086,611
21. The Lost Boys	1987	$32,222,567
22. Can't Buy Me Love	1987	$31,623,833
23. Endless Love	1981	$31,184,024
24. The Last Starfighter	1984	$28,733,290
25. Fast Times At Ridgemont High	1982	$27,092,880
26. Private Lessons	1981	$26,279,000
27. The Outsiders	1983	$25,697,647
28. Iron Eagle	1986	$24,159,872
29. Spring Break	1983	$24,071,666
30. Weird Science	1985	$23,834,048
31. Sixteen Candles	1984	$23,686,027
32. My Tutor	1983	$22,587,834
33. My Bodyguard	1980	$22,482,952

34.	License To Drive	1988	$22,433,275
35.	Class	1983	$21,667,789
36.	Fame	1980	$21,202,829
37.	Say Anything	1989	$20,781,385
38.	Some Kind Of Wonderful	1987	$18,553,948
39.	The Sure Thing	1985	$18,135,531
40.	For Keeps?	1988	$17,514,553
41.	Valley Girl	1983	$17,343,596
42.	All The Right Moves	1983	$17,233,166
43.	Zapped	1982	$16,897,768
44.	Private School	1983	$14,049,540
45.	Back To The Beach	1987	$13,110,903
46.	Real Genius	1985	$12,952,019
47.	She's Out Of Control	1989	$12,065,892
48.	Just One Of The Guys	1985	$11,528,900
49.	Where The Boys Are '84	1984	$10,530,000
50.	Better Off Dead	1985	$10,297,601
51.	Tuff Turf	1985	$9,369,329
52.	Bad Boys	1983	$9,190,819
53.	Mischief	1985	$8,692,426
54.	Secret Admirer	1985	$8,622,757
55.	Reckless	1984	$8,289,916
56.	Lucas	1986	$8,200,000
57.	Foxes	1980	$7,470,348
58.	Tex	1982	$7,400,000
59.	Class Of 1984	1982	$6,965,361
60.	Girls Just Want To Have Fun	1985	$6,326,051
61.	The Last American Virgin	1982	$5,829,781
62.	Paradise	1982	$5,588,800
63.	Dream A Little Dream	1989	$5,552,441
64.	No Small Affair	1984	$4,994,094
65.	Making The Grade	1984	$4,561,346
66.	My Science Project	1985	$4,122,748
67.	Loverboy	1989	$3,960,327
68.	The Heavenly Kid	1985	$3,852,271
69.	North Shore	1987	$3,832,228
70.	Three O'clock High	1987	$3,685,862
71.	Gleaming The Cube	1989	$2,777,280
72.	The Idolmaker	1980	$2,625,716
73.	Losin' It	1983	$1,246,141
74.	Private Resort	1985	$331,816

75.	Teen Witch	1989	**$27,843**
76.	Liar's Moon	1982	**N/A**
77.	Never Too Young To Die	1986	**N/A**
78.	Thrashin'	1986	**N/A**
79.	Hotshot	1987	**N/A**
80.	The Night Before	1989	**N/A**

Above: Randall Batinkoff & Molly Ringwald in "For Keeps" (1988)

Website Bibliography

Hollywood Teen Movies (www.hollywoodteenmovies.com)
Hollywood Cult Movies (www.hollywoodcultmovies.com)
Internet Actors Database (www.internetactorsdatabase.com)
Pick Of The Flicks (www.pickoftheflicks.com)
Internet Movie Database (www.imdb.com)
Box Office Mojo (www.boxofficemojo.com)

Posters & Photos

Movie Goods (www.moviegoods.com)
Hollywood Teen Movies (www.hollywoodteenmovies.com)

Author Contact Details

Email: hollywoodteenmovies@hotmail.com

Above: Teen stars from two generations
come together in "Back To The Beach" (1987)

CPSIA information can be obtained at www.ICGtesting.com
Printed in the USA
BVOW07s2138180314

348088BV00003B/14/P

9 781742 841557